MW01073786

WARRIOR
MAGIC

Ray Garcia Photography

ABOUT THE AUTHOR

Tomás Prower is a graduate of the University of California: Santa Barbara with degrees in global socioeconomics and Latin American studies. Born and raised in Southern California, his fluency in English, French, and Spanish gave him the opportunity to work for the French government as a cultural liaison throughout South America, with extended assignments in Buenos Aires, Santiago de Chile, and the Amazon jungle. Since then, he has been the External Relations Director for the American Red Cross, LGBT+ Programs Director for entertainment productions in Los Angeles, and a licensed mortuary professional in California and Nevada. Currently, Tomás resides in his hometown of L.A. as a writer and author of popular fiction and nonfiction works.

WARRIOR MAGIC

JUSTICE SPIRITUALITY AND CULTURE
FROM AROUND THE WORLD

TOMÁS PROWER

LLEWELLYN PUBLICATIONS
Woodbury, Minnesota

FIRST EDITION
First Printing, 2022

Cover design by Shannon McKuhen

Llewellyn Publications is a registered trademark of Llewellyn Worldwide Ltd.

Library of Congress Cataloging-in-Publication Data (Pending)
ISBN: 978-0-7387-6797-0

Llewellyn Publications
A Division of Llewellyn Worldwide Ltd.
2143 Wooddale Drive
Woodbury, MN 55125-2989

www.llewellyn.com

Printed in the United States of America

Other Books by Tomás Prower

This book is dedicated to Ares, god of war.
May he continue to fight alongside us, shoulder to shoulder in the heat
and mud of battle as we hold the line against injustice and push forward
toward something more than this.

CONTENTS

PRE-MISSION BRIEFING

*Wars are the most interesting times. It
shows the best and the worst in people.*
IAN "LEMMY" KILMISTER

War … what is it good for? Well, absolutely everything as far as history is concerned. With the extremely small exception of the recent past, everything, absolutely almost everything we currently know about the human race in every culture around the world, has been written by the sides victorious in armed conflict. It has shaped the world, the environment, the entire timeline trajectory of humanity. It has created the greatest atrocities human beings have ever committed while also having forged the most noble acts of heroism and greatest heroes that have ever risen from the ranks of us to become legends immortal.

Whether you like it or not, practically your entire understanding of the past has been shaped by war. Think back to your school textbooks and how they taught you all about everything that has ever happened through showcasing one war after the other, battle after battle, conflict after conflict, struggle after struggle. Times of peace are displayed as anomalous resting points in a temporal valley between two mountainous wars. Even right now as you read this, your country, your nation, your peoples, the very ideals you hold dear are either involved in a war or another is just beyond the horizon.

But why so much bloodshed? Why is it that the music and poetry of war have such an affinity for refrain? Is it because of governments and those who lead us? Is it because of the lack of justice or overzealous execution of it? Is it just the times, the unfortunate eras into which we are born? No.

War exists because humans exist. Injustice exists because humans exist. But by that same token, peace also exists because humans exist, and so, too, does justice. It is because of this fact that warriors are so important. Conflicts will come to tear you and the innocent down, and if you aren't prepared, aren't trained in the ways of the warrior, these conspiring forces *will* win.

War does not only exist on the battlefield, though. Being prepared isn't only a matter of being trained in physical combat. We all go through our own wars, our own defeats, our own victories. Everyone you meet is fighting a personal battle of some sort; just because they don't talk about it or let their internal war-weariness show doesn't mean it isn't there. As long as human beings are suffering and clamoring for justice, there will always be another battle to fight. And it's a battle we *have* to fight. After all, peace and justice are not fruits that fall from the tree once they are ripe; we have to either reach up and grab them or shake that tree to make them fall lest they wither and rot on the branch.

I'm not saying it's an easy feat. Hell, if it *was* easy, we would've done it already. I'm not even saying we will be victorious, but I can guarantee that it will be worse and we *will* lose if we don't even try. Missing a shot and not taking a shot both have the same outcomes. Whether it's a magic spell in aid of justice or on-the-ground activism, the possibility of success only exists if we actually get out there and try.

Of course, no one wants to be a warrior for the things warriors do. Ask any military veteran, and they'll tell you they didn't enlist for the sole purpose of fighting and killing. No, warriors are warriors because they hold people, ideals, and their version of justice (however they personally define it) so dearly that they want to protect them in an active way, even if it means risking their own life. People enlist and subject themselves to the horrors of war so that future generations won't have to.

Then, of course, there's the saying that "deep down, everyone wants peace." But that just isn't true. If truly no one wanted war, there would be no war. It exists *because* certain people want it. It brings them wealth and power, silences opposition, maintains their warped ideal of "justice" in this world, and countless other reasons. For every war that ever has been or ever shall be, someone wanted it, and they either forced or convinced others to want it too. There is no such thing as a war no one wanted.

That is where this book and the worldwide reconnaissance mission upon which we are about to embark come in. Because there will always be someone who wants a war, we must be prepared to fight one, and by looking into how spirituality, magic, and mysticism have played a part in them, those who are workers of magic, partners with the Divine, or have had just about enough of oppression in this world can all be a little better prepared in the forthcoming fight.

To do this, we will look at both the aggressors and defenders in eras of conflicts and social justice struggles around the world throughout human history and how both sides have incorporated active and passive spirituality into their arsenals. We will look at the deities and spiritual forces of the universe that have been called upon as allies in the war effort. We will look at the inspired mortals who rose to battle leadership or had the warrior mantle thrust upon them, leading their people to victory. We will look at the spells, rituals, and daily practices of everyday people actively engaged in combatting injustice. We will look into the mythos and at all things spiritual and mystical that have been used to fight the good fight.

And along the way, as we learn these arts of war, revolution, and social justice activism of our worldwide ancestors, we will also meet contemporary warriors. These living and breathing peers of ours from cultures throughout the globe will share with us their own stories in their own words of personal trials and tribulations, activities on the front lines of protests and underground movements, spells and meditations to bind the wicked and elevate the oppressed, rituals to strengthen our bodies and galvanize our souls, and everything else under the sun and moon that can and will aid us in our own battles internally and in the world at large.

As a person who can enact change in the material world, a person capable of manipulating the energies and natural forces of the universe, you are already a warrior whether you accept the outward label or not. Your skills and partnership with the Divine already make you responsible because you are response-*able*. Those who are not response-*able* can never choose peace for themselves because they lack the ability to forge their own futures; they simply have to live and deal with whatever the "victors" allow them to have. After all, a person who cannot fight back is not "peaceful," they're just "harmless."

But you, you're different. As a warrior, you have the capacity to fight back and the ability to say, "No, I do not accept this" and then do something about it. Only a warrior has the ability to shape the future, and therefore, all of history. Only a warrior can *choose* peace since only they have the strength and capacity, should they so choose, to not be peaceful.

So, if you're going to forge your own destiny and help bring about a better world for all those who cannot or do not have the power to choose it for themselves, then you might as well learn how to be the best warrior you can be. You're not in it alone; every other person reading this book is here training alongside you.

Let the ink on these pages open your mind to the international array of allies clamoring for justice; let their stories inspire you with hope and passion, and, most importantly, let yourself be powerful. You already are, though you may not know it or believe it. As you'll see, the power of a warrior comes in many shapes and forms, all of which play their part in the effort. Find your power in this book and learn to unleash it. All of the history yet to be written depends upon it.

PART 1

GREATER MIDDLE EAST

*To everything there is a season, and a
time to every purpose under heaven . . .
A time to love, and a time to hate; a
time for war, and a time for peace.*
ECCLESIASTES 3:1-8 (TANAKH)

1

CRADLES OF CIVILIZATION

Cultural

PREHISTORY

From our evolution into *Homo sapiens* in our cradle of East Africa to every inch of the earth that we have since ventured toward and renamed "home," warfare and violence of the organized, strategized kind have been a defining part of us. Granted, it wasn't the go-to first response that our earliest ancestors immediately began planning whenever they had problems with each other, but it was often a common last resort brought about by the most basic of human needs: survival.

The Origins of War

From the evidence we have, war was, since its origins, seen as a sub-optimal course of action; our prehistoric ancestors went to war only when they *really* needed to, most often when local resources were scarce. The benefits had to outweigh the costs, and when our low population, small-grouped ancestors were just starting out, these costs were always too high.

Of course, all forms of war are costly, especially in human life. To give some relative perspective, though, nowadays with our high-population metropolises, it's socially "easier" to up and declare and support war because not only are there a glut of people to fill in the jobs of those deployed to war, but there's also a large reserve of soldiers available to replace the sacrificial fallen. It's also, in a sense, "emotionally" easier to advocate for war since those who will be sacrificed on the front lines will often be unknown strangers to the vast majority of the population. There are just too many of us around in the twenty-first century for everyone to know everyone on a familiar level.

The smaller the group, the more devastating the loss of a group member and the more likely it would've been for all members to have developed emotional ties with that person, but in modern cities with populations in the *thousands* or *millions*, a single person's death (or even a hundred people's deaths) easily goes unnoticed by the community at large and makes no real dent in the community's ability to continue functioning. Having worked in the funeral industry myself, I can guarantee you there are *lots* of people dying all the time all around you in big cities, but because there are so many of us, no one outside of immediate family and friends really notices or is emotionally affected by the loss.

When talking about our earliest ancestors, however, who were living in small, low-populated communities wherein everyone was absolutely essential to pitch in for the survival of the group and no one was a total stranger from anyone due to everyone being only one or two degrees of separation from each other, every life was that much more intrinsically and emotionally valuable to the community—too valuable to risk for war. Plus, a more nomadic lifestyle and not being politico-economically tied to specific plots of land offered migration away from the threat of war as a preferred alternative. That is, of course, unless there was nowhere else to go because of ecological crises.

Climatic Competition

It wasn't until around 10,000 BCE that we humans learned how to manipulate the earth via farming to produce bountiful surpluses of food on a reliable schedule. Before then, in our hunter-gatherer days, our survival was reliant upon migrating around during any given season and whatever edible food was naturally growing. So, during times of climate change and eras of unseasonable weather patterns prior to 10,000 BCE, there was less food to find and to share. This competition for diminishing resources amid a growing population during our most ancient existence is believed to be humankind's earliest engagements into premeditated warfare.[1]

It has to be mentioned, though, that this topic on prehistoric warfare is highly controversial among modern anthropologists (because everything *prehistory* is a bit more based on theory than sociological hard evidence). Nevertheless, there recently have been some telling archeological finds that show a correlation in the rise of large-scale lethal aggression among our prehistoric ancestors whenever available food resources in a region were scarce. This is further compounded by correlations of a lot less evidence of similar large-scale lethal aggression whenever food was plentiful and abundant in that same region. Also, unsurprisingly, a similar correlational increase in prehistorical human violence can be seen in regions abundant in food if an unjust redistribution of that food led to inequality and hunger.[2]

1   Erin Blakemore, "What Was the Neolithic Revolution?" *National Geographic*, April 5, 2019, https://www.nationalgeographic.com/culture/topics/reference /neolithic-agricultural-revolution/.

2   Mark W. Allen et al., "Resource Scarcity Drives Lethal Aggression Among Prehistoric Hunter-Gatherers in Central California," *Proceedings of the National Academy of Sciences of the United States of America* 113, no. 43 (October 10, 2016): 12120–12125, https://doi.org/10.1073/pnas.1607996113.

Regardless of whether you agree with these proposed archaeological findings (keeping in mind that correlation does not always equal causation), there is an extra bit of fascinating information on war that has been so frequently documented that it cannot be denied. Premeditated, organized, strategized, lethal aggression between two groups has been found in other members of the animal kingdom, most notably among our closest cousins: chimpanzees. War is part and parcel of humanity, but it is not exclusively ours.

Ethnologist *célèbre* Jane Goodall in her groundbreaking research into these primates revealed a four-year-long deadly war between rival chimpanzee groups. Power struggles, internal competition for mates and resources, and the deterioration of established social dynamics (aka, the same usual suspects for human conflict) all led to full-blown warfare between members of a close-knit chimpanzee group that had split apart into two separate factions. More unnerving is how this infamous chimp war wasn't a one-off thing. Ever since Goodall's time personally witnessing this war in the mid-1970s, other scientists have had many opportunities to study many more similar killings between chimpanzees.[3]

MESOPOTAMIA

Civilization as we know it only really started when humans stopped roaming around and started settling in place because we learned to farm and have a reliable, predicable surplus of food that could be stored and saved for later. Thus crops, and more specifically the static plots of land on which those crops were grown, became *super* important; whoever controlled that land, controlled the food (and therefore the life and death of everyone reliant upon that food).

---

3   Rami Tzabar, "Do Chimpanzee Wars Prove that Violence Is Innate?" BBC, August 11, 2015, http://www.bbc.com/earth/story/20150811 -do-animals-fight-wars; Christopher Lile, "Science Update: Chimps Start Wars for Power and Benefit from Play," Jane Goodall's Good News For All, July 11, 2018, https://news.janegoodall.org/2018/07/11/chimps-start-wars -power-show-disgust-feces-benefit-play/.

Civilized Soldiers

Since not every able-bodied person had to spend their entire day procuring food for survival (the farmers took care of that for everyone), some people could dedicate their waking hours to new things such as the arts, astronomy, pottery, religious mediumship, and more. Of particular importance, though, were the people who spent their daily energies on perfecting combat and becoming adept in the art of killing in protection of this all-important land. Enter the warrior class.

Here in the historical region of the Middle East, now called "Mesopotamia," is where some of the earliest examples of such specialization in soldiering have been unearthed. Keep in mind, Mesopotamia wasn't just one single civilization. Rather, "Mesopotamia" is a catchall descriptor for the various civilizations that rose and fell between the Tigris and Euphrates rivers from approximately 5000 BCE to 539 BCE when the Persian Empire took over.

So, when you hear someone say "Mesopotamia," they're generally talking about a clumping together of the four big civilizations of that timeframe: Sumer, Akkad, Assyria, and Babylon. Though uniquely different, they all had a lot of similarities, especially in terms of their polytheistic spiritual beliefs wherein, more or less, the same gods and goddesses were worshipped but with different names and nuanced changes to their lore. And, of course, another similarity was their escalation of this thing called war, a thing in which the gods were heavily involved.

Hometown Heroes

Mesopotamia's religious beliefs were deeply intertwined with the warfare that went on all around them, though most of the spirituality of war revolved around the leaders of each military campaign. Originally, these leaders were elected in a sort of proto-democracy fashion whose rule would only last as long as the military campaign, but as these military leaders gained more and more clout and influence from more and more victories and conquered land, a system of hereditary rule began to take root, with the earliest kings being the (or the sons of) successful campaign leaders.

These leaders and their families often solidified their rule by presenting themselves as representatives of the gods, and while this idea of rulers justifying their position as being chosen by the Divine is common throughout many cultures throughout our history, the peoples of Mesopotamia were unique in that all the various rulers were believed to be the represented *military champions* of different gods, fighting on their divine behalf here on earth.

So, essentially, out on the battlefields of war, the kings (who were also the de facto military leaders) were seen as their god's mightiest warrior on earth, and when two kings' armies clashed, it was regarded as more of a proxy war between the gods so that the gods didn't have to fight each other directly. Whichever god's champion was victorious, then that god was victorious. To put it succinctly, wars were seen as solely matters between the gods, and humans just got involved because their champion kings were obligated to fight each other in place of the gods.

You might be thinking, what if two kings represented the same god? Wouldn't every military ruler want to represent the god of war or some other more powerful and tough god over a peaceful one? How did these kings choose their gods? Well, the answer is, they didn't; the city over which they ruled decided that for them.

The civilizations of Mesopotamia, similar to ancient Greece, were really just city-states that exerted influence over nearby territory, and each city was said to be the hometown of a certain god and to be where that god physically resided on earth. A king who rose to power in a specific city meant that they were the representative of the god of whose hometown city that was. (It might be easier to picture this by comparing hometown gods to something like high school mascots. You cannot choose your personal mascot whom you want to represent. Rather, the school you attend determines the mascot you represent because the mascot is tied with the school and not your personal choice of favorite animal or symbolism. If you want to change your mascot/god under whom you compete/fight, you have to change schools/cities.)[4]

Co-Op Mode

Just because warriors were seen as being little more than proxy-puppets on the battlefield doesn't mean that they were completely without self-determination. On the contrary, Mesopotamians saw themselves as cooperative partners with the gods. In fact, humans believed the gods brought them into existence in the first place so as to help them restrain the powers of chaos. Thus, humans were gifted with logic, reason, and the ability to control and bring order unto the physical world around them, all necessary in helping the gods keep chaos at bay and keep the universe organized. (They even regarded the knowledge of how to brew beer as a reward from the gods for helping them out in this eternal military struggle.)[5]

Still, even though humans were cooperative allies with the gods in the never-ending war against chaos (because how can you win a war against an abstract concept?), the city-states and civilizations of Mesopotamia were also constantly in conflict with one another over land and water rights. This inter-fighting kept the various peoples of the region divided and at each other's throats, all culminating in 539 BCE when Cyrus the Great defeated the last great Mesopotamian civilization of Babylon and expanded the Persian Empire (...but more on him after a quick stop in Egypt).

Prehistoric and Mesopotamian Takeaway:
ALLIES

There is no such thing as the self-made man. For every successful person out there, there have been *many* more people behind the scenes who contributed to that success, oftentimes even more so than the individual

4   Matt Hollis, "Rise of Sumer: Cradle of Civilization DOCUMENTARY," Kings and Generals, YouTube, 13:45, March 14, 2019, https://www.youtube.com /watch?v=MHpmLrWBjnM&list=PLaBYW76inbX4vEmC1vfsJDzQhs8M _ufQn&index=2&t=8s.
5   Joshua J. Mark, "Religion in the Ancient World," World History Encyclopedia, March 23, 2018, https://www.worldhistory.org/religion/.

person themselves. The people who manufacture the products, the marketing personnel, the people who gave or bequeathed the seed capital, the friend who gave them encouraging words and a place to stay when things were rough. No one ever did it alone.

This is *especially* true in warfare. Unless both sides agree to decide the fate of an entire conflict on a single hand-to-hand duel between two individuals, no war is won singlehandedly (and even then, who fashioned the armor and taught the individual how to fight?). You need allies if you want to be successful, if you want to win. In ancient Mesopotamia, even the gods needed allies. The all-powerful deities of all existence needed mortals to be their allies in the war against chaos. So, if the gods, these masters of the universe, could swallow their pride and ask for help, so can you.

So, your takeaway challenge here is to seek out allies. On a practical level, this means getting in touch with like-minded people to form a collective greater than the individual. Pick a cause, a social justice movement, a change you want to bring into the world, and ameliorate your power to manifest that vision by connecting with others. Join a social media page, start a Discord group, seek out your neighborhood community organizations. Get involved.

On a spiritual level, this means partnering with the gods or however you relate to the Divine. Perform meditations to get in touch with divinities you'd like on your side in the good fight or even do research into finding out which deities hold patronage over aspects of that specific change you want to bring into the world. There's a saying that goes: "If God be with you, then who could be against you?" It's very true; so start amassing your allies, both mortal and divine.

ANCIENT EGYPT

In the earliest times of ancient Egypt, most military personnel were really just the palace soldiers and personal guards of the pharaohs. The pharaohs, as the supreme spiritual leaders of all their people and the representatives of the gods on earth, needed to be protected. They were divine, yes, but they were also very capable of dying.

Laws & Order

Aside from governance, one of the pharaoh's main mystical duties was to keep order in the universe by acting as the intermediary between mortals and the Divine. Of course, once you make "order" a top priority, a slew of laws to define the parameters of "order" often ensue ... followed by a massive bureaucracy to keep the iron wheels of law and order functioning.

This sense of highly regulated organization gave the ancient Egyptians a slight superiority complex in which they saw their neighbors as the barbarian antitheses to "civilized" Egypt. Because their neighbors often lacked the same sophisticated level of urban bureaucracy that the ancient Egyptians had, these neighbors were regarded by the ancient Egyptians as agents of cosmic disorder whose disorganization flew defiantly in the face of the ancient Egyptian gods' desire for law and order in all the universe. And since it was the pharaoh's divine-appointed duty to maintain order in the universe, it was the pharaoh himself (and on multiple occasions herself) whose spiritual obligation it would be to lead his people on the battlefield against these foreign agents of disorder.[6]

Thanatophobia

Despite this divine duty, however, foreign wars weren't done very much. Lands away from the Nile's floodplain weren't very profitable, and even if the pharaoh wanted that unwanted land for some intangible reason like glory or honor, the costs of war did not outweigh the benefits. This was mostly because of the supreme fear of dying far from home that every ancient Egyptian had (especially the pharaoh).

You have to remember, death and the afterlife were *the* most important things in the life of an ancient Egyptian. If you've read my previous book *Morbid Magic: Death Spirituality and Culture from Around the World*, you know all about how mummification and preservation of the corpse was essential to having any semblance of an afterlife, but if you haven't, the Cliff's Notes version is that the ancient Egyptians believed that part of the soul

---

6   Garry J. Shaw, *War and Trade with the Pharaohs: An Archaeological Study of Ancient Egypt's Foreign Relations* (Barnsley, UK: Pen & Sword Books, Ltd., 2017), n.p.

was eternally tied to the human body, so if the body rotted away, a part of your soul rotted away too, and you needed your *entire* soul in order to experience an afterlife. Thus the afterlife fears of dying far away from home on a military campaign where no one could professionally preserve their corpse was too much of a risk for pharaohs.[7]

The Best Defense

It wouldn't be until the mid-seventeenth century BCE when foreigners called the *Hyksos* briefly conquered the ancient Egyptians that ancient Egypt would start becoming more of an aggressive superpower. Originally, it seemed too farfetched to the ancient Egyptians that peoples not as civilized or as blessed by the gods as themselves could possibly conquer their millennia-old civilization, but the pharaohs soon learned that you didn't really need law and order or even divine favoritism to be powerful—just military superiority would do it.

So after the Hyksos came into Lower and Middle Egypt and seized control from within, these foreign invaders were able to maintain their ruling power through their use of more advanced weapons and tactics. Eventually, ancient Egypt reconquered their lands from the Hyksos and, from then on out, placed more emphasis and focus on a proactive military with the mindset that the best defense is a good offense.[8]

Gods Among Men

After ancient Egypt liberated their occupied lands from Hyksos rule, the era of the New Kingdom began (sixteenth century BCE–eleventh century BCE), and, still traumatized from having been conquered, the pharaohs refocused their armies from a self-defense force to an imperialistic war

---

7   Anita Stratos, "Egypt: The Evolution of Warfare Part I," Tour Egypt, accessed April 11, 2020, http://www.touregypt.net/featurestories/war.htm.

8   Andrew Curry, "The Rulers of Foreign Lands," *Archaeology*, Archaeological Institute of America (Sept.–Oct. 2018), https://www.archaeology.org/issues/309-1809/features/6855-egypt-hyksos-foreign-dynasty; "How Three Rebel Queens of Egypt Overthrew an Empire and Gave Birth to a New Kingdom," *National Geographic History Magazine*, March 7, 2019, https://www.nationalgeographic.com/history/magazine/2017/07-08/rebel-queen-thebes/.

machine intent on conquering all neighbors before they could become a threat. During this time, the pharaohs began aligning themselves in art and inscriptions with the god of war, *Montu*.

This was also the time of some of Egypt's most legendary pharaohs: Nefertiti, Hatshepsut, Tutankhamun, Ramses II, and many others. However, to have a divine, absolute ruler with unquestionable power as head of both the military and the state was a double-edged sword. As a god on earth, if a pharaoh was wise, ambitious, and self-disciplined, then the empire experienced a mini golden age during their rule because no single person or interest group's corruptive selfishness, profiteering, or political maneuvering could be effective.

Conversely, if a pharaoh was apathetic, indulgent, or weak-willed, then their divine ordinances were more easily swayed by corruption. Moreover, if the divine embodiment of the gods on earth had a bad idea or a catastrophically fatal military strategy, then who was any mortal to tell them that their ideas were unwise? Luckily for the New Kingdom, many of their pharaohs were extremely capable, and the empire rapidly expanded, encompassing parts of modern-day Turkey in the north all the way to Ethiopia in the south.[9]

Middlemen Monopoly

Another, albeit unintended, side effect of pharaohs becoming more powerful during the New Kingdom was that it changed millennia-old practices on how the common people related to the Divine. In the past, ancient Egyptians understood that the pharaoh was a relatively balanced mix of both divine and human, and if everyday folks wanted to worship or get in touch with the Divine, they could have their own personal, direct experiences. As the New Kingdom pharaohs consolidated their power, however, they presented themselves as much more divine than human, and they

---

9   Dattatreya Mandal, "The Ancient Egyptian Armies of the New Kingdom,"
     Realm of History, June 16, 2017, https://www.realmofhistory
     .com/2017/06/16/10-facts-ancient-egyptian-armies-new-kingdom/.

began to exert more influence over being the only form of direct human communication with the gods.

So now, if commoners wanted to get in touch with the Divine, they'd have to do it through the pharaoh him- or herself, not through their own personal gnosis anymore. However, as the pharaohs were now more pre-occupied with war campaigns than administering to the spiritual needs of their people, the pharaohs began delegating this spiritual authority to appointed priests and mystics. While this delegation did, indeed, leave the pharaohs with more time to strategize and engage in war, it also made the pharaohs less powerful at home since they were no longer the only divine authority in government.[10]

Needless to say, the allowing of these priesthood special interest groups into government power (each with their own agenda) led to rampant cor-ruption and abuse of all sorts. Continuous wars of aggression that were farther and farther away were getting more and more expensive, and what-ever spoils could be plundered somehow began finding their way toward the pharaoh-appointed religious officials greatly more so than in times past. This growing wealth gap led to increasing internal strife and divi-sions, which weren't helped by the additional fact that all the nonstop foreign wars had given valuable experience and learn-by-losing military training to ancient Egypt's rivals.

Making matters even worse, later-generation pharaohs who earnestly wanted to fix all these problems found that they no longer had a strong central government behind them or the spiritual authority with which to enact changes. In focusing on war and having delegated much of their spir-itual duties to their priests and mystics, the divine authority to rule and command government no longer rested solely with the pharaohs. Power now had to be shared with various priesthood factions.[11]

10   Jan Assmann, *The Search for God in Ancient Egypt*, trans. David Lorton (Ithaca: Cornell University Press, 2001); Jacobus van Dijk, "The Amarna Period and the Later New Kingdom," in *The Oxford History of Ancient Egypt*, ed. Ian Shaw (Oxford: Oxford University Press, 2000), n.p.

11   Joshua J. Mark, "New Kingdom of Egypt," World History Encyclopedia, October 7, 2016, https://www.worldhistory.org/New_Kingdom_of_Egypt/.

All these factors led to ancient Egypt's decline and eventual fall. Had the pharaohs of the New Kingdom of ancient Egypt not been so expansion-oriented and not delegated away their spiritual authority, maybe history would have turned out differently. But then again, it was that same aggressive military expansion and fewer side-duties to distract them from warfare that brought ancient Egypt to its cultural and historic zenith. The sword cuts both ways.

Ancient Egyptian Takeaway:
SUSPICIOUS MINDS

There is no double-edged sword in a warrior's arsenal quite like suspicion. On the one hand, it's essential for survival because of the treachery, backstabbing, and capability to lie that we humans so ashamedly possess. On the other hand, it's the main ingredient in paranoia and can cause us to mistakenly turn on our allies and refuse much-needed help. It's a tightrope walk trying to balance the right amount of suspicion to have in our endeavors: too little will get us killed just as too much will self-sabotage all our efforts.

Ancient Egypt learned the double-edged nature of suspicion the hard way. Their defeat to foreign rule under the Hyksos didn't come solely from the invasion of an outside force bettering them in war. No, long before any of that, many Hyksos had infiltrated the halls of power in ancient Egyptian society to such an extent that ancient Egypt's fall was as much of an inside job as it was an outside one. Then, once the ancient Egyptians overthrew the Hyksos, they became so suspicious and paranoid of all their foreign neighbors and "outsiders" that they became an aggressive, imperialistic, conquering force, which then contributed to both their glorious zenith and their permanent downfall later on.

So, for your takeaway challenge here, learn to balance yourself on the political and mental tightrope walk that is suspicion. You can't go around trusting everybody and take everything everyone says at face value, but you also can't go around distrusting everybody and assuming that everyone has sinister ulterior motives and is out to get you. Learn to trust your gut more and place limits on your confidence until those who prove themselves trustworthy can be given more of it, but do be willing to adapt if logic and experience prove your gut otherwise.

This goes for your spiritual and self-improvement endeavors too. Don't just flat-out reject a book, piece of information, or bit of advice just because it comes from someone you don't know or don't personally respect. Facts are facts regardless of who says them, and even a broken clock is right twice a day. Similarly, don't just flat-out trust or believe what's written in a book, that piece of information, or that bit of advice just because it comes from someone whom you know or greatly admire. While not everyone is out to intentionally mislead you, not everyone has good, accurate information that's worthwhile (and even then, not everyone is right or wrong 100 percent of the time). Judge the quality of magic and information by two factors only: Is it objectively true? Does it work? After all, if something is not true or doesn't work, then it doesn't matter.

Deities & Legends

THE CODE OF HAMMURABI

The Code of Hammurabi is one of the most legendary and progressive legal documents in human history. Its importance cannot be overstated because before these transcribed laws, justice was arbitrary; the judgment and sentencing of any alleged wrongdoing varied from person to person (even the definition of what exactly was considered a "crime" was arbitrary). Once Hammurabi became ruler of the Babylonian Empire (around the early to mid-1700s BCE), he made sure that the dispensation of justice was standardized throughout his realm.

However, his code of laws was much more revolutionary than simply establishing regulations on justice. It also established progressive judicial theory for the times, such as the accused's presumption of innocence, the necessity of evidence to garner a conviction, and the regulation of pre-set punishments that befit the crime.[12]

This codification of the judicial system prevented excessive retribution, personal revenge, mob justice, and vigilantism, especially against minority groups. If you had a problem with someone, the courts had to pass objective judgment based on set criteria and could not sentence the guilty to a punishment that exceeded the damage that they caused (though this, of course, only applied to free men of the upper classes due to women, enslaved peoples, and the poor being regarded as not equal to wealthy free men and therefore not equally protected in the eyes of the law…a recurring worldwide theme we will unfortunately see again in our global trek).[13]

INANNA/ISHTAR

Among all the Mesopotamian gods, none are arguably more pervasive or popular in modern times as Inanna (Inanna being her original Sumerian name, though she was later re-named Ishtar by subsequent Mesopotamian civilizations once they came to power). Nowadays, she is known primarily for her role as a love and sex goddess, but in ancient Mesopotamia, she was equally revered and feared for her patronage of war.

Uniquely, rather than all-out battle, Inanna's specialty in warfare was political warfare. The halls of power during times of war are where she held prominence, not usually out in the killing fields amidst the mêlée, though it was an open secret that she loved the mess of war and was said that these bloody battles were a "feast" to her. This aspect of her is memorialized in

---

12   Ann Wolbert Burgess, Albert R. Roberts, and Cheryl Regehr, *Victimology: Theories and Applications* (Burlington: Jones & Bartlett Learning, 2009), 103–104.

13   Kristin Baird Rattini, "Who Was Hammurabi?," *National Geographic*, April 22, 2019, https://www.nationalgeographic.com/culture/people/reference /hammurabi/; "The Code of Hammurabi," The Avalon Project: Documents on Law, History and Diplomacy, trans. L.W. King, 2008, https://avalon.law.yale .edu/ancient/hamframe.asp.

artwork of the time wherein she is depicted in full armor regalia celebrating military victories.

It's up for debate just how bloodthirsty Inanna was actually perceived to be by the Mesopotamians since most instances wherein she is described as being very militaristic tend to be politically charged in context. So, uncertainty still remains as to whether Inanna being associated with war was propaganda by political leaders to gain popular support for war or if it was just another example of how when a people go to war (regardless of culture), their gods' warrior aspects start getting more attention because that is where the culture's attention becomes focused. Nevertheless, which is the source and which is the reflection as to the true nature of Inanna/Ishtar's bloodthirsty militarism, for now, remains subjective.[14]

MA'AT

Ma'at was the deific personification of justice, truth, balance, and morality in ancient Egypt. Her most prominent role in mythology and in the minds of the ancient Egyptians was as the counterbalance to the sum total of the morality of all your earthly deeds during the famous "weighing of the heart" ceremony. This ceremony was a postmortem spiritual trial that determined whether or not all your souls (because ancient Egyptians believed people to have multiple souls within them) could reunite after your death. This was tremendously important because if you failed the trial and your souls could not reunite, then you could not experience an afterlife, only an eternity of oblivion.

Depicted as a human woman wearing a headband with a single ostrich feather secured in it (also sometimes with feathered wings attached along her arms), it was that single ostrich feather that Ma'at would place on one end of the weighing scales during the trial, and on the other end was your

14   Yağmur Heffron, "Inana/Ištar (goddess)," Ancient Mesopotamian Gods and Goddesses, Oracc and the UK Higher Education Academy, 2016, http://oracc .museum.upenn.edu/amgg/listofdeities/inanaitar/; Patricia Kalensky, "Stele representing the goddess Ishtar," Louvre, accessed April 14, 2020, https:// www.louvre.fr/en/oeuvre-notices/stele-representing-goddess-ishtar (site discontinued).

heart (thought by ancient Egyptians to be the center of thought, memory, and emotion). If your heart weighed heavier than the feather (because it was laden with wicked thoughts and actions), then it would be eaten by a chimeric beast and you'd cease to exist. However, if your heart was as light as the feather, then your souls would reunite and you'd move on to the next stage in your afterlife journey.[15]

Beyond just this role, reverence for Ma'at was widespread throughout ancient Egypt. She was believed to not only be the symbol and patron of morality and order, but she also literally kept the forces of depravity and chaos in the universe at bay. This was not just a cosmic battle, though. She actively took part in upholding truth and justice in the physical world between humans too. So, both a healthy fear of her retribution and thankfulness for allowing civilized society to exist made her worship very popular.[16]

MONTU

In ancient Egypt, a handful of gods were associated with war and various aspects of warfare, but when it came to the dominion over war itself, none other than Montu was the most supreme. He was a falcon-headed (sometimes bovine-headed) deity who wore a plumed, red solar disk atop his head like a crown, symbolic for his most ancient origins as the manifestation of the scorchingly destructive effects of the desert sun (and therefore the divine scourge of the chief sun god, *Ra*). Later, Montu became seen as the lead enforcer for Ma'at, goddess of truth and justice. Nevertheless, in his earliest worship, he was also considered the patron of the city

---

15   Francesco Carelli, "The Book of Death: Weighing Your Heart," *London Journal of Primary Care* 4, no. 1 (July 2011): 86–87, https://www.ncbi.nlm.nih.gov /pmc/articles/PMC3960665/.

16   "Ma'at," Rosicrucian Egyptian Museum, accessed April 14, 2020, https:// egyptianmuseum.org/deities-Maat; A. Broadie and J. Macdonald, "The Concept of Cosmic Order in Ancient Egypt in Dynastic and Roman Times," *L'Antiquité Classique* 47, no. 1 (1978): 106–128, https://www.persee.fr/doc /antiq_0770-2817_1978_num_47_1_1885.

of Thebes, and because Thebes became the pharaonic capital of Egypt for a time, Montu also became patron of the pharaohs.

During times of war, pharaohs publicly associated themselves more with Montu, and he was evoked on military campaigns to bring about a successful conquest. However, Montu was also seen as a defensive protector. He was the god to whom the ancient Egyptians prayed to ensure their mighty empire not be conquered by foreigners, and he was the personal bodyguard of the supreme sun god, Ra, protecting him every night until the sun could once more rise into the sky. Neither blood-hungry nor chaotic, Montu's militarism and lethal force were generally regarded as neutral necessities to maintain balance in the universe, essentially doing the dirty work on behalf of the goddess of justice, Ma'at, and being the teeth by which her harmony and goodness could be realized and maintained.[17]

17   Jenny Hill, "Montu," Ancient Egypt Online, 2015, https:// ancientegyptonline.co.uk/montu/; Lillie Shelton, "The God of War," Johns Hopkins Archaeological Museum, accessed April 14, 2020, http:// archaeologicalmuseum.jhu.edu/the-collection/object-stories/egyptian -statuary-in-the-hopkins-archaeological-museum/the-god-of-war/.

2

PERSIA & THE JEWISH LEVANT

Cultural

PERSIA

In less than thirty years, the Persian Empire (more authentically known as the Achaemenid Empire from an ancient tribal ruler named "Achaemenes," after whom they called their civilization) rose from small obscurity in the Iranian highlands to become the most powerful force on earth. This power started to come about around 550 BCE when Cyrus the Great inherited the throne, and in addition to being ambitious, he was both a military strategist and administrative leader without equal.

One King to Rule Them All

Under Cyrus the Great's leadership and battle savvy, Persia quickly grew in territory, conquering the last great empire of ancient Mesopotamia: Babylon. While there have been many rulers and generals throughout history who have had similar successes, what made Cyrus stand out (and deserving of the oft-gifted title "the Great") is how he ran his empire of conquered peoples.

His strategy was unheard of at the time: tolerance. You see, in the Middle East, prior to Cyrus coming to power, if you were conquered by a foreign empire, you were no longer allowed to practice your native spiritual beliefs. Moreover, you could not govern yourselves; a foreigner from the religion and ethnic group of the ruling empire would be installed as the local ruler over the native peoples. And if that wasn't enough, another common practice would be to forcibly relocate you and your people to another region of the empire, effectively breaking your ties to the land and instilling political impotence since your kind had no connections or majority in this new locale. The harshness of all this was intentional. Any conquering empire's biggest worry is controlling the native peoples to prevent rebellion and revolution, and the empires of Mesopotamia believed that these oppressive control tactics were the best way to maintain dominance.

Cyrus, however, was completely revolutionary because he believed the exact opposite of all this. He believed that by disallowing people to practice their native spiritual traditions, govern themselves, and live in their own homeland, that would only make them *more* likely to revolt and be problematic (which sounds obvious now, but remember, the BCEs were a *very* different time). So, if Cyrus and his Persian Empire conquered you (or conquered the people who had conquered you), you were all of a sudden allowed to practice your own religion again, govern yourselves with your own native leaders, and stay on your own land (or even returned back to your homeland if you had previously been forcibly exiled).[18]

---

18   Steven Schroeder, "The Rise of Persia," Khan Academy, accessed April 18, 2020, https://www.khanacademy.org/humanities/world-history/ancient -medieval/ancient-persia/a/the-rise-of-persia.

The caveat to all this, though, was that in order to have such autonomy, you and your people had to accept Cyrus as the supreme ruler and "King of Kings" (a title that acknowledged the legitimacy of native kings, though placing the Persian king above them in rank). Due to the unprecedented level of tolerance that Cyrus became known for (and given the alternatives), many conquered peoples accepted this "Hobson's choice" of an offer. In fact, the written proclamation of Cyrus the Great on the right for the Jewish people to be freed from slavery and returned to their homeland is still considered by some archaeologists to be the world's first official human rights declaration, though there is still some debate on this.[19]

Zoroastrian Benevolence

What was it about Cyrus the Great that influenced him to have such a humanitarian outlook on empire building? One leading theory is that the Persian state religion of Zoroastrianism played a big part in it (whether or not the Persian "Kings of Kings" were Zoroastrian themselves is hotly debated, though the faith was, indeed, dominant in the empire and greatly influenced its administrative circles).

It's important to note that Zoroastrianism (with its earliest origins around the second millennium BCE) is still an actively practiced religion (with Queen lead singer Freddie Mercury probably being the world's most famous Zoroastrian of recent times), and, like any religion millennia old, the way it was back then, the way it is now, and the way each individual personally practices it is not exactly the same. Its traditional lack of a unified, organized structure has also contributed to giving it lots of internal variance throughout the eras.[20]

---

19   Kristin Baird Rattini, "Who Was Cyrus the Great?" *National Geographic*, May 6, 2019, https://www.nationalgeographic.com/culture/people/reference/cyrus -the-great/.

20   Vasudha Narayanan, "Freddie Mercury's Family Faith: The Ancient Religion of Zoroastrianism," The Conversation, November 3, 2018, https:// theconversation.com/freddie-mercurys-family-faith-the-ancient-religion-of -zoroastrianism-105806; William M. Malandra, "Zoroastrianism i. Historical Review up to the Arab Conquest," Encyclopedia Iranica, July 20, 2005, http:// www.iranicaonline.org/articles/zoroastrianism-i-historical-review.

Nevertheless, in general, Zoroastrianism is monotheistic (though it can be argued that it is simultaneously both mono- and polytheistic), is centered on the cosmic battle between good and evil, teaches of an impending apocalyptic judgment day wherein the good will go to a realm of paradise while the wicked will go to a realm of eternal suffering, and that humans have a part in shaping their own afterlife destiny by the morality of their earthly actions as opposed to just the caprice of the gods. If this all sounds familiar, then you're on the same wavelength as leading anthropologists and theologists because it's believed Zoroastrianism had a huge influencing effect on the other big monotheistic religions coming out of the region: Judaism, Christianity, and Islam.[21]

The major beliefs of a cosmic battle between the forces of good and evil and an afterlife destination dependent upon which side of the battle you took during your years on earth likely served as a motivating factor for the benevolence of Cyrus the Great (beyond its established practical application of mitigating rebellion). If all existence was in a battle between the forces of good and evil, and the Persian kings were the supreme military leaders of the known world, then it was their cosmic duty to lead the fight against evil within this world that they ruled. The humanitarian aspects toward those they conquered is often seen as Zoroastrian beliefs in action.[22]

No one stays on top forever, though, and Cyrus the Great's successors would become less tolerant as time went on. A mix of needing to solidify their increasingly dubious legitimacy to the throne, managing an ever-growing empire, increasing corruption, and more frequent military setbacks all resulted in the Persian kings resorting to more of an iron fist in governance to keep a solid grasp on the ruling power that was slipping through their fingers. Eventually, another "Great" would come and conquer

21   Joobin Bekhrad, "The Obscure Religion that Shaped the West," BBC, April 6, 2017, http://www.bbc.com/culture/story/20170406-this-obscure-religion-shaped-the-west.

22   Max Mallowan, "Cyrus the Great (558–529 B.C.)," in *The Cambridge History of Iran Vol. 2: The Median and Achaemenian Periods*, ed. Ilya Gershevitch (Cambridge: Cambridge University Press, 1985), 392–419.

this conquering empire, a Macedonian named Alexander, but we'll get to him a bit later.

Persian Takeaway:
ENOUGH

Look back at almost any successful revolution and you'll notice a trend: the tactics that won the revolution almost never aid in the aftermath of the war. Sure, one can conquer or liberate a people from atop a warhorse or from inside a tank, but to rule a people from atop a warhorse or from inside a tank does not have the same benevolent effects. Winning and ruling require completely different methodologies and mindsets.

This is true the world over. The anger and aggression of the oppressed greatly aided the lower classes of France to be victorious in the French Revolution, but that same anger and aggression continued on after victory, resulting in the horrific Reign of Terror. Mao Zedong's communist revolution may have started off with striving for social equality and overthrowing a brutal totalitarian dictatorship, but that same angry paranoia against oppression continued on after victory, culminating in the new communist leadership eventually morphing into a brutal totalitarian dictatorship of its own. The Persian Empire under Cyrus the Great, however, got it right. When the war was over, they switched gears toward tolerance, peace, and rebuilding. They did not continue the war after the war was over.

So, for your takeaway challenge here, practice identifying when enough is enough. Once you've beaten your enemy, don't keep attacking them because not only will it enrage that enemy toward more vengeance, it will also be seen by onlookers as if you are becoming the new oppressor. Of course, though, if the enemy gets back up with the intent of resuming their wicked ways, then yes, absolutely put them back in their place.

The same goes with spells and prayers. Once your target has paid for what they had done and sincerely learned their lesson, don't keep piling on that bad magic; it could drive them to such desperation that they become even more enraged, unpredictable, and harmfully dangerous (and if not toward you, then toward other innocents around them). Do what you've got to do to win the war, but learn to recognize when the war is over and when to acknowledge that you have done enough.

THE JEWISH LEVANT

The eastern shores of the Mediterranean were the crossroads of the world for much of written history. The lands now called Syria, Lebanon, Jordan, Israel, and Palestine have been traditionally called the "Levant" (derived from Latin meaning "to rise" since the sun rose from that eastern end of the Mediterranean). Many peoples have called this region of the world home, but one of the most well-known and lasting are the Jewish people.

Mass Exodus I: The Getaway

The history of Judaism is one of constant struggle, continued resistance against oppression, and revolution. Their faith and their culture have been in continued existence long enough to have lived on both sides of the extreme: oppressed and murdered by numerous empires and peoples (most notably and horrifically in the Holocaust) while also having been the ones who did the oppressing and killing of other peoples (from the ancient Canaanites to modern Palestinians).[23]

Still, their tales of resistance and fighting oppression are some of the most inspiring and memorable to this day, and their entire history is filled with such stories. By far, though, the most popular and influential story in Jewish history (and thus the one we'll focus on with our short time here)

---

23   "The Holocaust," History, updated January 25, 2021, https://www.history .com/topics/world-war-ii/the-holocaust; Rivon Krygier, "Did God Command the Extermination of the Canaanites? The Rabbis' Encounter with Genocide," Adath Shalom, accessed April 19, 2020, 1–11, https://www.adathshalom.org /RK/about_the_extermination_of_the_Canaanites.pdf; "Yehoshua – Joshua-Chapter 10," Josh. 10:28–43, *The Complete Jewish Bible*, Chabad.org, Chabad-Lubavitch Media Center, accessed April 19, 2020, https://www.chabad.org /library/bible_cdo/aid/15794/jewish/Chapter-10.htm; "Israel and Occupied Palestinian Territories," Amnesty International, accessed February 5, 2021, https://www.amnesty.org/en/countries/middle-east-and-north-africa/israel -and-occupied-palestinian-territories/.

is the tale of Moses freeing the enslaved Hebrews from Egypt and leading them to the Promised Land in the Levant.

It is still debated among researchers and archaeologists just how much of this epic story that comprises four out of the first five books of the Hebrew Bible (stretching from Exodus to Deuteronomy) actually really happened and how much is hyperbole. Biblical archaeology is always a bit murky since researchers usually have agendas to validate or invalidate. Nevertheless, what's most important is that this underdog story of a people oppressed by the powers that be successfully pulling off a daring escape with the aid of divine phenomena has inspired many other oppressed peoples around the world for millennia.

The full story has many happenings, but the streamlined version is that a Hebrew named Moses grew up in the lap of luxury after having been adopted and raised by ancient Egyptian royalty, but after seeing an enslaved Hebrew being severely beaten, he killed the Egyptian abuser and ran away and hid in the wilderness to escape murder charges. While out on the lam, God appeared to him, instructing him to return to Egypt and free the Hebrews so they could all resettle to the Promised Land in the Levant.

Moses does this, starting off by using his personal connections to directly ask Pharaoh to just let the Hebrews go. Of course, Pharaoh does not consent to releasing an entire free labor source just because an old friend who has been missing for decades after allegedly murdering someone asked him to, and so God steps in and flexes His authority by transforming the water of the Nile into blood. Pharaoh continues to refuse and God unleashes plague after plague, each one more severe than the last, until finally God kills every firstborn son in the land (except for those from Hebrew families who smeared lamb's blood on their doorway, the origins of "Passover" among the Jewish people).

Incidentally, Pharaoh's son dies from this, and, in his grief, he consents to free the Hebrews. However, Pharaoh changes his mind at the last minute and chases down the fleeing Hebrews, but Moses parts the Red Sea as a quick escape route and crashes the waters down upon Pharaoh's pursuing army. The Hebrews are freed, but they are a long way from the Levantine

Promised Land. This is where the story gets a bit more cynical, Moses has a meltdown, and the Hebrews snatch defeat from the jaws of victory.[24]

Mass Exodus II: Crimes and Punishments

This second half of the exodus from Egypt story is the one that is less told, but it holds many lessons on why it's important not to rest on your laurels and to continue the fight until the struggle is *officially* over (as well to never lose faith in the Divine). To put it into context, these former slaves had just witnessed their Egyptian oppressors be cut down by miracle after miracle and were now a free people. All they had to do was keep their faith in the God who performed these miracles (that they witnessed with their own eyes) and endure the long, arduous walk through the desert to the Promised Land, but the people, with their newfound freedom, proved to be their own worst enemy and self-sabotaged their goals while the finish line was in sight.

As the story goes, the people kept on complaining to Moses about all their various problems and discomforts associated with a long march through the desert. This wore Moses down emotionally because not only did he have to lead all these people through a harsh desert, but now he also had to listen to, be the judge of, and arbitrate every single offense, slight, wrongdoing, complaint, and petty accusation that the people had about each other since he was the only one through whom God communicated. So, Moses climbed up Mount Sinai to get advice from God on how to handle these newfound burdens on him. The end result was that God gave Moses a personally engraved set of guidelines (the Ten Commandments and a whole lot of other rules), and hopefully with these divine laws understood and obeyed by everyone, Moses could focus fully on getting them out of the desert.

Well, the problem was that Moses was up on Mount Sinai for forty days. Meanwhile, the people had no idea what was going on. Was he ever

24   "Shemot—Exodus," Exodus 1–14, *The Complete Jewish Bible*, Chabad.org, Chabad-Lubavitch Media Center, accessed April 19, 2020, https://www .chabad.org/library/bible_cdo/aid/9862/jewish/Chapter-1.htm.

coming back? Was he killed up there? Did he run off on his own? All sorts of doubts, worries, and rumors began to circulate, and the general consensus was that Moses would never be back and that God had abandoned them. So, they gave up on the two things that had gotten them this far (God and Moses) and started to worship other deities in the hopes that these new ones would finish leading them to the Promised Land.

When Moses did finally come down to the people, he had a complete meltdown. After all of his hard work, all of his personal suffering, and all of the magical phenomena that went down in Egypt on their behalf, his own people had dropped him like a hot potato. After everything they had seen and experienced, he could not believe that they had so easily and quickly lost faith in him and in God and were now worshiping a pagan calf deity just because it took longer than expected for him to communicate with the Divine (which he only did in the first place because they kept fighting with each other and demanding he solve all their personal problems).

He took this lack of faith in him to heart as extreme disrespect for everything he had done for them. It was the absolute last straw, and Moses went berserk. Giving in to full rage, he smashed the tablets on which the Ten Commandments were engraved and set fire to the newly made golden statue of the people's new god, but his rage did not stop there. Moses then assembled all the people who had stayed true to him and to God and led them on a mass execution spree, murdering every single person who had turned their back on him and on God.

With all opposition annihilated, Moses continued to lead the journey and eventually reached the Promised Land, but in an unexpected twist, they found it already occupied by native peoples with very strong defenses. *Again* the Hebrews gave up faith in Moses and in God, complaining that it had all been for nothing and refusing to go any further. As punishment for yet another mass lack of faith, God declared that this entire generation would have to die before the Promised Land will be given to them. So, Moses had to lead them back into the desert where they wandered endlessly for forty additional years, returning to the Promised Land once the children of the original expedition were now the adults.

The story ends on even more of a tragic note. During the extra forty years of wandering, Moses continuously had to put down internal rebellions and revolts and numerous other problems that the people kept instigating. It all came to a head when, in his frustration, Moses directly disobeyed God on how to manifest drinking water (God told him to speak to the rock from which it would spring, but a frustrated Moses just smashed the magic rock with his staff instead). For this, Moses was forbidden to enter the Promised Land upon their return. And, true to word, Moses led the Hebrews back to the Promised Land, but then personally went no further, handing the reigns of leadership to his successors (who subsequently conquered the native peoples by military force).

For all their efforts, Moses and the original Hebrews who escaped Egypt never arrived in the Promised Land, though they certainly had the opportunity to achieve this. Because of their continuous inter-squabbling and evaporation of faith whenever things became difficult or uncomfortable, their victory march across the desert devolved into a divine death march. Even Moses, their leader through it all, became frustrated with God right at the finish line and so, too, was doomed to never enjoy the fruit for which he spent his entire life laboring.[25]

As we well know, though, the Jewish people's arrival to and conquering of the Promised Land was not a happily-ever-after end to hard times. They would be conquered and reconquered, displaced, victimized, scapegoated, and become the targets of many empires' wrath for a whole host of flimsy reasons. Yet through it all, here they are: resilient, rebuilding, and surviving. Yes, at times the victim becomes the victimizer, and though the complete veracity of a people's religious history may be padded with self-aggrandizing propaganda, one thing's for certain: Jewish history is that of underdogs overcoming oppressors time and time again.

---

25   "Torah—The Pentateuch," Exodus 15–40, Leviticus 1–27, Numbers 1–36, Deuteronomy 1–34, *The Complete Jewish Bible*, Chabad.org, Chabad-Lubavitch Media Center, accessed April 19, 2020, https://www.chabad.org/library /article_cdo/aid/109864/jewish/Classic-Texts.htm.

Jewish Levantine Takeaway:
KEEPING THE FAITH

Faith is such an elusive thing, and yet it's the most important thing every warrior needs in their arsenal. Without faith in yourself, faith that you will win, faith that the Divine is on your side, faith that a better world is possible... how can you persevere through the arduous obligations of battle? If you go into battle not believing that you're going to win, you've already defeated yourself, and if you go into it thinking that the Universe is cosmically against you, then you've defeated yourself in yet another way.

This was the recurring difficulty of the Hebrew people within the extended story of their Exodus from Egypt. They kept losing faith and doubting both themselves and God to be able to get them through to their goal. When things were going well and miracles were manifesting, then their faith was at an all-time high, but when things got hard, that faith just vanished. But that's not faith. Faith is the ability to believe and trust in someone, in yourself, or in the Divine *when* things are tough. Anyone can have faith when things are going well, but true faith is only revealed when things are going poorly.

So, your takeaway challenge here is to keep the faith. Sure, you may *say* that you have full trust in the Universe, in God, in your friend, in your spouse, in your magical abilities, but do you really? Are you contradicting yourself by praying for the same thing or doing the same ritual over and over again out of doubt that the first several times didn't work? Are you always needing your romantic partner to demonstrate how much they care about you because you yourself don't really believe it? Are you surreptitiously scouring through people's phones, diaries, and social media archives to grant credence to your paranoia? You cannot have faith and be doubtful at the same time. Start noticing when you slip into doubt and then remind yourself to have faith, lest you sabotage yourself with your own self-invented distrust and worry.

Deities & Legends

ARCHANGEL MICHAEL

In Jewish scripture, Archangel Michael is one of the few angels mentioned by name, and though he doesn't play as large of a role in official Judaic texts as he would later on in those of Christianity, he does have many magical associations to him in the Jewish mystical tradition of Kabbalah (also spelled Qabalah). Particularly, he is frequently referred to as the "advocate of the Jews" and the angel of mercy and self-control. In fact, so popular were his intercessions and prayers for him to advocate to God on behalf of humans, rabbis and other spiritual Jewish leaders had to keep pleading with people to not use him as their main spiritual intermediary, insisting it was better to commune with the Almighty directly in personal prayer.[26]

In the Kabbalistic cosmos, Michael's position is at the right hand of God, symbolic of him being God's right-hand man. Magically, this also aligns with the tradition's correspondences wherein "right" (as opposed to left) is associated with mercy and kindness. Certain meditational exercises practiced by Kabbalists that are designed to open your heart up to the world and invoke a sense of inner peace regardless of the global calamities around you involve focusing one's mind, attention, and visualization on Archangel Michael.[27]

GEVURAH

Gevurah, in the Jewish mystical tradition of Kabbalah, is the concept of God's strength, usually in reference toward God's furious power in judging humanity on their goodness and wickedness. In technical terms, it is the red-colored fifth sephirah on the Kabbalistic Tree of Life denoting

---

26   Joseph Jacobs, M. Seligsohn, and Mary W. Montgomery, "Michael," *Jewish Encyclopedia*, 1906, http://www.jewishencyclopedia.com/articles/10779 -michael.

27   Rabbi David Cooper, "2193 The Archangel Michael," Rabbi David Cooper, November 8, 2010, https://www.rabbidavidcooper.com/cooper-print-index /2010/11/8/2193-the-archangel-michael.html.

the emotive attributes of creation, and while the magical symbology and significances of Kabbalah get highly detailed and nuanced, the simplified essence of Gevurah is as a counterbalance to *Chesed*, the sephirah of love and kindness.

This isn't to say that Gevurah, therefore, is all about hate and evil—not at all. While the love and kindness as symbolized through Chesed is meant to be boundless and infinite, Gevurah focuses on setting boundaries and placing limits on things. In Jewish mystical thought, certain things (good things) are intended to be unimpeded and unrestrained—things such as love for your neighbor, help toward others, and tolerance of differences. However, mystic Judaism, via the concept of Gevurah, also believes that certain other things have to be stood up to, not tolerated, and need a line to be drawn on where acceptability ends—things such as hate, prejudice, and violence.

On an active level, Gevurah is the practice of discipline and restraint. An outward practice of Gevurah is to judge wicked as wicked and place restraints on it, not to tolerate intolerance or bad behavior. An inward practice is to objectively judge your own wants and desires and call them out for what they are, restraining the ones that would negatively affect yourself and others even if you personally want and desire them.[28]

MITHRA

Mithra is the Zoroastrian deity of light, pastures, gift-giving, contracts, agreements, and oaths. Among the pantheon of divine figures in Zoroastrianism, Mithra is especially exalted because he is the principal assistant of *Ahura Mazda* (the highest supreme deity) as his chief defender of truth

---

28   Rabbi Shimon Leiberman, "Kabbalah #11: Gevurah: The Strength of Judgment," Aish.com, accessed April 20, 2020, https://www.aish.com/sp/k /Kabbala_11_Gevurah_The_Strength_of_Judgment.html; Alan Morinis, "Path of the Soul #8: Strength of a Hero," Aish.com, accessed August 5, 2021, https://www.aish.com/sp/pg/48909227.html.

and goodness in the universe (often allied by *Sraosha* and *Rashnu*, divinities of Obedience and Justice, respectively).[29]

Rightness of action was the main focus of Mithra's attention in regard to humans. He was the supernatural force that made sure you always kept your word, lived up to your promises, and chose the path of morality should you come to a decisional crossroads. Because of this, Mithra was beloved by the poor and served as an equal-opportunity arbitrator who judged merit based on actions, not status or wealth. If you freely entered into an agreement with someone, then Mithra would judge you based only on your fulfillment of the agreement in which you freely entered, not upon outside circumstances beyond your control.[30]

Later on in Roman times, Mithra would be adopted into the Roman pantheon as "Mithras" and become the center cult figure of a mystery school among the Roman military (especially the legionaries) called the Mithraic Mysteries. Nowadays, there is not much conclusive evidence of what was involved in the Mithraic Mysteries (because the initiates were very good at keeping their mysteries, well…a mystery), so the exact specifics aren't known, but it is generally believed that Mithras gained popularity among Roman soldiers from their battles with the pirates in the Levant who were particularly devoted to Mithra—wartime interactions that then spread his worship to the rest of the Roman army.[31]

VERETHRAGNA

In ancient Persian mythology, Verethragna (also called Bahrām) was the deity of victory and of smiting resistance. Though technically a neuter name in the original Avestan language of early Iran (and therefore gender-

29   Martin Luther King, Jr., "A Study of Mithraism," *The Papers of Martin Luther King, Jr. Volume I: Called to Serve, January 1929–June 1951* (Berkeley: University of California Press, 1992), 211–225, https://kinginstitute.stanford.edu/king -papers/documents/study-mithraism.

30   "Mitra, Mithra, Mithras Mystery," The Iranian, in D. Jason Cooper, *Mithras: Mysteries and Initiation Rediscovered* (Newburyport: Red Wheel/Weiser, 1996), 1–8, September 11, 1997, https://iranian.com/1997/09/11/mithra/.

31   Joshua J. Mark, "Mithra," World History Encyclopedia, February 11, 2020, https://www.worldhistory.org/Mithra/.

less), Verethragna is often depicted as a male (because patriarchy of ancient times and whatnot). They were seen as a warrior deity, super aggressive, and always victorious in the fight against evil and against whatever was trying to resist them.

In modern Zoroastrianism, however, Verethragna has lost many of their associations with militarism and battle; instead, they are more closely aligned with intellectual and moral victories as opposed to physical ones. Devotees of theirs are believed to be favored in the pursuit of victory through persuasive rhetoric (such as arguments, judicial hearings, or any other scenario in which the goal is to convince or persuade others).[32]

32   G. Gnoli and P. Jamzadeh, "BAHRĀM (Vərəθrayna)," Encyclopedia Iranica, updated August 24, 2011, http://www.iranicaonline.org/articles/bahram-1.

3

THE ISLAMIC CALIPHATES

Cultural

The Price of Power

By the time the Prophet Muhammad was born around 570 CE, almost all the other well-known "big" organized religions that survive today were already well established with large followings (Hinduism, Judaism, Buddhism, Taoism, Confucianism, Christianity, etc.). Still, against the odds, this then-obscure Islamic faith from the deserts of Arabia has become, in our time, one of the most popular and geographically expansive world religions.

So, how did this happen? Yes, brute military conquest got the ball rolling, but to form a devotedly lasting faith that would stand the test of time among various cultures and peoples throughout the rise and fall of various empires takes more than the point of a sword. No, a new kind of battle tactic had to be perfected, a less direct one that still exists today: economic warfare in the name of religion.

Let's face it, money makes the world go 'round and it bestows power on those who have it. Even if your rivals have a more powerful force than yours, having more money can easily allow you to endure a more drawn-out conflict, entice enemies to switch to your side, and arm your troops with the latest and most technologically advanced weapons you can buy or fund to research. In the middle of the first millennium CE, the leaders of Islam figured this out and found that hitting people economically in their wallets could be just as (if not *more*) effective in getting people to convert than hitting them physically on their bodies.

Taxing Situations

To prevent rebellion and revolts (in addition to gaining converts), the Islamic Caliphates took a page from Cyrus the Great's strategy guide and treated their conquered subjects with humanity, respect, and a level of self-rule.

Rare for any empire anywhere in history, neither your national origin nor your skin color really mattered. Of course, this was by no means an all-peoples-are-equal utopia, and much sexist and racial prejudice did exist, but in the Caliphates, it was the religion to which you adhered that was your most important demographic feature. Therefore, if you wanted to move up in society and climb the ladder of success, you had to be a Muslim. Because of this, many of the most ambitious and driven people in the empire voluntarily converted to Islam as well as many of the downtrodden and oppressed whose Islamic conversions allowed them to finally attain a level of social respect and influence.[33]

33   John D. Szostak, "The Spread of Islam Along the Silk Route," University of Washington, July 29, 2002, https://depts.washington.edu/silkroad/exhibit/religion/islam/essay.html.

To compound this incentive for their subjects to convert to Islam of their own will (even though the converts' intentions were probably insincere), the rulers of the Islamic Caliphates not only offered economic and social-climbing incentives, they also employed economic punishments for not being a Muslim in their empires.

This was done primarily through taxes. Maybe you didn't aspire to great power and just wanted to live a simple kind of life, but even with this absence of ambition, you were still financially better off if you converted to Islam. Non-Muslims in the empire were often subjected to higher taxes. So, just to avoid paying more in taxes, many people converted to Islam.

It should be said, though, that most people did not convert and just settled for paying higher taxes and being restricted from elite positions in society, instead choosing to keep their traditional faith. This was allowed because it benefitted the ruling Muslim elite to not have the entire population convert to Islam since that would mean less tax revenue and more competition for positions of power. Nonetheless, it was still quite effective and pioneered an early form of minority upliftment and passive religious warfare fought through economics.[34]

Brain Drain

It's important to remember that until Europeans began their "Age of Exploration" in the fifteenth century, the Islamic Caliphates were at the center of the world's global trade network between Africa, Europe, India, and East Asia. Practically all intercontinental trade in the world passed through here, as well as all the intangible aspects of the known world, which included various cultures, languages, ideas, religions, points of view, spiritual traditions, and scientific thoughts. Rather than take up

---

34 Eman M. Elshaikh, "The Rise of Islamic Empires and States," Khan Academy, accessed April 21, 2020, https://www.khanacademy.org/humanities/world -history/medieval-times/spread-of-islam/a/the-rise-of-islamic-empires-and -states; Christian C. Sahner, "How Did the Christian Middle East Become Predominantly Muslim?" University of Oxford, September 17, 2018, http:// www.ox.ac.uk/news/arts-blog/how-did-christian-middle-east-become -predominantly-muslim.

arms against all of these potential "threats" to traditional Muslim rule and worldview, the Caliphates' Islamic faith encouraged them to embrace this diversity.

Knowledge is power, and so by combining the intellect of all the known world's greatest civilizations who were passing through their territory, Islamic empires became very powerful, especially in a relatively less tolerant time when neighboring Christianity allowed no other opinionative thought that even slightly disagreed with Christian worldview. Compounding this, Europe had collapsed into the Dark Ages, and China was still far enough away geographically to not be too regionally influential. This left the Islamic Caliphates as some of the smartest, most advanced, and open-minded cultures around at the time (stretching from modern Spain to the western edges of India). By not dismissing a person's ideas based off of their skin color, national origin, religious faith, or any other prejudiced determiner, these empires of Islam were able to benefit from the best of human innovation and ingenuity.

They also became a magnet of sorts for the most intelligent and ambitious people of other empires who sought to escape from being persecuted and limited in their homelands. Thus, the brain drain had begun, and the Caliphates' progressive social acceptance attracted the world's best and brightest (which consequently left other empires less competent and less capable of internal administration since all the smarter and most qualified people were emigrating to the empires of the Caliphates, thus making the Caliphates' gains against their rivals that much more exponential).[35]

Conservative Chokehold

Usually, the biggest test of any empire is how they handle transitions of power. Whether it be from president to president, from dynasty to dynasty,

---

35 Department of the Arts of Africa, Oceania, and the Americas, "Trade and the Spread of Islam in Africa," in *Heilbrunn Timeline of Art History* (New York: The Metropolitan Museum of Art, 2000), https://www.metmuseum.org/toah/hd /tsis/hd_tsis.htm; "The Spread of Islam," Khan Academy, February 16, 2017, https://www.khanacademy.org/humanities/world-history/medieval-times /spread-of-islam/v/spread-of-islam.

or even from a monarchy to a republic, these periods of internal change are vulnerable times. In the case of the Islamic Caliphates, the transitions of power became more and more illegitimate as time went on, and the leaders began embracing a more socially conservative rule so as to stamp out public dissent of their new ill-gotten regimes.

Though these new, more conservative Caliphate rulers did understand that the strength of their empires was sustained by their diversity and tolerance of different religions and ethnicities, they were more concerned about their personal welfare than that of their empire at large. They embraced conservative values more and more because they needed more and more absolute authority to combat growing internal political divisions that sprung from their dubious legitimacies to the throne.

During the twelfth century CE, blind faith and religious orthodoxy began to supersede reason and scientific inquiry within the Caliphates, and so the persecution of non-Muslims grew. This led many of the non-Muslim thinkers, philosophers, businesspeople, and scientists to flee in a reverse brain drain. As a result of this, less-learned and less-qualified people came to fill the positions of power and leadership left vacant by emigration.

Corruption, financial mismanagement, military losses, and poor decision-making quickly ensued, leaving the Caliphates a shadow of their former glory. Islamic Arabia's golden age officially ended in 1258 CE when the Mongol Empire delivered the killing blow by conquering Baghdad and running the Tigris River black from the ink of all the Islamic books of knowledge thrown into it, lost forever to history.[36]

---

36   Don Liebich, "What Can the Islamic Golden Age Teach Us About Migration and Diversity?" Boise State University, accessed April 22, 2020, https://www .boisestate.edu/sps-frankchurchinstitute/publications/essays/can-islamic -golden-age-teach-us-migration-diversity/; Glenn McDonald, "The Rise and Fall of Islam's Golden Age," Seeker, September 4, 2016, https://www.seeker .com/the-rise-and-fall-of-islams-golden-age-1997288472.html.

Islamic Takeaway:
HIT 'EM IN THE WALLET

Even more effective than physical assaults, attacks upon a person or group's finances are some of the most devastating tactics a warrior can pursue, and this fact is just as true today as it was during the Islamic Caliphates. Think back to all the peaceful, nonviolent revolutions that are held up as models of integrity and "high-road" rebellion. Their success was not because a bunch of people got together and took a moral stand, convincing the powers that be to just do the right thing. No, they were successful because they were economic attacks against their oppressors, causing their enemies to suffer financially.

Gandhi's nonviolent resistance in India centered on Indians manufacturing their own goods and necessities so that they weren't reliant upon British products and so that Britain's economic profitability in India would grind to a deficit, thus economically forcing them to leave. Martin Luther King, Jr.'s civil rights revolution was catalyzed by boycotts and sit-ins against products, industries, and businesses that chose to align with the oppressors and discriminate against people of color.

The same things go on today. A company, a presidency, an institution only changes if it is economically advantageous for them to do so. Back when LGBTQ+ rights were "controversial," most companies and politicians didn't want to say anything lest they upset potential customers, donors, or voters, but once it became economically and politically beneficial to "be on the right side of history," only then did public figures sign petitions in favor of queer rights to the Supreme Court, companies produce "queer-focused" products, and left-wing presidents "evolve" on their personal opinions of the queer community. Is it all insincere? Absolutely! But the point is that beneficial change for the queer community only came about when it did because it was now economically and politically advantageous for the powers that be to grow a pair of morals and ethics.

So, your takeaway challenge here is to start enacting revolution through your wallet. Your purse is just as powerful as your fist and your vote. If a company or public personality is involved with hate groups or refuses to take a stand against injustice, do not support them with your money. You don't have to publicly attack them; you can simply let them wither into bankrupt obscurity by not giving them your money or your time. Money is power, and to those whom you give money, you also give power.

Magically, money is also the most immediate and effective tool you have. You want to manifest anything in your life, manipulate people to do your bidding, or help (dis)empower others? Money can make it all happen. You can literally force your will upon a person or entity if you throw enough money at (or withhold enough from) them. So, start treating money like the powerful, magical weapon it really is, and use it to bolster the good and punish the wicked.

Deities & Legends

AL-LĀT

In pre-Islamic Arabia, al-Lāt was the warrior goddess of the military and of love, and as worship of her spread, she also became associated with solitude and mercy as well as vengeance and the looted spoils of war.[37]

Devotion to her was so strong in Arabia during the early days of Islam that the nascent monotheistic faith tried to incorporate her into Islam so as to more easily convert her pagan followers. In doing so, she was reinterpreted to be the daughter of Allah, and in some legends, the consort of Allah. However, the Prophet Muhammad later changed his mind and decided to no longer placate the pagan Arabs by twisting Islam to become more compatible with their beliefs, thus disavowing al-Lāt in the process.[38]

---

37   Osama Shukir Muhammed Amin, "Goddess Al-Lat and an Elderly God from Hatra," World History Encyclopedia, June 4, 2019, https://www.worldhistory .org/image/10861/goddess-al-lat-and-an-elderly-god-from-hatra/; Robert G. Hoyland, *Arabia and the Arabs: From the Bronze Age to the Coming of Islam* (New York: Routledge, 2001), n.p.

38   "Al-Lāt," Encyclopedia Britannica, July 20, 1998, https://www.britannica.com /topic/al-Lat.

Still, in his quest to spread Islam and suppress al-Lāt's deep follow-ing, the Prophet Muhammad specifically called for the destruction of her temples and statues, which were widely eradicated during his lifetime. Later on, his previous approval of al-Lāt was written off in legend as the "Satanic verses" incident wherein he was tricked by Satan into supporting her (though modern Muslims do not give credence to this incident due to Islam's teachings about how the Prophet is theologically immune to demonic trickery).[39]

ARCHANGEL JIBRĀ'ĪL

Archangel Jibrā'īl (better known to the non-Arabic world as the Arch-angel Gabriel) is one of Allah's supreme and most important angels. In Judaism, Christianity, and Islam, he primarily plays the role of God/Allah's messenger to the prophets, revealing divine decrees and import-ant new information humanity must know. Some of his most memorable revelations include interpreting the visions of Daniel from his eponymous book in the Hebrew Bible, announcing to the Virgin Mary that she was to become miraculously pregnant, and revealing the Qur'an to the Prophet Muhammad for him to write down and from which to establish Islam.

Regarding Islam in particular, Archangel Jibrā'īl is regarded as a military leader and the Prophet Muhammad's main mentor in both spirituality and warfare. In addition to being the angel who smote Sodom and Gomorrah (according to Islamic texts), he aided Muhammad's military campaigns throughout Arabia, most especially at the all-important Battle of Badr wherein the Prophet won a decisive victory against the military forces of pagan Arabs thanks to Archangel Jibrā'īl's participation in personally lead-ing thousands of angel soldiers in the fight as allies (though non-Muslims give the credit of Muhammad's stunning victory to his own ahead-of-his-

---

39   Abū Ja'far Muḥammad ibn Jarīr al-Ṭabarī , *The History of al-Tabari, vol. 9: The Last Years of the Prophet*, trans. Ismail K. Poonawala (Albany: State University of New York Press, 1990), n.p.

time advanced knowledge of guerrilla warfare, insurgency tactics, and use of intelligence-gathering).[40]

JIHAD

In our modern world, "jihad" has become a loaded word. To many non-Muslims, the mentioning of "jihad" conjures up warped and deep-rooted fears of terrorist organizations and a holy war of grisly violence by Muslims against all non-Muslims. Conversely, some Muslims (with only a superficial understanding of their own faith and a dangerous devotion to firebrand leaders) interpret it as a sort of mafia-esque kiss of death, a declaration of sanctified and justified fatal violence against another person or entity. But what is a jihad *really*? To understand Islam and shed preconceived prejudices of it as a war-hawk religion, jihad is an important concept to comprehend correctly.

In official Islamic belief, "jihad" essentially means "struggle/striving"—as in, the internal struggle of self-improvement, the struggle to build a better society, and, yes, the struggle to defend Islam (with force, if necessary). Essentially, it is the struggle of goodness against wickedness in every form imaginable (and naturally, the leader deciding what is good and what is wicked sets the rules for all those who follow them).[41]

Jihad is divided into two categories: the "Greater Jihad," or the inward struggle of ever striving to become a better person, and the "Lesser Jihad," or the outward struggle of combatting and defending good people from the forces of oppression and injustice (though controversy exists among different denominations of Islam as to whether or not the Prophet Muhammad

---

40   Christine Huda Dodge, "Angel Jibreel (Gabriel) in Islam," Learn Religions, February 5, 2018, https://www.learnreligions.com/angel-jibreel-gabriel-in-islam-2004031; "Jibrīl," Encyclopedia Britannica, updated May 4, 2020, https://www.britannica.com/topic/Jibril; Richard A. Gabriel, *Muhammad: Islam's First Great General* (Norman, OK: University of Oklahoma Press, 2007), 86–107.

41   Alexandra Poolos, "World: The True Meaning of the Islamic Term 'Jihad,'" Radio Free Europe/Radio Liberty, September 20, 2001, https://www.rferl.org/a/1097473.html.

himself made these categorizations). As the hierarchy implies, the Greater Jihad of self-improvement is the most important while the Lesser Jihad of active defense is secondary.[42]

This "Lesser" one is the one that has become problematic. In the Qur'an, Allah sanctioned warlike violence so that the early Muslims (who were living in a violent era of history) could justifiably defend themselves from people who were literally trying to kill them because they were a minority religion. Even so, physical violence was (and still is) seen as a last resort only if all other options have been exhausted.[43]

Should it come down to violence being absolutely necessary and the only option left remaining, participating in the Lesser Jihad has strict rules of engagement, many of which coincide with the twentieth-century edicts of the Geneva Convention. These rules include not harming noncombatants; not being the aggressor; prohibitions against harming women, children, and the elderly; just treatment of prisoners of war; no poisoning of wells (which would be the then-equivalent to modern chemical warfare); ceasing all violence as soon as the enemy surrenders; and so on.[44]

Though a jihad technically can mean Allah-endorsed violence, it's strictly relegated for self-defense when no other option is available and heavily regulated as to when and to how far a person can exert such violence. Sadly, though, what can be classified as "self-defense" is as endless as our ability to do the mental gymnastics necessary for self-justification. Pretending to play the victim is a powerful weapon, and many people,

---

42   "What is the Truth About American Muslims?" Interfaith Alliance and Religious Freedom Project of the First Amendment Center, accessed April 26, 2020, https://www.tolerance.org/sites/default/files/2017-06/What_is_the _Truth_About_American_Muslims.pdf.

43   Brian Handwerk, "What does 'Jihad' Really Mean to Muslims?" *National Geographic*, October 24, 2003, https://www.nationalgeographic.com/news /2003/10/what-does-jihad-really-mean-to-muslims/.

44   "Jihad," BBC, updated August 3, 2009, https://www.bbc.co.uk/religion /religions/islam/beliefs/jihad_1.shtml.

nations, and faiths have endorsed violence under the dishonest pretext of being "attacked" first. Like anything, victimhood and justification are all a matter of what you believe and what you can convince others to believe ... not necessarily what is true.

4

GREATER MIDDLE EASTERN MAGICAL COMMUNITY

SUMERIAN STRENGTH & EMPATHY

For our first guest warrior here in the Greater Middle East, I've invited Markus Ironwood to recount his personal experience on the battlefields of life. To get a general sense of this warrior whom I met while on a book tour in Minnesota, the best way I can describe him to you would be as a gay, coffee-fueled, witch astrologer with a drag queen alter-ego by the name of "Swamp Witch Stephanie" (who is also a purveyor of natural anointing oils and self-care products if you check her out on Instagram @swampwitchstephanie or even on Markus's own non-drag account @markusironwood). However, I know him best as a fierce devotee of Sumerian goddesses.

The reason I've asked him here is so that he can share with you how his dual devotion to the strength of Inanna and to the radical empathy that was shown to Ereshkigal not only aided him in social activism but also in his own personal battles with his family. The gods of ancient times are still around, and they're willing to help us if we're willing to ask them for it.

Inanna is the Sumerian Goddess of Love, War, and Justice. She was the Queen of Heaven and Earth. She was also my mythic guide through much of my undergraduate years. Her story is one of facing the darkness of the past and expressing radical empathy. As a student in the Women's Studies program at the University of Minnesota, Duluth, we were confronting our own systemic oppression while academically and politically engaging with the struggles of the world at large. Inanna helped me find my own courage to face the horrors of patriarchy and find strength in empathizing with others.

Working with Inanna was a private affair. I found comfort and strength in lighting a small candle before a framed image of her. I would offer water from a stream that ran by campus to her and other spirits, a practice I still keep to this day. Sitting in meditation, I would ask for understanding, for justice to be upheld, and to be able to bear witness to the all that was asked of me. Watching people get brutalized by their governments for their race, class, or gender takes a deep emotional toll. It was my spirituality and the fellowship I found in the community that fueled my strength in continuing my education, participating in protests, and regularly speaking with legislators.

Beyond the strength of Inanna was the radical empathy shown to Ereshkigal. In the underworld, Ereshkigal was Inanna's sister and was treated with great compassion by two genderless spirits. In the throes of imprisonment, they cried when she cried and screamed when she screamed. They were with her in her pain. Being one of the oldest stories we have on record, this is a clear example of how we are capable of truly "feeling-with" another person. When we see each other suffering, we are able to be there with and help another person through their suffering. This touched me deeply seeing the oppression, pain, and suffering of women and the environment on the daily. We are able to help others heal.

I'm not always good at showing empathy, though. I can be critical or judgmental. It's a character trait I've worked on for most of my life. My relationship with my brother has been contentious for most of my life. There was a very long period of time when he wanted to join the U.S. military. While I want to support my family in their choice of career, I've studied the industrial military complex and know it to be a sexist, colonizing, and capitalistic system. It was very hard to support my brother in this choice. It made me so mad that he couldn't see the army for the system I knew it to be. I couldn't understand why anyone would want to support it, let alone be a part of it. I had some very deep soul searching to do and many times wrestled with myself.

I wasn't always kind with my words, as he wasn't always kind. It took a long time, years after working with myths of Inanna and Ereshkigal that I had to radically accept my brother. I had to show my brother the support and empathy that I would want to be shown. I talked with family members about this, and I brought it to my altar. I couldn't move on with my relationship with my brother unless I let him go just as Ereshkigal had to let Inanna go, even if the wounds felt so deeply personal. I'm happy to say that even though my brother and I still don't agree on many things, our relationship these days is the best it's been in our entire lives.

I still strive for Inanna's courage and power and for being able to exemplify the same empathy that was shown to Ereshkigal.

—Markus Ironwood

WHO BY FIRE?

For our next guest, I've brought along one of the most passionate eco-warriors I know, David Freedman. When I first met him in Palm Springs, California (where he has written many of the city's energy, renewable energy, and water conservation policies while on the city's Sustainability Commission), his passion for the environment and the natural world around us was immediately evident. The encyclopedic intelligence with which he spoke about these subjects really left me quite impressed (I later learned he had a 30-year career as a corporate lawyer in New York and Paris before retiring in Palm Springs, explaining his acumen in rhetoric).

The reason David is the perfect person to give us advice on our global trek here is because he credits his Jewish faith as the source of his environmental activism. When I approached him in the infamous summer of 2020 to share with us about being a Jewish eco-warrior, he said that he just had to write about the unprecedented wildfires that were raging at that time all throughout California. As you'll see, Judaism places great emphasis on protecting the natural world, and David's encyclopedic knowledge of Jewish Scripture will help us understand this connection a bit better.

"Mi ba-esh—Who by Fire?" These words in Leonard Cohen's song come from the Jewish high holidays prayer U-Netaneh Tokef, listing the fates of life and death that may await us in the new year. These words take on a deeper and darker meaning during 2020 Labor Day weekend in California, as wildfires scorch the state amid yet another record-breaking heatwave. During the high holidays and the month of Elul preceding them, Jews are called upon to engage in teshuvah, which U-Netaneh Tokef tells us is one of the ways to transcend the harshness of our future. Teshuvah is usually translated as "repentance," but the literal meaning is "return," to the right path. My teshuvah this holiday season is to research and advocate for energy policies that will return us to a path of environmental sustainability and avert the harsh future of a state continuously on fire.

Jewish texts rooted in the commandment to pursue justice in Deuteronomy 16:20 and the principle of tikkun olam, or "repairing the world," provide a strong foundation for my environmental activism. Rosh HaShanah, the Jewish New Year, is called the birthday of the world, so my path of return first takes me to the story of the world's creation and the original model of environmental sustainability—the Garden of Eden. We learn in Genesis 2:15 that God places Adam in the Garden of Eden to till and tend it. That verse recalls the stirring music Leonard Bernstein wrote for the end of his operetta Candide reminding us of our duty to "Make Our Garden Grow." In Kohelet Rabbah 7:13, a rabbinic interpretation (midrash) of the creation story, God tells Adam: "Take great care that you do not damage and destroy My world, for if you do there is no one else to put right what you have destroyed." And, as we saw in recent climate protest signs, there is no Planet B.

Other Biblical verses demonstrate a reverence for the environment. Deuteronomy 20:19–20 *forbid cutting down fruit trees when besieging a city, leading the rabbis to establish a general prohibition of needless destruction known as* bal tashchit. *The modern concept of the circular economy, which focuses on reusing, recycling, and repurposing products instead of throwing them away, fits well within this principle of* bal tashchit. Leviticus Chapter 25 *sets out the rules for the land to have its own sabbath, a year of complete rest for it every seven years. Work in the fields is also forbidden in the jubilee every 50 years, a celebration remembered in American history through the excerpt from* Leviticus 25:10 *inscribed on the Liberty Bell in Philadelphia: "Proclaim Liberty throughout all the land unto all the inhabitants thereof."* Leviticus 25:23 *and* Psalm 24:1 *remind us that the land is the Lord's. As in the Garden of Eden, we are its caretakers.*

As the smoke and fires rage nearby and throughout California and countless trees go up in flames, I am reminded of the conclusion of the Torah service when we chant Proverbs 3:18 *comparing the Torah to the Tree of Life, which* Genesis 2:9 *places in the middle of the Garden of Eden. In* Deuteronomy 30:19, *which we read in this week's Torah portion in anticipation of* Rosh HaShanah, *Moses tells the Israelites assembled before him that he has put before them life and death, blessing and curse, and he exhorts them to choose life. The* U-Netaneh Tokef *prayer offers us a similar choice between life and death, blessing and curse. In devoting my retirement years to protecting our environment and speaking for the trees, I, too, choose life.*

—David Freedman *(17 Elul 5780)*

PRE-ISLAMIC MAGIC DURING THE PANDEMIC

Rounding out or guest warriors here in the Greater Middle East is Bader Saab, an Arabic witch, journalist, and columnist who has a Master's degree in Digital Research and writes a pre-Islamic folklore blog called *A*

Modern Day Sha'ir on Patheos Pagan. I met him through the circuits and junkets of promoting one of my previous books, and it was his journalistic side as a book reviewer that led to us meeting, which then led to a fascinating friendship.

The reason I've asked him to meet us here is because of his unique personal experience of growing up in a conservative Arabic family while becoming fascinated by and allying with the pagan pre-Islamic goddesses of Arabia on his personal journey to becoming a witch. So, I'll bow out now for a bit and let Bader tell you about being a warrior for his own pre-Islamic Arabian goddesses amidst the global COVID-19 pandemic that shut down the world and struck someone close to him.

Although I come from a traditional, conservative Arabic family, I was taught basically nothing about religion and beliefs, which made me want to learn about the first faith that caught my attention: NeoPaganism. However, there was always something lacking, until I started reading about pre-Islamic folklore. When I discovered the three daughters of Allah and the role of the Sha'ir, it all clicked. A "Sha'ir" is basically a priest who was believed to work with the Gods and the jinn (spirits of place, fire, and wilderness). They also used poetry for magic, inspiring their tribe during wars and making fun of their enemies.

With so much information missing, I've had to read as much as I could before trying anything. Mostly I read about Allah's daughters: Al-'Uzza, Al-Lat, and Manat. They are said to watch over humanity after Their father decided to stand back following the creation of all that exists, including His daughters, who also work under His permission. He's still watching. Nothing happens without His permission, but His daughters have the active role.

I find dark deities and their myths more appealing, so I naturally favored Manat first, the oldest sister, the pre-Islamic Goddess of time, fate, and death, but when my mother became ill during the COVID-19 pandemic, I had several reasons to fear. Despite her being a very healthy person by not using much oil or salt, avoiding foods with preservatives, exercising daily, and always choosing natural ingredients, the sickness left her unable to leave her bed. Not a chance would I let the virus win. So I asked Al-'Uzza for help. She's the youngest sister, the Goddess of war, protection, and healing, also named al-Zahra, the planet Venus (though that's not always so). Coincidentally, my mother's severe sickness came on a Thursday, so I decided to wait until Friday and act on the hour of Venus.

That Thursday night, however, I prayed to my ancestors in front of my family tree. With my hands and my mother's name written down, I asked them to protect her and be with her, that nothing and no one harm her, and to keep our home safe. I focused only on that as I breathed deeply, until I saw and felt golden and black sand falling on me, running through my arms, and finally onto my mother's name. I also felt my family behind me, attentive and supportive, which made me shiver more than once. I remained like that until the images stopped and then went to bed.

I did the heavy work on Friday. With a pencil, I wrote my mother's full name in Arabic at the bottom of a piece of paper, and Al-'Uzza's at the top. When the right time came, I lit a white candle, and prayed to the Goddess intuitively in verse and Arabic as I marked Their names with a golden crayon and made a circle with dried rose petals that touched Their names. Again, I prayed for my mother and home to be protected, healthy, and safe.

At the center of the circle, I put a single petal topped by a rose quartz, and with my hands on both sides of the paper, I visualized pink energy coming from my hands, all while still praying to Al-'Uzza in my limited Arabic. I went to bed when I felt it was enough and left it all like that until next morning. Surprise. Mom felt better enough to work from home, cook, and exercise. I knew Al-'Uzza had listened, and so I thanked Her that night. While I don't give all the credit to magic and religion, Mom was suddenly feeling better after the rituals, so I must have done something right.

—Bader Saab

PART 2

SUB-SAHARAN AFRICA & LANDS OF THE AFRICAN DIASPORA

Peace is costly, but it is worth the expense.
KENYAN PROVERB

5

SUB-SAHARAN AFRICA

Cultural

Divided We Fall

When looking at the mysticism of war and social justice struggles in Sub-Saharan Africa, it's important to remember that human conflict was not something suddenly introduced here when Christian Europeans first started arriving. No, war is a very human trait. Our tendency to self-divide among tribe/color/faith and any other demographic we can justify to ourselves and others is as old as us. A utopian *Lost Horizon* culture living in its own self-isolated Shangri-La of never-ending peace is a nice fantasy, but it has always been just that throughout all of human history the world over…a fantasy.

So, even before Christian Europe began setting its sights on Sub-Saharan Africa and unquestionably making things more horrific, the countless native peoples here had already been at war with each other for a long, long time. What made matters worse for Sub-Saharan Africa (and a military advantage colonizers and politicians have exploited here into the present) is that the native peoples did not stop fighting amongst each other once the new and more militarily powerful enemy of Europe entered the game.

In an ideal situation (and one often romanticized in works of fiction), the bickering indigenous peoples of a land, as underdogs to a looming foreign threat, would recognize that they needed to put aside their differences and unite together to fight this more powerful foe. Individually, each tribe stood absolutely no chance at winning, but if they all joined together and teamed up in arms, then they stood at least a chance. Sadly, this never really happened here. Not only did many of the native peoples of Sub-Saharan Africa continue to fight their own wars with each other, but some of them even sided with the colonizers as a way to snuff out their centuries-old local rivals. World history could've been quite different, but because oppressed and targeted peoples could not put aside their own religious and cultural differences, history turned out as it did.[45]

Fight Like a Woman

In the Dahomey Kingdom of West Africa (in what is now Benin), the religious beliefs of the native people allowed a unique military force to emerge and give France all hell in her attempt to colonize them. This was a highly elite, highly deadly special forces cadre of all-women warriors whom the Europeans regarded as equivalent to the legendary Amazons, earning the Dahomey Kingdom the nickname of "Black Sparta." These

---

45   Benjamin Talton, "African Resistance to Colonial Rule," African Age, 2011,
      http://exhibitions.nypl.org/africanaage/essay-resistance.html.

fierce female fighters would later be immortalized in Marvel Comics' *Black Panther* franchise as the "Dora Milaje" on page and on screen.[46]

In many ancient conflicts around the world, having women warriors was not all that uncommon. Once civilization and urban settlements around agriculture started becoming predominant, though, the patriarchal male "superiority" over females started entrenching itself around the world. However, sexist ideas like the inherent weakness of women and the need to protect them as one would a valuable piece of property (because women were often seen as no more than property) did not exist here. You see, in the Dahomeys' native religion of Vodun (native African predecessor of Vodou/Voodoo in the Americas), it was understood that both male and female were created equal in power, stemming from the creation myth wherein a supreme male deity and supreme female deity needed to come together and use both of their powers to create the universe.[47]

With a spiritual outlook promoting gender equality, women were specifically sought after as the ideal warriors for the kings and queens of Dahomey. Only women could be allowed in the palace after dark (out of the fear kings had that their male soldiers would try to usurp the throne by killing them in their sleep), and there were already elite all-women hunting groups called *gbeto* from whom to conscript for the royal guard.

Eventually adding to the high ratio of women in the military was the imbalance of a lot more women to men in the kingdom due to strong males being prized in the slave trade and spirited away to the Americas more often than females. Also, more women readily volunteered to be

46   Fleur Macdonald, "The Legend of Benin's Fearless Female Warriors," BBC, August 27, 2018, http://www.bbc.com/travel/story/20180826-the-legend-of -benins-fearless-female-warriors.

47   Zama Mdoda, "WHM: Dahomey Amazons Were Bad-Ass African Warriors," AfroPunk, March 8, 2019, https://afropunk.com/2019/03/dahomey-amazons -african-warriors/.

warriors anyway since the job also came with the coveted side perks of free alcohol, tobacco, and their own personal slaves.[48]

When the French came to colonize West Africa, they had a hard time subduing the Dahomey Kingdom thanks to these female warriors. Not only were French soldiers not expecting (and therefore unprepared) that these women would fight so viciously and be so skilled in war, but a lot of them also could not bring themselves to harm or kill women—chivalric sympathy that the female fighters tactically exploited to their advantage. After losing too many battles, though, the French Foreign Legion supplied their soldiers with a large enough force to adequately address the situation, and in 1894, the Dahomey Kingdom was finally conquered and added to colonial French West Africa.[49]

Like Water for Bullets

One of the surviving magical tactics of war that tribes in Zimbabwe and the Congo have utilized against their enemies since Neolithic times is the use of a revered potion believed to make a person invulnerable to enemies' projectile weapons by magically transforming the incoming weapons into harmless water. Called *dawa* by peoples of the Congo, it is a concoction made from the sap of several different specific vines that was poured over a warrior who then received a ritualistic sealing of the energy with magical symbols drawn on the forehead before they entered battle.

This and similar potions had been part of Central and Southern African warrior culture for millennia against arrows and javelins, and so when guns were introduced, it was believed that those who had been anointed

48   David Geggus, "Sex Ratio, Age and Ethnicity in the Atlantic Slave Trade: Data from French Shipping and Plantation Records," *The Journal of African History* 30, no. 1 (March 1989): 23–44, https://doi.org/10.1017/S0021853700030863; Mike Dash, "Dahomey's Women Warriors," *Smithsonian Magazine*, September 23, 2011, https://www.smithsonianmag.com/history/dahomeys-women -warriors-88286072/.

49   Ruslan Budnik, "Dahomey Amazons—The Only Elite All-Female Warrior Regiments," War History Online, October 10, 2018, https://www .warhistoryonline.com/instant-articles/dahomey-amazons.html.

by this potion would have all bullets also turn into water upon impacting their body since guns fell into the category of projectile weapons.

Of course, European bullets never did transform into water, and despite the fact that the warriors who had used this potion were dying from bullet wounds, the belief in this magic was so engrained in these cultures from millennia of use that it was believed the human, not the potion, had failed. Usually, the dead were blamed for committing a taboo that broke the spell's effectiveness. Specifically, these taboos were: eating, having sex, or feeling fear. So, when a bullet did not turn into water upon impact, it was assumed the dead warrior must've done one of those three taboo things after having been ritualistically anointed by the potion, not that the magic potion had been ineffective.

Even in the mid-1960s when Che Guevara traveled to the Congo to help the native peoples in armed resistance against European and American-backed right-wing military takeovers of their homelands, he made special note in his diary about these very potions that the soldiers believed would make them invulnerable to bullets. At first, he was upset that the people were unwisely endangering themselves from "superstition," but he eventually accepted their faith in this magic as more of a boon than a detriment because he recognized that, if anything, it instilled them with a sense of self-power and courage to give their all in battle that they wouldn't have had otherwise.[50]

The Ethiopian Exception

Once Europeans gained a strong foothold in Sub-Saharan Africa, it became a scramble amongst themselves to stake out a claim on as much land as possible for their respective countries. However, one place that managed to repel European colonialism altogether was Ethiopia. What was Ethiopia's secret? Religion and modernization. Already having a growing

---

50   Heidi Holland, *African Magic: Traditional Ideas that Heal a Continent* (Johannesburg: Penguin Books, 2011), n.p.; Christian Locka, "Cameroon Has Been Using Witchcraft to Fight Boko Haram," The World, January 11, 2017, https://www.pri.org/stories/2017-01-11/cameroon-has-been-using-witchcraft-fight-boko-haram.

amount of Christians in the kingdom by the fourth century CE, this made them unpopular for Europeans to declare war against due to being brothers and sisters of the faith. They had also modernized and became an imperialist power in their own right.[51]

A union of various tribes (by peace and force) allowed Ethiopia to become a Christian empire and expand its sphere of influence, all the while buying guns from the Europeans and training their warriors on how to use them effectively. In addition, Ethiopia hired Europeans to develop a network of transportation infrastructure within the country, to introduce electricity and telephone services, and to establish modern banking, postal, and school systems.[52]

Then, in the late 1800s, Italy (who was late to the bandwagon of colonizing Africa) saw this "still-unclaimed" piece of the continent as a territory they could colonize without inciting a war with another European power. However, this happened during the reign of Ethiopia's King Menelik II, a powerful Christian military leader who was no stranger to modern warfare or Europeans and who had already conquered many of his neighbors and had financial investments in various U.S. and European business ventures.

Once Italy officially sent troops to Ethiopia, Menelik II deftly used this foreign aggression as a rallying cry behind which all the peoples he had conquered could unite together in African solidarity against this European

51   Christopher Hass, "Mountain Constantines: The Christianization of Aksum and Iberia," *Journal of Late Antiquity* 1, no. 1 (2008): 101–126, http://users.clas .ufl.edu/sterk/junsem/haas.pdf.

52   Marjolein 't Hart, "Why Was Ethiopia not Colonized During the Late Nineteenth-Century 'Scramble for Africa'?" in *A History of the Global Economy: From 1500 to the Present*," ed. Joerg Baten (Cambridge: Cambridge University Press, 2016), 1–2; Todd Johnson, "Menelik II: Independence in the Age of Imperialism," NBC News Learn, May 1, 2020, YouTube, 3:27, https://www .youtube.com/watch?v=wf2EYcKDEq8.

power. The Italians were decisively beaten, and Ethiopia remained the free, non-colonized exception in Sub-Saharan Africa.[53]

Sub-Saharan African Takeaway:
ADAPTATION

When it comes to power, many people have used (and often still do) the Darwinian ideal of "survival of the fittest" as an excuse to justify needing to be the baddest guy on the block, the most physically strong, and the most alpha-male dominant person in the room. Others equate "fittest" as "smartest" and use it to justify looking down upon those who are less academically adept as themselves. The irony of all this is that Darwin's "survival of the fittest" conclusions were never about "fittest" equaling physical strength or intelligence. As a university professor from the 1960s once elucidated: "According to Darwin's *Origin of Species*, it is not the most intellectual of the species that survives; it is not the strongest that survives; but the species that survives is the one that is able best to adapt and adjust to the changing environment in which it finds itself."[54]

The peoples of Sub-Saharan Africa lived the truth of this evolutionary observation from both ends of reality. Those who did not (or could not) adapt to the new paradigm shift of European colonization (in military technology, in putting aside historic rivalries, etc.) became colonies and enslaved and shipped en masse to the Americas. Meanwhile, Ethiopia adapted itself to the new circumstances of the times and remained sovereign and free, with the only exception being during WWII when the country was occupied by the Axis powers. So, it is not always about being the

---

53   Nigel Tussing, "African Resistance to European Colonial Aggression: An Assessment," *Africana Studies Student Research Conference*, February 12, 2017, https://scholarworks.bgsu.edu/cgi/viewcontent.cgi?article=1056&context =africana_studies_conf.

54   "The Evolution of a Misquotation," Darwin Correspondence Project, University of Cambridge, accessed September 5, 2020, https://www .darwinproject.ac.uk/people/about-darwin/six-things-darwin-never-said /evolution-misquotation.

strongest or smartest that makes one powerful and ensures survival; it's our ability to adapt to new situations in an ever-changing world.

So, for your takeaway challenge here, perform a deep meditation into your own life to objectively inspect where your adherence to "the past," "tradition," "personal preference," and all other rigid, limiting beliefs are preventing you from adapting to the reality of the current world around you. Besides, "tradition" is just peer pressure from our ancestors. They lived in a very different time, and what may have worked for them then does not guarantee it will work or be what's best for us now.

Even outside of yourself, as a warrior for justice, no two opponents are the same, and if you cannot adapt your battle strategies to the enemy at hand, you will become predictable and be at a disadvantage. The same goes for your spiritual endeavors. If doing that ritual or saying that prayer over and over again is not working, adapt and do something else. If you want to learn a type of magic or perform a spell that your spiritual tradition either disallows or just doesn't have in their repertoire, then that doesn't mean it's off-limits to you. Go beyond the limits of your tradition and seek out the knowledge they can't (or don't want to) give you. Though there may be good reasons for your tradition not exploring certain knowledge, the limitations of your "tradition" are only your limits if you accept them as so.

When you cease to learn new information or are insistent on doing things the way you have always done them, you are, in effect, disempowering yourself from more effectively enacting change in the modern world. After all, the world is going to keep on turning and changing regardless of your opinions or preferences, and if you can't adapt to that, including to things you don't like, you won't survive.

Deities & Legends

NZINGA MBANDE

Nzinga Mbande was the seventeenth-century monarch of the Kingdoms of Ndongo and Matamba of the Mbundu people in what is now Angola and ruled during the growing boom of the Atlantic slave trade.

Born the princess of a despot king, she was her royal father's favorite child, and he effectively taught her how to govern. This direct tutelage helped her develop a strong capacity for diplomacy, a skill for which her brother (who succeeded the throne after their father) appointed her ambassador to Portugal. Her time as ambassador proved fruitful as she endeared herself to her subjects by successfully negotiating peace treaties with the Portuguese. Such acceptance by the people ultimately led to her smooth transition as their next monarch after the death of her brother (which she is assumed to have had a hand in, though no reliable sources can firmly confirm or deny it). [55]

Cleverly, she would tactically convert to Christianity (the religion of her European enemies) so as to make any aggression against her and her people less popular in the eyes of other European superpowers. Her interactions with Portugal, now as monarch rather than ambassador, were particularly noted for her refusal to be treated as less than. When on a diplomatic mission to meet with the local Portuguese governor, for example, rather than having to stand or sit on the floor like a servant (since the governor refused to give her a chair because she was an African woman), she defiantly sat atop one of her powerful bodyguards who was on their hands and knees beneath her, allowing her to demonstrate without words that *she* was the strongest, most dominant person in the room regardless of her physical gender or skin color.[56]

---

55 Orquídea Moreira Ribeiro, Fernando Alberto Torres Moreira, and Susana Pimenta, "Nzinga Mbandi: From Story to Myth," *Journal of Science and Technology of the Arts* 11, no. 1 (September 10, 2019): 51–59, https://doi.org /10.7559/citarj.v11i1.594.

56 DHWTY, "Queen Nzinga: A Courageous Ruler Who Set Her People Free," Ancient Origins, March 26, 2020, https://www.ancient-origins.net/history -famous-people/queen-nzinga-ruler-who-set-her-people-free-006235.

Moreover, she was widely believed to be what we would equate to in modern times as a transgender male and began to exemplify this most strongly once becoming the official monarch. (It is important to note here that queerness in the Kingdoms of Ndongo and Matamba in the 1600s was an entirely different concept against which twenty-first-century Western definitions of "transgender" don't line up well. Out of modern respect, I'll use our modern English-language masculine pronouns for him here on out now that we've reached the part of his story wherein he historically began demanding that he be addressed with masculine titles and vocabulary.)

The era of his rule was especially noted for the social acceptance of third-gender peoples and other gender variances beyond the traditional binary of male/female. For himself, personally, in addition to terminology and labels, he actively dressed in what would be considered "male" clothing and behaved in accordance with his culture's social mores of masculinity. Most strikingly, though, was his personal harem of male concubines, whom he referred to as his "wives" and forced them to dress in their culture's traditionally "female" clothing.[57]

Beyond diplomacy and administration, Nzinga was also highly skilled in the arts of war. Guerrilla warfare, in particular, was his strong suit, which proved effective against the Portuguese when they cancelled their peace treaties with him and intended to enslave his people and ship them off to Brazil. With their superior technology, the Portuguese were, at first, very successful, but because of Nzinga's charisma, command of guerrilla warfare, and never giving up armed resistance, Portugal was unable to fully subdue Nzinga's people.

---

57   Mikael Owunna, "Drawing a Portrait of L.G.B.T.Q. Life," *The New York Times*, June 16, 2018, https://www.nytimes.com/2018/06/16/us/lgbtq-africans -share-their-stories.html; Leslie Feinberg, *Transgender Warriors: Making History from Joan of Arc to RuPaul* (Boston: Beacon Press, 1996), 34; Bharat Mehra, Paul A. Lemieux III, and Keri Stophel, "An Exploratory Journey of Cultural Visual Literacy of 'Non-Conforming' Gender Representations from Pre-Colonial Sub-Saharan Africa," *Open Information Science* 3:1 (January 15, 2019): 1–21, https:// doi.org/10.1515/opis-2019-0001.

Nzinga himself was no backstage general; rather, he actively led and fought alongside his troops and recruited runaway slaves into his forces. As a direct consequence of his leadership and dogged determination to never give up armed resistance even in the face of insurmountable odds, the Portuguese eventually deemed the Ndongo and Matamba kingdoms as more economically costly than what the territory was worth to them and gave up colonial expansion into Nzinga's lands. After Nzinga died peacefully in his sleep in his eighties, however, Portugal resumed the war. Later in the 1970s, Nzinga's memory would be a driving inspiration in the successful, armed independence movement of the modern nation of Angola.[58]

OGUN

Among the Yoruba people of Nigeria and Benin (as well as religions that derive from traditional Yoruba beliefs like Santería and Vodou) Ogun is the *Orisha* (deity) of iron and war. He is an archetypal blacksmith divinity who is patron of soldiers and metalworking (especially weapons) and is usually depicted as the stereotypical "masculine ideal" (muscular, virile, handsome, honorable, courageous, and a born leader).

Though he is fierce, he is often depicted as a friend to humanity, particularly in teaching humankind how to forge iron into tools so as to clear away jungle, to farm more easily, and to defend themselves from enemies. Nevertheless, Ogun is also a god of creation as much as he is of destruction. In the same way he taught humans how to forge weapons from the metal of everyday work tools, so, too, did he teach humans how to melt down weapons and re-forge them into everyday work tools for when peace returned to the land.

Outside of blacksmiths and soldiers, though, Ogun's most fervent modern devotees are mechanics, taxi drivers, truck drivers, and all those whose trades revolve around automobiles. Perhaps most controversially (to those outside the faith, that is), annual sacrificial rituals of dogs are made to

---

58 Jessica Snethen, "Queen Nzinga (1583–1663)," BlackPast.org, June 16, 2009, https://www.blackpast.org/global-african-history/queen-nzinga-1583-1663/.

Ogun by some devotees, the dogs' blood being used to bless their vehicles and tools of the trade so as to ensure protection and a profitable year.[59]

SHAKA ZULU

Shaka kaSenzangakhona was the chieftain of the Zulu Kingdom during the early 1800s in what is now eastern South Africa and has since become one of the most legendary African leaders and warriors in history. He has become *such* an emblematic icon of African strength and pride that much of his recorded life is now a tangled mix of truth and fiction. Nonetheless, he was known at a young age for his strength, intellect, resolve, and aggressiveness and was regarded by those in power as an unusually ambitious shepherd boy.

In his twenties, he was drafted into the military and revolutionized warfare in the region. Rather than armies simply hurling spears at each other from a distance and then pausing the violence to venture into the no-man's-land between them to collect their weapons before running back to their respective sides and hurling those same spears again (as per tradition), Shaka commanded that his troops unbalance their enemies by breaking with tradition and charging into close-quarters combat, even designing a new spear that could be readily used as both a projectile and effective stabbing weapon. This ingenuity won him victory after victory, gaining him so much respect that, after Shaka's father passed him over by choosing a younger son to be royal heir to the throne, regional chieftains from neighboring tribes supplied Shaka with troops to ensure by force that he would be the new Zulu chief as originally planned.[60]

As chieftain, he expanded Zulu territory at lightning speed, massacring his enemies, displacing the native peoples from their homelands, and also

---

59   Robin Brooks, with Hyacinth Simpson, "Ogun: God of Iron," Ryerson University, 2012, https://www.ryerson.ca/olivesenior/poems/ogun.html; Afolabi Sotunde, "Ogun: Sacrifice to the Iron God," Reuters, September 23, 2015, https://widerimage.reuters.com/story/ogun-sacrifice-to-the-iron-god.

60   Truman R. Strobridge, "Shaka: Zulu Chieftain," History.net, October 2002, https://www.historynet.com/shaka-zulu-chieftain.htm.

establishing a solid empire composed of various cultures and languages. He even established all-female regiments in his armies.[61]

Unfortunately, later on in his life, Shaka's mother died, and his grief over her irreparably broke his psyche. He began making bizarre decisions and decrees such as the random executions of hundreds of people as well as the outlawing of milk and farming. Due to this insanity, he was assassinated by his own family, though by the time of his death, he had established a powerful regional empire.[62]

However, it would be his reverence for native tradition over foreign innovation that would ultimately lead to the fall of the Zulu Empire half a century later. His friendliness with the Europeans had allowed him the opportunity to be one of the first native-African empires to obtain the latest rifles and firearm tactical training, but he eschewed them as inferior to traditional African weapons and tactics (especially those he invented himself, so there was somewhat of a prideful bias). This left the Zulu technologically in the past for decades on end, ultimately leading to them being conquered by the British only about fifty years after Shaka's death.[63]

TANO

In the traditional religion of the Ashanti people (in what is now Ghana and Côte d'Ivoire), Tano is the god of the eponymous Tano River who was often most popular among his people in times of adversity and struggle. These associations came about from a legend in which Tano and Death engaged in a singing contest, but since neither one proved to be demonstrably better than the other, they agreed to a compromise as to the prize that they would share.

Depending on which story you prefer, there are two different legends as to what that compromise ultimately was. In the first version, whenever

---

61   Kenneth P. Vickery, "Shaka Zulu: Creator and Destroyer," The Great Courses Daily, July 18, 2017, https://www.thegreatcoursesdaily.com/shaka-zulu/.

62   "Shaka Zulu Assassinated," History, updated September 21, 2020, https://www.history.com/this-day-in-history/shaka-zulu-assassinated.

63   Donald R. Morris, *The Washing of the Spears: The Rise and Fall of the Zulu Nation* (Cambridge: Da Capo Press, 1998), n.p.

Tano would visit the human world, he would always have to be accompanied by Death and vice versa. In the other version, the fate of someone suffering from an illness or grievous injury would be up for grabs depending on which of the two reached the person first. If Death got to them faster, the person would die, but if Tano got to them faster, they would live. Thus, in times of war or danger, the people prayed to Tano, knowing that he accompanies Death and hoping that he'd more speedily come to their side than Death.[64]

64   Patricia Ann Lynch, *African Mythology: A to Z*, rev. Jeremy Roberts (Broomall: Chelsea House Publications, 2010), 122.

6

LANDS OF
THE AFRICAN
DIASPORA

Cultural

THE CARIBBEAN

The Atlantic slave trade lasted centuries, and throughout it, count-less people and families were displaced from their homes in Sub-Saharan Africa to be taken thousands of miles away to the New World. Not so much an intended form of slow genocide (though it amounted to such) as it was unfettered human capitalism at its most masochistic.

Profits over People

The key cog to all this immensely profitable international trade was the enslaved peoples taken from the African continent. To the money-hungry

Europeans and colonists of the New World, the peoples of Sub-Saharan Africa and their enslaved descendants in the Americas were not seen as human, but rather beasts to be made docile so as to fulfill their place in the machine of profit production. Having "free" (aka: brutally forced) laborers kept production costs down for the New World plantations, which then led to increased profits in Europe since European industries could buy New World raw materials at a cheaper price than if plantation owners had to actually pay their workforce.

Without the enslaved peoples from Africa, profit margins would've been dramatically lower, and thus the businesses of Europe and the colonial Americas wanted to keep their supply of free labor firmly under heel. However, those they oppressed found ways to adapt their homeland magic to this new, cruel world and developed a mighty resistance against the landowners and businessmen of the Americas as we'll see here.

Control Channels

Having a sense of control over one's self or one's destiny is a primal human longing, but when you're enslaved, all sense of control and self-determination is gone. This often leads to hopelessness and a surrender to the status quo. So, the first and most important thing needed for any warrior or revolution is that sense of being able to be in control of one's self. For the enslaved African peoples taken to the British West Indies (the Bahamas, Jamaica, Barbados, and other now-English-speaking islands of the Caribbean), they took back their control through a belief in magic called *Obeah*.

Obeah is difficult to describe since it's neither an organized religion nor are there definite standards as to what it definitively is and is not, but in the most general sense (because how can we talk about it otherwise?), it's a system of magic developed by the enslaved African peoples in the British colonies of the Caribbean (somewhat akin to Vodou and Santería of the French and Spanish Caribbean colonies, respectively).

A person who practiced Obeah was seen as a cosmic channeler, a mystic medium who could interact with the spirit world and provide services to their people. An enslaved person cannot get justice or their desires met by colonial society, but they *can* bypass that racist society and get it from the Obeah medium of the community. Knowing that they could channel this higher power that cosmically outranked their slave masters, the power of these mortal "masters" seemed not as all-encompassing as white society wanted them to believe.

Communal Obeah rituals were often held at night so as to not be seen by plantation owners, and these rituals served (in addition to magic) as a communal bonding experience between the oppressed and a rare moment wherein they could exist as masters of their own free society, even if just for a little while. Eventually, emboldened by their Obeah practices, a full-scale slave revolt (Tacky's Rebellion) erupted in Jamaica in 1760. After it was put down, Obeah evermore took on a drastically more political meaning in its continued use on the island to both the white colonists who saw it as a form of "savage" resistance magic and to the enslaved people who saw it as a powerful political and spiritual force to overturn the system (as Tacky's Rebellion almost achieved).[65]

Subversive Survival

Over in the Spanish colonies of the Caribbean, slave resistance often came in the form of Santería. A blend of African Yoruban traditions with Spanish Catholicism and the beliefs of indigenous Caribbean peoples, Santería was a subversive way for enslaved Africans to keep their traditions alive, albeit in secret.

Since an enslaved person could not outright worship their traditional African deities in the open, those in Spanish colonies associated Catholic saints with different Yoruban deities (known as *Orishas*), and so to their Spanish masters, it may have looked like they were praying to a statue of a Catholic saint, though in reality they were actually praying to an Orisha, just in a masked way (hence the name "Santería" from the stem "santo," Spanish for "saint"). Over the years, the coded separation between Catholicism and

---

65   Kirsten Raupach, "'Black Magic' and Diasporic Imagination," *Current Objectives of Postgraduate American Studies* vol. 3 (2002), http://dx.doi.org/10.5283/copas.67.

traditional Sub-Saharan beliefs became muddled, developing into Santería as we still know it today.[66]

Santería survived centuries of oppression thanks in large part to its reverence of the natural world and following nature's divine illustration. For example, in a severe storm, it is always the rigid, tall, defiant trees that are turned over, but the more flexible ones willing to bend a bit to the raging weather might live through it all to see the sunlight once again. Santería did this via codifying Catholic saints, giving it the ability to adapt and bend, and thus it still thrives today.[67]

When the Saints Go Riding In

One of Santería's most striking and iconic practices was used as an effective tool against the system: ritualized possession (think less Linda Blair and more high-intensity modern dance). This sacred form of trance possession is when an Orisha comes down into someone's body and begins controlling them (referred to as "mounting" them, in reference to how a rider would get control of a horse), thus allowing the spiritual world to more concretely affect the material world through the use of this human vessel. Usually, this ritual takes place in rhythmic drum circles, allowing the ecstasy of dance and primal percussions to facilitate the individual's openness to being ridden by an Orisha.[68]

This direct connection with the gods provided the most valuable asset in any resistance effort: hope. Knowing that there was a greater power above that of their earthly masters and knowing that this greater power was actively interested and engaged in the daily wants, needs, and lives of people who were enslaved was profoundly inspiring. Through a trance ritual, one could ask the Divine (via the possessed individual) for advice on

---

66 Migene González-Wippler, *Santeria, the Religion: Faith, Rites, Magic* (St. Paul, MN: Llewellyn Worldwide, 2002).

67 Cynthia Duncan, "Resistance and Change in Cuban Santería," About Santería, accessed May 7, 2020, http://www.aboutsanteria.com/resistance-and-change-in-santeriacutea.html.

68 Cynthia Duncan, "Trance Possession," About Santería, accessed May 7, 2020, http://www.aboutsanteria.com/trance-possession.html.

health, love, family, and anything else. So, through this direct connection to the *highest* power, that fire of hope in the souls of each devotee was kept alive and burning through the magic of Santería.[69]

Death Becomes Them

When living under such inhumane conditions as slavery, survival becomes paramount. You cannot combat oppression if you cannot even survive it, and so it's a testament to these African diasporic religions for having endured centuries of such hard times to still be vibrant today. However, it was not all passive resistance. There were plenty of active spells against the colonial slave owners in these syncretic magical systems of the New World, and one faith in particular that has gotten a lot of sensationalized press when it comes to supposed aggressive magic is Vodou (aka: Voodoo in its distinctly different Louisiana version).

Vodou arose in the colonies of the French Caribbean (most especially Haïti) as a syncretic mix of native West and Central African beliefs and French Catholicism, often existing in a coded form similar to Santería. Associations of death and the macabre have distorted outsiders' view of Vodou as evil or sinister, but when you have a religion that is highly focused on communing with the ancestors, reaching out to the dead is just a benign feature of getting in touch with them. (If you've ever said a prayer to a dead relative, you've effectively done the same thing.)

Arguably one of the most sensationalist forms of necromantic Vodou magic is that of the zombie. Much of the modern lore about zombies being brain-eating hordes of the insatiable dead that we're familiar with now largely come from the landmark '60s horror classic *Night of the Living Dead*, though that's all twentieth-century pop-culture fantasy. *Real* zombies (and yes, they're real, but not in the way you may think), were historically not mindless, reanimated corpses, but rather, they were individuals who were

---

69   Vanessa M. Navarro, "Aché, Music, and Spiritual Experience: The Concept of Aché and the Function of Music in Orisha Spirit Possession," (master's thesis, Florida State University, April 11, 2013), 16–17, https://fsu.digital.flvc.org /islandora/object/fsu:183842/datastream/PDF/download/citation.pdf.

drugged and taken mental advantage of by an unethical *bokor* (Vodou sorcerer for hire). It should be said, though, that zombification of *anyone* has always been a taboo among Vodou practitioners, and whenever it *did* occur, it was always on the fringes of the religion by the most immoral and unsavory of practitioners.

Though it seemed preternatural, the creation of a zombie was really all about biochemistry. A malicious bokor would create a magic powder (whose active ingredient is the lethal nerve toxin *tetrodotoxin*) and drug an unsuspecting person with it, using just enough of a dose to render them limply immobile but fully aware of what's going on (similar to sleep paralysis). The toxin also slows the heart pulse and breathing rate to an imperceptible level, and in a time before modern medical diagnostic devices, the drugged person would be perceived as and declared dead.

Soon after burial or entombment, the malicious bokor would go fetch the person and drug them again, this time with jimsonweed (*Datura stramonium*), which would render them ambulatory, albeit disorientated, psychologically passive, and extremely susceptible to suggestion (more in line with a Jeffrey Dahmer zombie than a George A. Romero one). As long as the victim is continually kept in this drugged state, they feebly follow the commands of whoever gives them orders without resistance, and because they had "officially" died in the eyes of the community, the community believed they had risen from the dead and was now a zombie under the control of an evil Vodou necromancer.[70]

A Fate Worse Than Life

Slavery was already the worst hell, and the idea of it continuing after death was the ultimate horror to enslaved peoples. It was also the ultimate abuse of power. In a psychological sense, "magical" zombification was a continuation of the chain of abuse that allowed the powerless to feel powerful, albeit in a sadistic way. When a person is abused by some-

---

70   Marc Lallanilla, "How to Make a Zombie (Seriously)," Live Science, October 24, 2013, https://www.livescience.com/40690-zombie-haiti-are-zombies-real .html.

one whom they cannot respond against, they often turn their rage toward someone weaker who cannot respond against their own abuse (such as an employee who is abused by their boss taking it out on their own spouse and kids … and children who are abused by their parents taking it out on pets and animals and other "weaker" kids through bullying). An enslaved person absolutely cannot respond against the horrific abuse of their masters and have no one else lower than them on whom to unleash their rage and over whom to feel powerful … except the unresisting dead.

Making the malicious magic of zombification even more sinister was how it, in effect, mirrored the kind of forced family separation cruelty exhibited by slave owners. For the enslaved Africans in the French Caribbean, it was commonly believed that after one's death, the soul would return to Africa where they could finally be free and with their ancestors. If a deceased person was turned into a zombie, however, that return to Africa, return to family, and return to freedom was denied to them, only to be replaced by continued slavery for the soul among the plantations in the Caribbean, except this time the slave master was not a white man but a fellow enslaved African exerting his magical power over the powerless dead.[71]

Enslaved Africans, themselves, were already living a zombie-esque life since they lacked free will and existed only to obediently serve the ones who owned and controlled their bodies. If, however, a downtrodden enslaved person could raise someone from the dead who'd be bereft of free will (or just drug them enough to be nonconsensually compliant), then that oppressed person could have ultimate power over this "undead" individual and be a master in their own right. It was the ultimate Vodou taboo:

---

71   Mike Mariani, "The Tragic, Forgotten History of Zombies," *The Atlantic*, October 28, 2015, https://www.theatlantic.com/entertainment/archive /2015/10/how-america-erased-the-tragic-history-of-the-zombie/412264/.

the abused victim becoming the very monster that had victimized them, the enslaved person becoming a slave master themselves.[72]

THE DEEP SOUTH

The horrors of slavery in the New World were not solely relegated to the Caribbean. Up and down the Atlantic coast of North and South America, enslaved peoples from Africa were transported from their homelands to work the plantations of many colonial empires. One major destination was what is now known as the Deep South of the United States. Here, spiritual resistance and revolts of the oppressed took on a different approach thanks to the multicultural metropolis of New Orleans and the fervent Protestantism of "American" values.

On Pins and Needles

One of the more infamous aspects of Vodou magic is the Voodoo doll. Now, most people think of these dolls as tools of spiteful magic, but in reality, they were mostly used for healing purposes born out of a necessity for survival.

More frequently used in Louisiana Voodoo than Haïtian Vodou, these dolls did, indeed, represent a specific person who'd be the target recipient of whatever spellwork was being done, but very rarely was it to inflict pain. Usually, the doll was utilized as a proxy for a patient and the pinpricks in it represented pinpoint precision attacks against whatever was ailing them (more in line with remote acupuncture than impalement). Keep in mind, enslaved people had no access to doctors (and those granted their freedom rarely had the funds to hire a good one), and so turning to your local Voodoo priest(ess) was the next best thing. Through this doll, they could remotely receive the healing that was denied to them by their oppressors.

Sometimes, however, the dolls didn't represent a specific person but rather a spiritual entity. They served as vessels in which to house various

---

72   Kyle Bishop, "The Sub-Subaltern Monster: Imperialist Hegemony and the Cinematic Voodoo Zombie," *The Journal of American Culture* 31, no. 2 (June 2008): 141–152, https://onlinelibrary.wiley.com/doi/pdf/10.1111/j.1542 -734X.2008.00668.x.

ancestors and divinities (known as *Lwa*) so as to have more accessible connection to the spirit realm right at home. Of course, when Louisiana plantation owners saw these human-shaped dolls, sometimes with pins sticking out of them, they freaked out and immediately assumed it was some sort of barbaric "black" magic, and since the ruling powers write history, Voodoo dolls became associated with evil and harm.[73]

Southern Charm

Over in the non-Catholic plantations of the United States, enslaved peoples developed a unique magical system that adopted traditional West and West-Central African spirituality with the fervent Protestantism of the Deep South, becoming what we now know as Hoodoo (as well as Conjure and Rootwork). Unlike Catholicism-infused Santería and Vodou/Voodoo, the Protestantism within Hoodoo geared its focus less on interacting with and invoking various specific saints and deities and more on working directly with an omnipresent, abstract God-like supreme force as well as relying more on the magic of Scripture (sometimes as direct spells in and of themselves) and seeing biblical figures like Moses and King Solomon as magical conjurers.

Even from its outset, though, Hoodoo was a political force born and bred out of and in response to the inequality of the times. It was not a unified faith system; rather, it was just the magical folk practices of enslaved African peoples living in the Deep South, and its traditions and methodologies often varied from plantation to plantation. They adapted to the land and used whatever was around locally as substitutes for traditional spellworking ingredients that could only be found in Africa. Thus, scavenged plants, minerals, animal bones, and Bible passages (the only literature allowed for enslaved people, if at all) became mainstays in the practice. In

---

73   James Duvalier, "The Importance of Dolls in Voodoo," James Duvalier, accessed May 8, 2020, http://jamesduvalier.com/importance-dolls-in-voodoo/; Catherine Beyer, "Are Voodoo Dolls Real?" Learn Religions, January 25, 2019, https://www.learnreligions.com/are-voodoo-dolls-real-95807.

doing this, the enslaved Africans and their descendants managed to sub-vert the ruling-class system by establishing their own system, which was impossible to suppress since it primarily utilized the two things that could not be taken away from them: the local environment and the oppressors' own sacred texts.

Once government-sanctioned slavery did end in the United States, Hoo-doo continued to be a boon to oppressed African communities. It allowed practitioners to make a living in an excluded world and accrue financial gain and local respect right in the face of Jim Crow while also helping to keep remnants of the traditional African spirituality of their ancestors alive.[74]

African Diasporic Takeaway:
SELF-CARE

You cannot be a warrior for justice or for the oppressed if you cannot even care for yourself. A sick and injured warrior is not only an ineffective fighter, but they also have the potential to be a liability to those actively in the good fight. Place the oxygen mask over your own face first before assisting others. Hell, even Jesus Christ emphasized this in his "speck in the eye" parable of Matthew 7:3–5 (which also serves as a condemnation of hypocrisy). No matter how you look at it, you have to make sure that *you* are healthy and self-aware enough before you can adequately help others.

Revolution is not all about attack; self-care and focusing on self-improvement are just as vital as action on the battlefield. To the enslaved peoples of Africa in the New World, they used their faith, their magic, and their passed-down wisdom to care for and continually heal themselves from the daily existence of their supremely monstrous life. If they couldn't survive to live another day, then they couldn't be there to fight another

---

74   Chris Newman, "African Spirituality's Influence on the Slave Experience in America" (thesis, Ohio State University, December 2016), 1–28, https://kb.osu.edu/bitstream/handle/1811/78339/AfricanSpiritualityInAmerica _ThesisPaper.pdf?sequence=1&isAllowed=y; Katrina Hazzard-Donald, *Mojo Workin': The Old African American Hoodoo System* (Champaign, IL: University of Illinois Press, 2012), n.p.

day. And you know what? They made it through the other end of that nightmare. Legalized, systemic slavery is a thing of the past, but the traditions and descendants of those slaves are still alive today. Yes, there are many more forms of slavery still to fight, but the modern descendants of those enslaved people are here to fight them because their ancestors survived through the worst of it with daily self-care.

So, your takeaway challenge here is to take some time to care for yourself. Say a prayer, perform a ritual, do whatever it is in your tradition you need to do to turn that healing magic toward your own self. And be sure to follow that up with real-world action like exercise, a healthy diet, and seeking the help of a licensed professional if you need them.

But even if you are strong and healthy, are you doing self-care for other aspects in your life? Just as you can't effectively nurse others back to health if you're severely ill, you cannot effectively lift others out of poverty if you're financially insolvent, cannot give good relationship advice if you're embittered in loneliness, and cannot inspire others toward greatness if your own life is lived so mundanely. Passionate people like to give their all to a cause and run themselves to exhaustion, always trying to help and "do" something, but if you want to be a more effective warrior, a more powerful ally, and be able to offer others a helping hand day after day, make sure you prioritize your own self-care.

Deities & Legends

BOSOU KOBLAMIN

Bosou Koblamin is a popular war *Lwa* (deity) in Vodou traditions because of his signature tendency for extreme violence. Knowing just how vicious and frenzied he can get, he's not a Lwa to whom devotees petition on a daily basis; rather, he is usually reserved for extreme and dangerous situations such as war or protection from violent criminal activity (especially at night). Still, because of his unpredictability, he is not very reliable, though he is still popularly called upon because of his sheer power and associations with breaking the chains that metaphorically bind you.

Like similar deities without a moral compass, Bosou Koblamin has devotees from all walks of life. Outwardly, he is depicted as being a man with three horns symbolizing strength, wildness, and violence.[75]

BWA KAYIMAN INSURRECTION CEREMONY

Of all the modern nations in our world, Haïti holds the honor of being the only one to not only have won its independence through a successful slave revolt but also be both founded and continuously governed by formerly enslaved people of color. According to legends, the catalyst tipping point that led to full-blown insurrection was a clandestine Vodou ceremony.

Around the mid-1700s, Haïti became the crown jewel in France's colonial empire due to it being the most profitable plantation colony in the New World thanks to its prodigious production of the most high-income generating cash crop of the time: sugar (sugar being the eighteenth-century equivalent in value to what petroleum oil would be in modern times). For this reason, France wanted to keep particular control over its biggest profit producer, but their extreme cruelty to maintain such desperate control over Haïti is what incidentally instigated an equal-yet-opposite intensity of a reaction from those they oppressed.

Under these desperate conditions, the leaders of various enslaved Africans groups from various plantations gathered together at a site on the north coast of Haïti called Bwa Kayiman (more familiar nowadays by its French spelling "Bois Caïman") to hold a Vodou ceremony headed by the legendary Mambo Mayanèt and Houngan Boukman ("Mambo" and "Houngan" being the titles for a Vodou priestess and priest, respectively). This ceremony was held for the specific purpose of petitioning and sealing themselves in a spiritual pact with the *Lwa* (spirits/divinities) for aid in obtaining freedom from their oppressors. Within days, revolutionary

---

75   Jan Chatland, "Descriptions of Various Loa of Voodoo," Webster University, accessed August 8, 2021, http://faculty.webster.edu/corbetre/haiti/voodoo /biglist.htm.

violence erupted all along the northern coast, and by the next year, the formerly enslaved Africans of Haïti would control one-third of the colony.

As an unexpected response to this, white plantation owners in Haïti appealed to Great Britain and the nascent United States, not their native France, to help turn the tide of the rebellion. The plantation owners (correctly) assumed that France was in no condition to offer assistance to their own colonies due to being in the throes of the recent French Revolution. Remember, though, whether as a monarchy or an instable republic, France *relied* on that Haïtian sugar money to fund their economy, and the thought of Britain or the U.S. gaining control of that crown jewel of a sugar colony was out of the question.

So, the Republic of France declared all free people of color in Haïti to be granted the same rights as white, full-French citizens (a desperate attempt to get the rebels to want to continue being a French colony and not an independent nation or a colony of another empire). This, however, backfired as the white rulers governing Haïti refused to acknowledge any mixed-race or non-white people to be equal to them, thus further fueling even more rebellious zeal among the revolutionaries. After over a decade of fighting, the revolutionaries won and, in 1804, established Haïti as the first independent nation of the Western Hemisphere to abolish slavery and be governed by formerly enslaved peoples, thus fulfilling the alliance they made with the Lwa for help in that Vodou ceremony at Bwa Kayiman to overthrow their oppressors and achieve freedom.[76]

MARIE LAVEAU

The Voodoo queen of New Orleans, Marie Laveau was a famously popular free creole woman in nineteenth-century Louisiana. Her life has become intertwined with rumors and legends due to her efficacy in Voodoo magic that was respected by peoples of all races and levels of income. With such power, she often utilized it to subvert the system by being an outspoken community activist as well as lifting up enslaved Africans and

---

76   Mambo Chita Tann, *Haitian Vodou: An Introduction to Haiti's Indigenous Spiritual Tradition* (Woodbury, MN: Llewellyn Publications, 2012), 24–26.

gathering intelligence on New Orleanian aristocratic society and slave owners.

To be able to fund her activism, she worked as a high-end hairdresser to New Orleans' wealthiest families. However, it wasn't just money that she got from this beautician service; she also got all the gossip and insider information about the goings-on in upper-class society. Additionally, she recruited their enslaved servants to spy on them and report back with information (sometimes by paying these spies, other times by exchanging a magical service for them such as healings).[77]

With her wealth, influence, and intelligence network, Marie bought the freedom of many enslaved Africans and helped initiate them on their way out of the Deep South through the Underground Railroad. She was also very involved in prison activism, medical triage assistance during epidemics in the city, and staging public Voodoo ceremonies, which she knowingly got away with because of her intimidating spiritual reputation as a powerful Voodoo priestess just as much as her sociopolitical connections. Even now, she is still remembered and greatly honored (her tomb being a sacred pilgrimage site among the faithful), and it was her unabashed outspokenness and public activism that cemented her legacy to survive and thrive into the twenty-first century.[78]

77   Ina Johanna Fandrich, *The Mysterious Voodoo Queen, Marie Laveaux: A Study of Powerful Female Leadership in Nineteenth-Century New Orleans* (Lafayette, LA: University of Louisiana Lafayette Press, 2012), n.p.; Denise Alvarado, *The Magic of Marie Laveau: Embracing the Spiritual Legacy of the Voodoo Queen of New Orleans* (Newburyport, MA: Weiser Books, 2020), n.p.

78   Jordan Flaherty, *Floodlines: Community and Resistance from Katrina to the Jena Six* (Chicago: Haymarket Books, 2010); Adrian Shirk, "The Voodoo Priestess Whose Celebrity Foretold America's Future," Zócalo Public Square, November 28, 2018, https://www.zocalopublicsquare.org/2018/11/28 /voodoo-priestess-whose-celebrity-foretold-americas-future/ideas/essay/.

7

SUB-SAHARAN & AFRICAN DIASPORIC MAGICAL COMMUNITY

CHANT OF REVOLUTION

When thinking of someone to invite to give us some warrior wisdom from traditional Sub-Saharan African and African diasporic faiths, one of the first people that popped in my mind was the *Vodouisant* Randy P. Conner. If you don't recognize Randy by name, perhaps you know him through his numerous publications (among them *Cassell's Encyclopedia of Queer Myth, Symbol, and Spirit* as well as *Queering Creole Spiritual Traditions: Lesbian, Gay, Bisexual, and Transgender Participation in African-Inspired Traditions in the Americas* to name just a couple). Oh, and he knows what he's talking about since Randy also has a doctorate in the humanities concentrating on philosophy and religion while also being a full-time instructor at Moraine Valley Community College in Illinois (professor of such courses as African

& Middle Eastern Humanities, Native American & Caribbean Humanities, World Mythology, and more).

To help rally the troops and instill inspiration into our warrior souls, Randy came up with the suggestion of offering us a magical Vodou chant right in line with the kind of inspirational, spiritual firepower we would need in the good fight, specifically, one to invoke the aid of Ezili Dantò (a fierce Haïtian Vodou *Lwa* who has been often associated with vengeance and revolution). So, without further ado, here's a chant for you and for all your revolutionary endeavors.

> *Ezili Dantò,*
> *We chant the praise-hymn you have given us,*
>
> Nou chante lwanj-kantik ou te ban nou an
>
> Set koud kouto, set koud pwenyad
> Prete'm dedin a pou m'al vomi sang mwen
> Sang ape koule
>
> *Seven stabs of the knife, seven stabs of the sword.*
> *Hand me that basin. I am going to vomit blood.*
> *The blood runs down.*
>
> *There you stand with your raisin skin, with tribal marks on your cheeks.*
> *Your hands are rough. In your indigo, hooded cape, bordered by gold,*
> *cloaking a blood-red gown, you are handsome and stern.*
>
> *You love women as you love men. When you love women, you are called*
> madivin, *my divine one. You also love men who love men, the* massissi.
>
> *You dwell in the deepest part of the woods. You rarely venture to the city.*
> *Once you did, and when you saw how your people were being oppressed,*
> *tortured, enslaved, you shouted so loudly that the earth trembled. A*
> *wicked man, a slaveholder, grabbed you and cut out your tongue.*

In 1791, you appeared in Haïti. There you encouraged your people to commence the Revolution. There you encouraged the Polish mercenaries, hired by the French, to turn against them and fight on the side of your people.

Li kòmanse Revolisyon an.
Li goumen pou pèp li a.

She starts the Revolution.
She fights for her people.

I offer you pork griyon, *in memory of the black pig that was sacrificed, popcorn with peanuts and bread, pimentos and yams, and pineapple floating in burgundy. I offer you cigarillos.*

Ezili, we need your fighting spirit now!

We are not enslaved, but we dwell in an era in which white men rule, rich men who oppress us, rattling the death-rattle of the patriarchy.

Camouflaged troops gas us,
Beat us, shoot us,
Abduct us in unmarked cars.

Ezili, we need your fighting spirit now.

Gather with us.
March with us.
Shout with us,
"Black Lives Matter!
Queer Lives Matter!"
until people of color are free
and LGBTQ people are free,
Let us not say, "All lives matter"
until we are respected as equals
And granted justice.

Ezili Dantò, we need your intervention now.

—Randy P. Conner (dedicated to the
memory of Mama Lola, my spiritual
mother, 1933–2020)

DOUBLE HOODOO DEFENSE

One form of modern warrior wisdom that we have not encountered thus far in our global trek is that of a good old-fashioned spell. Given the era in which we currently live, I thought it crucial and of particular importance to have our first all-out spell be taught to us from a Black female perspective…a voice that, despite relatively recent gains, still all too often goes unheard or is silenced in our modern world. For our first spellworking teacher in particular I've invited the practicing Hoodoo Stephanie Rose Bird to come and teach us a thing or two about contemporary magical self-defense.

To those of you already in the know, Stephanie's magical acumen might be familiar through her prolific output of seven books on African American culture and spirituality (her most recent being *365 Days of Hoodoo: Daily Rootwork, Mojo & Conjuration*). If not, well, then let me tell you that she's the real deal, a practicing Hoodoo with a passion for African American folklore and mythology. For us here now, she has put together two step-by-step instructional guides for performing Hoodoo protection magic. After all, you can't keep the peace with only positive thoughts.

I am a Hoodoo and I also practice Green Witchcraft and Shamanism. Most all that I do is built on the African wisdom of my ancestors. Wisdom is important to me and I've attempted to play my part in the dissemination of Earth Wisdom by having my seven, and still counting, books published.

My first book, Sticks, Stones, Roots & Bones, *found its title in the natural elements of Hoodoo and serves as a double entendre, with a real-life foundation in fighting the bullying and racism I experienced as a youth. You may be familiar with the following saying: Sticks and stones may break my bones but names will never hurt me. It not only popped up* and asserted itself in my first Hoodoo book's title and concept, but it is also an affirmation.

By nature, I am a peaceful person. I have always tried to approach racists and bullies with empathy. Knowing what I know from my magickal paths, particularly Hoodoo, has led me to a dualist approach to troublesome and would-be harmful people as well as entities. This essay speaks about and shares some different tools I, as a Hoodoo, employ in war matters and keeping the peace. This is all the more relevant as I write, in the enormous shadow of the very significant Anti-racist and Black Lives Matter movements.

There is a lot more to Hoodoo than I can squeeze into this space. Luckily there are some prominent features of Hoodoo that fold easily into the conversation of this book. Hoodoo is elemental and alchemical. Harvesting from these two broad powerful aspects of Hoodoo enables us to approach war and give us the tools for living in peace.

Protect Me Powder

One important arm of Hoodoo is Protection Magick, much of which is Foot Track Magick.

Since your feet carry powerful intent of your will with them, some spells, such as this one, reinforce the power of your feet. This powder gets its oomph from using well-known power elements like red pepper, gun powder, and Sulphur.

Gun powder incorporates yet another category of magick, Sympathetic Magick. If your feet become as strong and powerful as guns, you will be very hard to stop. This potent combination obviously will help you step over malicious things put in your path. With Protect Me Powder, you can go about your day, step high, and be empowered.

You will only need the following four ingredients:

- Red pepper
- Gunpowder
- Sulphur
- Shoes

Mix the first three ingredients.

Add to soles of shoes.

Wear.

Be protected from evil doers and evil spirits.

Body Guard

We all need a good body guard from time to time. Any practicing Hoodoo would agree protection is a necessary, if not essential, part of the Hoodoo practice. Here is a traditional protective body guard, in the form of a mojo bag that draws on the melding of potent High John the Conqueror Root, chamber lye, silver, and Hoyt's Cologne. Try to create this when the moon is full.

You will need the following ingredients:

- *Lidded Glass Jar*
- *High John the Conqueror Root*
- *Silver Dime (minted 1964 or before)*
- *Chamber Lye (your urine)*
- *Purple Ribbon*
- *Red Flannel*
- *Hoyt's Cologne*

First thing in the morning, collect chamber lye in the jar. Add the silver dime and High John the Conqueror Root to this jar. Screw the lid on tightly; soak overnight. The next morning, remove the dime and root and pat them dry with a paper towel or rag. Place these curios inside a red flannel (mojo bag). Pull the drawstring tightly and fix with knotted purple ribbon. Feed the bag; through the exterior of the flannel drop on several drops of Hoyt's Cologne. Tie this mojo around your waist. Now feel safer under the confluence of alchemical elements from which your body guard has been made.

—Stephanie Rose Bird

BLACK MAGIC WOMAN IN MODERN AMERICA

In addition to chants and spells, another important lesson is that of perspective itself, and it's something that can only really be taught to us by people who are different from us and who carry different ways of seeing and interacting with the world around them. So, to continue the Black representation within this section of the world, I've asked another modern magical worker of African descent to come and speak to us directly on what it's like to be a Black, magic-practicing woman right here and now in modern America.

In order to give such insight, back in the seemingly apocalyptic summer of 2020 I approached my fellow author friend Najah Lightfoot to come and share with us how she gets through this thing called life during a time and in a place wherein to be Black is to still be persecuted by your fellow citizens and your own government. Najah's wisdom is also critically recognized, too, if being a multi-award-winning author is a standard by which to judge (her book *Good Juju: Mojos, Rites & Practices for the Magical Soul* even won the 2020 Coalition of Visionary Resources award as well as the 2019 New York City Big Book award). So, while I personally cannot directly speak about the Black, magical female perspective of life in today's U.S.A., Najah certainly can, and here's her advice of perspective and insight for us all.

> *These are unprecedented times. At the time of this writing, the world is experiencing the global pandemic known as COVID-19 or the Coronavirus. There is a spotlight upon racism in the United States, whose flame was lit when George Floyd was murdered in Minneapolis, MN on May 25, 2020.*
>
> *To say these times have been stressful would be an understatement. Daily, people are faced with restrictions, which include social distancing, and wearing masks, and there are protests happening in the United States and across the world to battle police brutality and racism.*
>
> *So how does a Black woman, an African American woman, such as myself cope? How do I use my magickal spirituality and training to get through these hard times?*
>
> *Daily practice. Gentleness. Easy does it and one day at a time.*
>
> *I've been trained as a Hoodoo Practitioner. I hold sacred the Divine Feminine and the Divine Mother Goddess. I'm an initiate of Vodou. I'm a practicing Witch, and a sister Fellow of Sojourner Truth Leadership Circle,*

sponsored by Auburn Seminary. As such there is much at my disposal to help me cope during these trying times. Yet I too am not immune to the suffering and conflict. For surely these times have brought heaping table- spoons of tribulation to the daily lives of myself, my family, my friends and loved ones.

But even in these dark times, I can call upon the strength of ten thou- sand women. I can call upon the Divine Mother Goddess, my Ancestors and the Lwa to help guide and sustain me. In my daily practice I call upon the Archangels for protection, through the ritual of the Lesser Banishing Ritual of the Pentagram. I pour water to those who have gone before me; family members and people who have made significant contributions to the world.

I acknowledge the directions of East, South, West, and North, every day. I give thanks and gratitude every day. And these rituals, which have become my daily spiritual and magickal practice, help me get through the tough times, as well as celebrate the good times.

And once a month during the Full Moon, I light candles to the Divine Marie Laveau, and recite the "Charge of the Goddess" as written by Mother Witch Doreen Valiente. During these rites I take time to feel the power and presence of the Full Moon and thank her for being a symbol of the Divine Mother Goddess, who shines her light upon us in the darkness.

—Najah Lightfoot

PART 3

EUROPE

Though justice be thy plea, consider this:
That in the course of justice none of us
Should see salvation. We do pray for mercy,
And that same prayer doth
teach us all to render
The deeds of mercy.
WILLIAM SHAKESPEARE
(THE MERCHANT OF VENICE,
ACT 4, SCENE 1)

8

ANCIENT GREECE & ROME

Cultural

ANCIENT GREECE

When people think of ancient Greek warriors, the image of red-caped, chiseled-ab, stoic Spartans (à la the film *300*) comes to mind, and though a lot of that imagery is emphasized for Hollywood spectacle, the foundational facts of it all were quite true. In Sparta, militarism and physical fitness were worshiped like a religion, and the continuous self-improvement to become the perfect soldier was pursued with as much fervor and focused effort as a Zen monk would put toward attaining enlightenment. Part of this was due to spiritual reasons and part was due to reasons more practical.

Glory Days

Spiritually, throughout all Greek city-states, it was important to achieve glory. By accomplishing something glorious and worthy of being remembered, you ensured access to the Elysian Fields upon your death, a heaven-like realm of comfort and ease. All other afterlife destinations were either torturous or monotonously boring; so if you wanted to spend eternity being even remotely happy, you had to achieve glory. In Sparta, the only true glory was on the battlefield, and so being the perfect soldier was your only chance to enter paradise.[79]

Meanwhile, on the practical side, Spartans needed to be tough warriors because of just how dependent their society was upon slave labor and social inequality. This kind of social system is always rife with uprisings and rebellions, but rather than slowly give tiny concessions to placate the oppressed into obedience (as is tradition in modern industrialized nations), Sparta saw to it that their land-owning ruling classes were *such* perfect soldiers that no one in the lower classes dare try to challenge them or the status quo.

The Cult of Militarism

The standard for being a perfect soldier, however, had its costs. You see, it's not just that weakness was not tolerated in ancient Sparta; it was not allowed to even exist, period. Highly controversial to us today (though a universally common practice of the ancient world among cultures that worshipped militarism), eugenics was employed to weed out the "weak" and ensure that Sparta would be entirely composed of only healthy, able-bodied humans.[80]

Babies born deformed or unhealthy in any perceived way would be left out to die of exposure. Since Spartans were very much of the mentality that a group is only as strong as its weakest link, this practice was believed

---

79 Ernest L. Abel, *Death Gods: An Encyclopedia of the Rulers, Evil Spirits, and Geographies of the Dead* (Westport, CT: Greenwood Press, 2009), 74–77.

80 Mary Harrsch, "Eugenics in the Ancient World," Brewminate, February 17, 2017, https://brewminate.com/eugenics-in-the-ancient-world/.

to prevent any "weak links" in their society, ensuring only the strongest and "genetically best" humans would live to become Spartan citizens. Unsurprisingly, though, this practice also led to a huge population disparity between free Spartans and the people they enslaved. With so many "unfit" babies being killed for the supposed sake of genetic advancement, the surviving populace of free citizens were vastly outnumbered by the amount of enslaved people they had, and thus free Spartans needed to be that much more skilled in military tactics to keep the enslaved majority firmly under heel.[81]

In Sparta, it was actually against the law for Spartan citizens to do any farming (though they owned all the land), thus those they enslaved and those they subjugated as *helots* (state-owned serfs that did not have their own freedom yet had a small measure of self-determination unavailable to privately owned slaves) had to be used on a massive scale just for Spartans to be able to eat. Consequently, because Spartans didn't have to do any of the daily labor, they could devote their time entirely toward military training and honing their fighting techniques, something soldiers of other Greek city-states couldn't do since they had day jobs in the fields and marketplace that occupied most of their time.[82]

Ironically, this made Sparta paradoxically both the most equal and unfree city-state in ancient Greece. All landowning free men were seen as equals on par with the democratic ideals of their rival city-state Athens. Spartan women also had freedoms and liberties that surpassed those of women in Athens or elsewhere: they could actively influence government decision-making, receive a good education, have a measure of self-determination, participate in athletics, own property rights, choose with whom they wanted to have sex, and more. Nevertheless, Sparta was more reliant upon slavery than other Greek city-states (which makes the Spartan fight against Persian oppression

81   David J. Galton, "Greek Theories on Eugenics," *Journal of Medical Ethics* 24, no. 4 (1998): 263–267, https://jme.bmj.com/content/medethics/24/4/263.full.pdf.

82   Mark Cartwright, "Sparta," World History Encyclopedia, May 28, 2013, https://www.worldhistory.org/sparta/.

in *300* and other such romanticized histories all the more ironic, since those freedom fighters were the biggest slave owners around).[83]

Brawn vs. Brains

Sparta's devotion to warrior culture also made it unique in its spiritual outlook. The war god Ares was greatly admired and honored among Spartans as the ideal soldier: passionately all-in in battle, physically powerful, and resilient amid setbacks. Outside of Sparta (*especially* in Athens), Ares was not well respected, seen as a brute who lets his emotions get the better of him in battle and loves all the worst aspects of war; they much preferred the cool-headed, strategic, and noble grace of Athena over Ares.[84]

This value preference of Spartan muscle versus Athenian intellect made them ideological rivals. They were also the two most powerful Greek city-states and were always at each other's throats for regional supremacy. This escalated into what is now known as the Peloponnesian War between the two of them, the long-awaited conflict pitting the Athena-esque academic and philosophical superiority of the Athenians and all they stood for against the Ares-esque brute strength and physical superiority of the Spartans and all they stood for. When the dust settled and the war was over, Sparta had won (the classic outcome you'd expect if stereotypical academics and jocks got into a physical beatdown).

Born for Greatness

Though one side may come out victorious in war, sometimes the effort is not worth the cost, and both sides end up losing in the long run. This was true of the Peloponnesian War, which left both Sparta and Athens greatly weakened, allowing a tribe from the northern backwoods called Macedon to swoop down and conquer all the ancient Greek city-states.

---

83   James C. Thompson, "Women in Sparta," Women in the Ancient World, accessed April 28, 2020, http://www.womenintheancientworld.com /women%20in%20sparta.htm.

84   Edward Whelan, "Ares: The Greek God of War," Classical Wisdom, July 29, 2020, https://classicalwisdom.com/mythology/gods/ares-the-greek-god -of-war/.

This was the empire of Alexander the Great who, upon his death at age thirty-two, had created one of the largest empires of the ancient world and became one of the greatest military leaders of all time, all while never having been defeated in battle.[85]

Everything about Alexander's early life vetted him to become the success that he ended up being. Not only was he the wealthy son of royalty and personally tutored by Aristotle (one of the wisest people in *history*), but his father was also, in his own right, a military genius and developed a powerful, trained army that Alexander inherited. More so, however, his spiritual psychology is believed to have played just as big of a role, and this magical way of seeing the world was imbued in him by both his parents.

Parental Advisory

It's important to remember that Alexander was only half-Macedonian. His mother was from another empire on the outskirts of Macedon that was seen as a poor backwater in comparison to Macedon (which, itself, was seen as a poor backwater by Athens and other Greeks), and so to instill in him an internal sense that he was no less important or less special than any purebred Macedonian, Alexander's mother would tell him that his *real* father was Zeus. Granted, Alexander's mom was quite religiously passionate and ambitious herself, so it's still not fully agreed as to whether she truly believed she was impregnated by Zeus or if it was just her little-white-lie way of making sure her son felt special, but it's undeniable that she passed on her driven ambition to Alexander by insisting that he achieve something worthy of his divine heritage and not settle for mortal mediocrity.[86]

This helped shape Alexander's psyche to believe that he was not only capable of greatness but also *destined* for greatness. Even his father, King Philip II, believed himself (and thus Alexander) to be a descendant of

---

85   Bill Yenne, *Alexander the Great: Lessons from History's Undefeated General* (New York: St. Martin's Press, 2010), n.p.

86   Kenneth R. Thomas, "A Psychoanalytic Study of Alexander the Great," *Psychoanalytic Review* 82, no. 6 (December 1995): 859–901, https://www.ncbi.nlm.nih.gov/pubmed/8657823.

Herakles (better known by his Roman name Hercules). So, if believing in yourself and having unwavering faith in your capabilities to achieve greatness are the essential psychological foundations for greatness, then Alexander's parents gave him this in spades.[87]

Nevertheless, Alexander the Great, for all his unprecedented achievements, was still a mortal, and when he died from disease while on campaign, his empire immediately fragmented in a vie for power amongst his elite generals. This left the Greek world weak and allowed a new Mediterranean power to grow to prominence, one whose grandeur would even surpass the glory that was Greece: ancient Rome.

ANCIENT ROME

Rome had a lot of commonalities with Greece in terms of spirituality and culture. The biggest difference, though, was how much respect, honor, and admiration Romans had for warfare and brute strength compared to that of most Greeks. Greece was a powerful world force by the time Alexander died, yes, but the Greeks (except Spartans, because they're always the exception) admired the battlefield of the mind more so than the battlefield of combat.

A Tale of Two Deities

The difference in fundamental ideology between Greece and Rome can best be seen in how the two civilizations worshipped two particular gods of war: Mars and Minerva (Ares and Athena, respectively, to the Greeks). To most Greeks, Ares was abhorred as a brute and regarded as someone not to be admired due to his lust for carnage and enjoyment of being in the mêlée of battle. Rather, they preferred Athena, someone who kept her emotions in check and who didn't so much get her hands bloodied by battle as she strategized and stage-managed her fighters from far behind the front lines, going into actual combat only occasionally.

---

87   Donald L. Wasson, "Alexander the Great as a God," World History
     Encyclopedia, July 28, 2016, https://www.worldhistory.org/article/925
     /alexander-the-great-as-a-god/.

Conversely, the Roman Mars was elevated to a position of utmost respect. No longer was he simply a deity of battle, he was now the ideal male, a symbol of masculine virility who used his great strength to both conquer and protect. As for Athena, she initially took a back seat upon becoming Minerva before eventually becoming more prominent again as time went on, but we'll get more in-depth on the two of them when we arrive at the "Deities & Legends" section.[88]

A Religion of War

Rome was a culture of expansionary war and benefitted from hyping up its own grandeur. Very early on, the *idea* of Rome as a mythologized concept was propagated to her citizens as a way of instilling and promoting a sense of inherent self-importance in them simply due to the fact that they were Romans. Today, we call that nationalism—the sense of pride and duty that comes not from personal achievement, but rather from being born in and belonging to a certain ethno-cultural group (or political nation). With Rome now a mythologized *idea*, it became almost a form of worship to fight for her, to make her stronger, to make her richer, to make her more influential. Thus, to become a soldier and fight for Rome was seen as a divine duty and a way of honoring all the gods of Rome.[89]

Through prowess on the battlefield and expanding Rome's interest in foreign lands, racking up wins abroad endeared generals to the people, and with enough popular support, a military leader could overshadow the ruling emperor in power simply through clout. This, coupled with the fact that the worship of the military made the military just that much more spiritually influential, led to the necessity of all Roman rulers to have the support of the military in order to usurp the throne, to prevent others

---

88 Mark Cartwright, "Mars," World History Encyclopedia, January 16, 2014, https://www.worldhistory.org/Mars/; Mark Cartwright, "Minerva," World History Encyclopedia, January 7, 2014, https://www.worldhistory.org /Minerva/.

89 Colin Martin, "The Gods of the Imperial Roman Army," *History Today* 19, no. 4 (April 1969), https://www.historytoday.com/archive/gods-imperial-roman -army.

from usurping it from them, and to have the publicly perceived spiritual support of the gods that the military conveyed. When it came to the Praetorian Guard (the emperor's personal military), loyalty often came down to money, and whoever the Praetorian Guard thought would be more financially beneficial to them, they'd ensure that person be emperor.[90]

Paths of Power

A very lasting effect of the Romans' worship of their military, which is still so often the case among our modern world's militaries, is how becoming a soldier and fighting for Rome was the main path to power and social mobility for the poor and lower classes. You might not think it, but this was absolutely revolutionary for the times. You see, before a general named Gaius Marius reformed the Roman army to include men from all economic backgrounds, only the wealthy upper classes could become soldiers. After all, if fighting for Rome on the battlefield was an honored sacred duty, then prevailing thought was that only the "best" of society could be allowed to participate in such martial worship.

The way the Republican-era Romans saw it, only the upper classes could benefit from war (which is arguably still true) since land conquered by Rome could only be bought and utilized by people with a lot of money. Furthermore, they thought that only the wealthy could be loyal soldiers since poor people would have less of an incentive fighting for a state that kept them systemically oppressed and impoverished. The downside to all this was that only a very small percentage of the population could then be soldiers, and as Rome grew, more soldiers were needed to expand farther and keep the peace in ever more conquered territory.

Marius solved this need for soldiers by controversially allowing the lower classes to enlist, and, to ensure their loyalty, he guaranteed that every soldier, upon full-service retirement, would be given a plot of land

---

90   Evan Andrews, "8 Things You May Not Know About the Praetorian Guard,"
History, August 29, 2018, https://www.history.com/news/8-things-you-may
-not-know-about-the-praetorian-guard; Lyn Goldfarb and Margaret Koval,
"The Roman Empire in the First Century," PBS, 2006, https://www.pbs.org
/empires/romans/empire/soldiers.html.

from conquered territory. Suddenly, a person with no money and no education living in the slums of Rome could now have a viable pathway to honorably serving the gods, owning land, and making a profit for his children and future generations.

This changed absolutely everything. Rome now had plenty of soldiers to be even more expansive, and since plots of land were awarded by generals and not the central government, military leaders (like Julius Caesar) suddenly held more real power and loyalty than anyone in actual government. Thus ushering in the era of Imperial Rome, though as an unintentional consequence (that would later lead to Rome's own downfall), Rome now had to *constantly* expand because it needed new land to gift to each wave of retiring soldiers. Never-ending growth is not sustainable, and it not only broke the Roman bank to fund "forever wars" but it also led to revolts and revolution from the lower classes who weren't given their plots of land as promised when Rome wasn't expanding or was on the back foot...except now these lower classes were trained military professionals more capable of actually seizing power.[91]

Ancient Greek & Roman Takeaway:
CULT OF PERSONALITY

Take a look at almost all the movers and shakers of the world nowadays and throughout history and you'll notice that these influential leaders of men were often not the strongest of men, not the smartest, not even the nicest...and yet they held so much power and achieved so much. What they all had in common, though, was their ability to inspire others to believe in them, to trust in them. Power, after all, doesn't come from being powerful; power comes from others' perception of you as powerful.

Alexander the Great and the generals of ancient Rome knew this strategy well. They understood that their troops' meager salary or bestowment

---

91   Philip Mathew, "Marian Reforms," World History Encyclopedia, September 14, 2020, https://www.worldhistory.org/article/1598/marian-reforms/; Matt Hollis, "Marian Reforms and Their Military Effects Documentary," Kings and Generals, December 13, 2018, YouTube, 14:19, https://www.youtube.com /watch?v=UIRS_PMeVVY.

of medals (or worse, forced conscription) wasn't what kept them fighting with full enthusiasm when times got tough. Rather, their troops persevered through the terrors of war because they believed in their leaders to be powerful people with a vision to change the world and the capability to bring about that change.

That's the spark of fire that wins battles and makes gods out of mortals. Conversely, that's also the same spark that ignites infernos of horror such as hate crimes, genocides, and mass killings. After all, being charismatic and influential is only a good thing if the charismatic influencer is a good person.

So, your takeaway challenge here is twofold. First, develop an image of power that others can recognize. Second, self-investigate to see if you're blindly following anyone simply because of the charismatic cult of personality they've built up around them. For this latter effort, be honest with yourself and do the research necessary to see if your idol, your favored politician, your celebrity influencer, your religious leader is walking their talk (and if you agree with both their walk and their talk). Even your idols (*especially* your idols) need to be held accountable, always.

As for developing a recognizable sense of power, this is important even if you aren't comfortable being in a leadership position. If you want to be of service to the cause and make an impact in this world at all, you have to possess a certain amount of power (physically, intellectually, influentially, spiritually, etc.) to assist in that change. Even if that "power" is being seen as that reliable person who always get the job done, that is enough. It doesn't have to be something grand, but it does have to be recognized by others because that is how you influence your allies and the next generation of warriors for the cause. Remember, you don't have to *be* strong, but you need to *appear* strong because I guarantee you that someone, somewhere, is looking up to you whether you know it or not.

Deities & Legends

ATHENA/MINERVA

Athena is the Greek goddess of (among other things) war, wisdom, and crafts. She was highly favored over her half-brother Ares as the preferred war deity throughout most of ancient Greece. Her preference for strategy, staying level-headed in conflict, and outsmarting her opponents were seen as traits superior to Ares's emotionally charged brawl tendencies (though she definitely could throw down if need be, as evidenced in Homer's *Iliad*).

In most Greek myths, she not only always comes out the victor over toe-to-toe fights with Ares (meant to symbolize the dominance of stoic strategy over emotionally fueled actions as well as propaganda of Athenian self-perceived superiority over Sparta), but she also plays the part of the protagonist who helps heroes and is on the winning side of conflicts (again, Athenian bias might have something to do with that).[92]

In Rome, she was renamed "Minerva" and initially lost much of her popular following, though she was still a major goddess. Truly, though, Minerva was more of an amalgamation of the Etruscan goddess Menvra and Greek Athena than she was a pure appropriation of Athena. In addition to keeping the martial and intellectual aspects of Greek Athena, Roman Minerva was also a patron deity of medicine, and though she was honored with a place next to the king and queen of the gods (Jupiter and Juno), she was initially less popular than Mars among the more hawkish Romans until influential generals and politicians began returning her to prominence.[93]

ARES/MARS

Ares is the Greek god of war, courage, battle lust, and civil order. While his half-sister Athena represented more of the intellectual strategy of war and battle, Ares represented the physically combative fighting that takes

---

92 "Athene," Theoi, accessed April 29, 2020, https://www.theoi.com/Olympios /Athena.html.

93 Christopher Muscato, "The Roman Goddess Minerva: Importance & Mythology," Study.com, January 12, 2016, https://study.com/academy/lesson /the-roman-goddess-minerva-importance-mythology.html.

place on the front lines of a conflict. Among the ancient Greeks, he was reviled for his enjoyment of combat and for giving over to passion and emotions amid the throes of battle as opposed to staying detached, calm, and collected like Athena. Because of this, Ares was not really a popular deity (except among the Spartans), though the Greeks did acknowledge the "bad boy" attraction that his stereotypical untamed masculinity, muscular physique, and sense of determination had by making him the most lusted-after and favored secret lover of none other than the goddess of love and beauty herself, Aphrodite, who could easily have her pick of anyone in the universe.[94]

Modern worship of Ares is still not as popular as that of Athena since the civility of the modern world upholds indirect diplomatic and economic warfare as more prestigious and preferable than physical action or taking to the streets. However, among those who do respect and worship him, it is his protective nature and defense of the weak that made them devotees.

Lesser-known myths about Ares involve him apprehending cruel tyrants who put their personal desires over the needs of the downtrodden and of the greater good, empowering women via active support of the fierce Amazons, and avenging sexual abuse victims by killing their rapists (conversely, Athena punishes rape victims and holds them responsible for having put themselves in such a position in the first place, as in the infamous "Medusa" myth in Ovid's *Metamorphoses*). Moreover, Ares's willingness to fight alongside soldiers in battle as a brother-in-arms is seen by many to be more inspirational and admirable than a behind-the-scenes master of puppets who stays a safe distance away and makes others fight for them (*cough, Athena, cough*).[95]

---

94   "Ares," Theoi, accessed April 29, 2020, https://www.theoi.com/Olympios /Ares.html.

95   Christobel Hastings, "The Timeless Myth of Medusa, a Rape Victim Turned Into a Monster," Vice, April 19, 2018, https://www.vice.com/en_us/article /qvxwax/medusa-greek-myth-rape-victim-turned-into-a-monster; Rebecca Buchanan, ed., *Dauntless: A Devotional for Ares and Mars* (Bibliotheca Alexandrina, 2017).

In Rome, he was renamed Mars (linguistic root from which we get the word "martial," having to do with war and the military such as "martial law," "martial arts," "court-martial," etc., as well as the calendar month "March") and given patronage over the life-sustaining bedrock of human civilization: agriculture. He was also elevated to the status of second-most important god (after Jupiter) and seen as not only the protector of Rome, but also as the epitome of Roman manhood: strong, courageous, resolved, and virile ("virility" tying in with the fertility undertones of his new patronage over agriculture). Because Rome was politically and economically reliant upon constant conquering, Mars held high prominence among the rulers, the people, and especially the military. [96]

SOL INVICTUS

Sol Invictus (Latin for "unconquered sun") is the Roman god of the sun and patron deity of soldiers. He was an existing deity since the dawn of the Kingdom of Rome, but it wasn't until the waning years of Imperial Rome that he became really influential after Emperor Aurelian promoted him to the ranks of a major deity. This, however, was a strategic political move more so than divine inspiration or personal devotion.

Aurelian became emperor in 270 CE during a time when Rome was on the brink of collapse due to peasant rebellions, foreign military pressure, and civil wars, and so to unify the fragmenting empire, he tactically promoted Sol Invictus as a sort of singular supreme god over all other gods (more akin to monotheistic religions than a Jupiterian king of the gods).

The idea was to have the people de-fragment and unite together in solidarity under a unified religion devoted to Sol Invictus (a prime deity for this strategy since every religion in the empire already held the sun as sacred or had a similar solar deity of their own). Moreover, by tactically aligning himself heavily with Sol Invictus in speech and art, Aurelian hoped that this

---

96 "Martial, (adj.)," Online Etymology Dictionary, accessed June 5, 2021, https://www.etymonline.com/word/martial; Patti Wigington, "Mars, Roman God of War," Learn Religions, December 10, 2018, https://www.learnreligions .com/mars-roman-god-2562632.

overt push for unified devotion to one supreme deity would also covertly get everyone to support him as their one supreme ruler. It worked, and through the propagandized worship of the hyper-militaristic and hyper-nationalistic Sol Invictus, Aurelian helped bring Rome back from the edge of destruction for a while longer.[97]

SPARTACUS

Spartacus is the legendary leader of the third (and last) massive slave revolt in Roman history. His story has since been made into the landmark Stanley Kubrick and Kirk Douglas film *Spartacus*, and though the documented accounts of his leadership of the slave resistance are contradictory, almost all reliable sources agree that he was a great martial leader.

The more reliable accounts say that Spartacus was originally a mercenary from Greece who was hired by the Roman military, but after his desertion, he was captured and sold into slavery as a gladiator in southern Italy. There, he led a prison break and managed to escape with about seventy other enslaved gladiators and much of the compound's armor and weapons. By guiding his men to defense-favored terrain, he managed to repel repeated attempts by the Roman army to capture them. Word got around about his victories over mighty Rome and inspired other enslaved people to also revolt and join up with him, swelling Spartacus's ranks to about seventy thousand.

Spartacus treated his followers well, making sure to equally split any spoils of war and treat everyone humanely. He also began actively attacking towns and estates throughout southern Italy in order to free more enslaved people and garner supplies to feed and arm his followers. But now that Spartacus was directly targeting the wealthy elite, the consuls and senators in Rome (all members of the landed aristocracy themselves)

---

97   Patrick Hurley, "Aurelian," World History Encyclopedia, March 20, 2011, https://www.worldhistory.org/Aurelian/; George Wolfgang Forell, *History of Christian Ethics, Vol. I: From the New Testament to Augustine* (Minneapolis: Augsburg Publishing House, 1979), 94; James Grout, "Sol Invictus and Christmas," Encyclopedia Romana, 2020, https://penelope.uchicago .edu/~grout/encyclopaedia_romana/calendar/invictus.html.

suddenly took the matter more seriously and sent large legionary forces to put down the rebellion... all of whom were defeated by Spartacus.

After three years of Spartacus running havoc among the southern Italian upper class, the wealthiest man in Republican Rome, Marcus Licinius Crassus, took total control of the Roman military and personally led an unprecedentedly large force to stifle the resistance. Knowing that Crassus's army far outnumbered his own and was composed of much better fighters, Spartacus negotiated with some pirates to transport his people off the Italian peninsula and away from Roman reach, but the pirates betrayed him by taking the money and not providing the ships. Disadvantageously pinned against the sea, Spartacus's troops suffered devastating losses against the Roman army, and not too long after, the rebellion was permanently put down with Spartacus's death in battle in 71 BCE.

Crassus made an example of the enslaved rebels by crucifying six thousand of them along the road between their original gladiatorial prison and the gates of Rome. Nevertheless, Spartacus's slave rebellion fundamentally changed Rome's internal politics and became a major impetus for the fall of the Roman Republic and the rise of the Roman Empire. Many socialist movements from the 1800s onward have particularly cited Spartacus's rebellion as an inspirational example of the lower classes uniting together in armed opposition against the oppressive aristocracy.[98]

98 Peter Voller, "Spartacus Rebellion—Roman Servile Wars," Kings and Generals, February 26, 2020, YouTube, 20:16, https://www.youtube.com/watch?v =RvaXBKUDG-Y; Owen Jarus, "Spartacus: History of Gladiator Revolt Leader," Live Science, September 17, 2013, https://www.livescience.com /39730-spartacus.html.

9
PAGAN EUROPE

Cultural

CELTIC HOMELANDS

For our mission here, "pagan Europe" refers to the native peoples of Europe outside of classical Greece and Rome and outside of Christian Europe. While these peoples were eventually Christianized, their complete conversion was not instantaneous, with pagans and Christians living side-by-side for centuries amid varying levels of hostility and cooperation.

History or Their Story?

The Celts (pronounced "kelts") are often regarded as a very war-like people throughout history. Even today, their ferocity in battle and proud, warrior culture is wistfully reminisced by many and reviled and stereo-typed as barbarous by many others. Regardless, why are the Celts so asso-ciated with violence and warfare? Well, like all of history, the "facts" of what went on in days gone by are often written by the winners, and in this case, the Romans.

Much of the earliest documentation we have about the Celts comes from Roman sources, and the reason we need to bring a brick of salt into this "history" is because the Romans mostly encountered Celtic peoples through warfare. So, if you're writing about a foreign culture that you and everyone you know have only met on the battlefield amid vicious combat, then the things that get written are often about how vicious and combat-ive those people are. Making matters murkier is that many Celtic tribes did not write down their own history, using oral tradition instead, which became lost or muddled through Christian evangelism. Still, there are some things we can safely infer about the Celts that don't rely solely on the word of their victorious enemies.

Aquatic Offerings

Now, when we talk about "Celts," most people think of the peoples of Ireland, Scotland, Wales, Cornwall, and French Brittany because that is where Celtic culture still thrives. However, before the Christianization of Europe, "Celts" was a very broad term for large numbers of indigenous peoples who lived throughout Western and Eastern Europe (from Spain to Bulgaria) that shared close linguistic, cultural, ethnic, and religious sim-ilarities. One similarity they had in regard to religion and war was the offering of war bounty into bodies of water.

Votive offerings to the gods and the spirits of the land were a common practice, but while most offerings were buried, those offerings pertaining to war were given up to the water. Lakes, bogs, rivers, and various other bodies of water were where military gifts to the Divine were given. These ranged from swords and other weaponry to elaborate shields and armor. In particular, the River Thames in modern England was a hotspot where archaeologists often continue to find Celtic war offerings to the gods. In fact, this common Celtic practice is believed to have influenced the King

Arthur legends about the Lady of the Lake, wherein Arthur receives his famous sword Excalibur from a magical woman lurking in the depths of a body of water.[99]

Furor Celtica

A recurring theme in the warrior cultures of the Celts is just how intensely they would throw their entire mind, body, and spirit into battle. This "Celtic fury" was seen by their enemies as a sort of temporary insanity wherein the Celts would give themselves entirely over to the battle-frenzy bloodlust of combat, losing all sense of rational humanity and thus making them more unpredictably deadly. Not only was this an effective tactic on the battlefield, but it also served a religious purpose.

Armed conflict was seen as a preeminent way to show one's value to the Celtic gods. By being brave, fierce, and victorious in military combat, your standing in the eyes of the Divine would move up, and thus you'd be more favored and likely to be aided by the gods should you petition their help for anything you desired. Also, being seen as a strong and valuable warrior was often the best way to gain respect and prestige in the eyes of the clan. With successive victories under your belt (and the socio-psychological benefit of being *perceived* by others as favored by the gods as evidenced by those victories), you'd be more inclined to be selected as a leader if not *the* chief of the clan (and all the side-benefits that came along with it). Once again, becoming a warrior was the best way to honor the gods and climb the social ladder.[100]

Adding to the infamy of this much-feared Celtic fury is the fact that many Celtic tribes often purposely decapitated their defeated enemies. So, if you were there in battle against them, not only would you see these

---

99 "Iron Age Celts: Religion & Belief," BBC, accessed May 1, 2020, https://www.bbc.co.uk/wales/celts/factfile/religion.shtml; Miguel A. De La Torre and Albert Hernández, *The Quest for the Historical Satan* (Minneapolis: Fortress Press, 2011), n.p.

100 Dattatreya Mandal, "Ancient Celtic Warriors: 10 Things You Should Know," Realm of History, October 18, 2016, https://www.realmofhistory.com/2016/10/18/10-facts-ancient-celts-warriors/.

"wild" men going absolutely insane with enraged strength, but you'd also see them carrying the severed heads of your comrades.

To the Celts, though, this was not for the psychological shock value of body desecration in and of itself, but rather, it was to enhance their own spiritual power. Admittedly, more research needs to be done for any definitive answers, but the current prevailing theory is that the head was the part of the body in which many Celtic tribes believed the soul resided. By having an enemy's head, they thus had their enemy's soul to use as a physical amulet that spiritually empowered them and warded off evil and misfortune amid battle.[101]

VIKING AGE SCANDINAVIA

As mythologized and reminisced as it is today in popular media, the Viking Age only lasted from around the early ninth to mid-eleventh century CE, but despite only existing in this relatively small window of time, the Norse peoples of this age left deep scars throughout the face of Europe that ever after greatly influenced the way history unfolded.

Going Berserk

The Scandinavian Norsemen from this era are prominently depicted as barbarous enemies who, like the Celts, were almost universally noted for their psychotic ferocity in battle that plunged into all-out insanity, and the name for being under the influence of this fury was called "berserk" after the Viking warriors known as "berserkers" (warriors wearing bear skins, believed to give them bearlike strength).[102]

Beyond just the all-in, seemingly superhuman strength akin to Celtic fury, going berserk included visibly disturbing fits such as the uncontrolla-

---

101   John C. Koch, ed., *Celtic Culture: A Historical Encyclopedia* (Santa Barbara, CA: ABC-CLIO, 2006), 895–898; Thomas Garlinghouse, "Ancient Celts Decapitated Their Enemies and Saved Their Heads, Archaeologists Say," *Discover Magazine*, February 12, 2019, https://www.discovermagazine.com /planet-earth/ancient-celts-decapitated-their-enemies-and-saved-their-heads -archaeologists-say.

102   "Berserk (adj.)," Online Etymology Dictionary, accessed May 1, 2020, https:// www.etymonline.com/word/berserk.

ble chattering of teeth, the face becoming purple, and even the biting and gnawing upon a berserker's own shield and skin like a rabid dog would do. Seeing this absolutely terrified their "sane" enemies, often weakening them psychologically before any fighting even began. As to what "going berserk" actually was, there are two prevailing theories.

The religious theory is that these Norse warriors were engaging in a type of spiritual possession to give them a leg up in battle. By invoking the instinctive ferocity of a powerful animal (such as a bear) and mimicking their bestial behavior, a warrior could increase his physical potency. The physio-biological theory is that purposely ingesting hallucinogenic plants (most likely mushrooms or bog myrtle) led to this desired effect of true, uninhibited madness on the battlefield.[103]

Aggressors

A lot of the bad rap these Norsemen got in the Viking Age had a lot to do with the fact that they were usually the aggressors in warfare. They were always prodding into other people's homelands and rarely were involved in a war of self-defense for their own homeland against invading foreign powers. Naturally, it's hard to be seen as anything but the bad guys when history is being written by all the people you've victimized over the years. Still (like everything), nothing happens in a vacuum, and there's a reason for the Vikings' piracy and conquest of foreign lands. When we get down to it, it was for both practical and spiritual reasons.

On the practical side, these raids brought in a lot of wealth to the various chieftains back in Scandinavia. If you wanted to conquer (or defend against) your homeland tribal neighbor, you needed warriors to back you up, and in order to have warriors fighting for you, you needed to pay them. A very profitable way to gather a lot of gold without instigating any domestic wars would be to get it from overseas. And it wasn't just the chieftains who'd benefit, either. The actual Viking warriors who went

---

103 Joanna Gillan, "Viking Berserkers—Fierce Warriors or Drug-Fuelled Madmen?" Ancient Origins, May 26, 2019, https://www.ancient-origins.net/myths-legends/viking-berserkers-fierce-warriors-or-drug-fuelled-madmen-001472.

overseas could amass personal wealth from the spoils of war that they plundered. With more wealth, they could become more influential back at home—once *again* showing that the best way to climb the socioeconomic ladder was to become a warrior.[104]

The spiritual reason for the Vikings' warfare aggression is thought to be their fears of the afterlife. Similar to the ancient Greeks, the default afterlife for Norse pagans was seen as dark and horrific. Nevertheless, an optimal afterlife of never-ending drinking, feasting, and carousing in the halls of Valhalla was a possible alternative … but only for those who died in battle or from battle wounds.

Thus, to ensure that your ever after in the hereafter was a good one, you needed to keep putting yourself in situations where you could potentially die from armed conflict, thus the high frequency of Viking raids. Also, in an ironic twist, if a Norse warrior was always victorious and unbeaten in battle, then that made them less likely to enter Valhalla since they were less likely to die in or because of losing a fight. Thus, for these veteran warriors who lived to a ripe old age, there was a real fear of not getting into Valhalla. This fear sometimes caused them to self-inflict axe and sword wounds while on their deathbed as a last-ditch attempt to fool the psychopomp Valkyries into thinking they had died from battle wounds.[105]

Nothing lasts forever, though, and around 1066 CE, the Viking Age had ended. Not only was it becoming less and less profitable to go on overseas raids, but their targets had learned their tactics by then and knew how to better repulse them on the battlefield. Most influentially, though, the Norse peoples weren't pagans anymore. Scandinavia had been effectively

104   Lise Brix, "Why Danish Vikings Moved to England," ScienceNordic, February 23, 2017, https://sciencenordic.com/denmark-society—culture-videnskabdk/why-danish-vikings-moved-to-england/1442885; Daniel McCoy, "Viking Raids and Warfare," Norse Mythology for Smart People, accessed May 1, 2020, https://norse-mythology.org/viking-raids-warfare/.

105   Gro Steinsland and Preben Meulengracht Sørensen, *Människor och makter i Vikingarnas värld* (Stockholm, Ordfront, 1998), n.p.; Snorri Sturluson, *The Poetic Edda*, trans. Lee M. Hollander (Austin, TX: University of Texas Press, 1986), n.p.

Christianized, and with most of Europe also Christianized, it became less popular among the Norsemen to brutally attack their brothers and sisters of the faith. Plus, all the looting, killing, and pillaging didn't align well with the new "love thy neighbor" teachings of Jesus Christ as it had with the more morally ambiguous and battle-ready deities of Norse mythology. Still, across the Baltic Sea there did exist one last kingdom that defiantly stood alone as a bastion of state-supported paganism against Christian encroachment: Lithuania.[106]

THE PAGAN BALTIC

Eastern Europe often gets left out when it comes to world history, but it was here where continental pagan spiritual resistance against the onslaught of Christian evangelism endured the longest. Outlasting all their contemporaries, the Baltic kingdom of Lithuania was the last bastion of state-supported pagan resistance amid the rising tide of Christianity, and they refused to submit without a hell of a fight.

Lots of Fortune

Paganism in the Baltic region of Eastern Europe held many similarities with paganism elsewhere in Europe. Aside from a polytheistic pantheon of deities, nature was regarded as inherently divine, and through the spiritual ability to commune with the unseen forces of the natural world, one could influence destiny. Of particular popularity here in the Baltic was fortune-telling via the casting of lots (usually through etched dice), and this sacred method of divination was notoriously utilized and depended upon by the region's warriors and soldiers (for whom mystical foresight into the future could not only lead to victory on the battlefield but also save them from a massacre).

Sometimes, the casting of lots proved invaluable, as exemplified in 1323 CE when a Baltic pagan warrior warned his brothers-in-arms of the ill

---

106 William R. Short, "What Happened to the Vikings?" Hurstwic, accessed May 1, 2020, http://www.hurstwic.org/history/articles/society/text/what _happened.htm.

omen he received from his divinatory dice. Because of his warning (and the fact that his fellow pagan soldiers believed in the divinatory power of casting lots), they retreated from their planned advance and "coincidentally" avoided a very deadly ambush that was awaiting them.

Other times, however, the casting of lots proved disastrous, as exemplified in 1290 CE when, while en route back home from a victory, the dice of a worried Baltic warrior predicted woe and death for him and his fellow soldiers. Consequently, this warrior was so freaked out by what he read in the dice that he kept yelling and loudly warning everyone about the prediction, ignoring their pleas for him to be quiet. Sure enough, this continual barrage of panicked yelling alerted their enemies of their whereabouts, leading to a fatal ambush proving the dice had, indeed, accurately foretold the future, albeit the prophecy was self-fulfilling.[107]

Teutonic Shift

By the dawn of the thirteenth century CE, paganism in Europe had been firmly placed under heel by Christianity. Yes, some peoples of Europe still practiced the "old ways" in clandestine secret, but paganism as a state-sanctioned and supported spiritual tradition no longer existed…except in a single kingdom on the Baltic Coast called Lithuania.

Medieval Lithuania, though heavily pagan, was initially not anti-Christian. The ruling kings (even Lithuanian Christian kings) were historically tolerant of all faiths and all forms of native paganism in their realm, but this was a liberalism against which the Vatican in Rome held a grudge. To deal with this inexcusable Lithuanian tolerance, Pope Innocent III expanded the "infidel" scope of the Crusades to include the Baltic pagans in 1204 CE. Adding to the anti-pagan pressure was the fact that neighboring Catholic Poland had petitioned the Teutonic Knights (a Germanic

---

107 "Baltic Paganism, Superstitions and Spells in the Grand Duchy of Lithuania," *Lithuania Tribune*, April 1, 2019, https://lithuaniatribune.com/baltic-paganism -superstitions-and-spells-in-the-grand-duchy-of-lithuania/.

crusading order of Catholic warrior monks) to help secure their borders against pagan Lithuania.[108]

With the intensely militaristic Teutonic Knights on their southern flank (and other monastic knights of the "Livonian Order" on their northern flank), the first grand duke of Lithuania, Mindaugas, tactically converted to Catholicism in the early 1250s so as to remove the threat of Crusader invasion from his territory and gain for his people the protective blessing of the Pope. Still, the situation remained tense because not only did Mindaugas continue to openly worship his pagan gods, but he also refused to persecute non-Christians in his majority-pagan realm. Eventually in 1261 CE, Mindaugas ceased his spiritual masquerade completely by openly denying the validity of Catholic teachings and forcibly expelling all Christians from his land.[109]

Friendless Fears

Religious conflicts continued plaguing the successors of Mindaugas after he was assassinated. Caught between the Catholicism of Western Europe and the Eastern Orthodoxy of Eastern Europe, no longer was being nondenominational Christian enough, as both factions of Catholic and Orthodox Christians demanded that each Lithuanian king pick a side. By the 1300s, the Lithuanian kings had solidified into a third option: open paganism, and it was a choice that brought the ire of all factional denominations of Christendom upon them and sanctioned the Teutonic Knights to wage a full-on Crusade against this last pagan kingdom in Europe.

This pressure from all sides (including recent Mongol invasions) eventually became insurmountable. Lithuania needed allies, but there were no more pagan kingdoms left with whom to ally against all of Christian

---

108   "Battle of Grunwald 1410—Northern Crusades Documentary," Kings and Generals, December 28, 2017, YouTube, 11:54, https://www.youtube.com /watch?v=VeBOJ0bAI6Q.

109   S. C. Rowell, *Lithuania Ascending: A Pagan Empire within East-Central Europe, 1295–1345* (Cambridge: Cambridge University Press, 2014), 51–52, 120–121, 131; Gabriel Ignatow, *Transnational Identity Politics and the Environment* (Lanham: Lexington Books, 2007), 100.

Europe and invading nomads from the steppes of Asia. Knowing this, Jogaila (the then-grand duke of Lithuania) chose neighboring Poland with whom to ally and converted to Catholicism, sealing the alliance by marrying the Catholic queen of Poland in 1386 CE. This marriage united Lithuania and Poland into, effectively, one Catholic kingdom. Thus, these wedding vows successfully accomplished what knights, monks, and popes had been trying to do for centuries: permanently Christianize the last pagan kingdom of Europe.[110]

European Pagan Takeaway:
THE COMPLETE HISTORY

History is written by the winners, and whatever you were taught about the past, you were taught it because it is the version of history that is most beneficial to the social and financial powers that be wherein you grew up. This is true regardless of where you are in the world.

China does not teach its citizens about the infamous Tiananmen Square student rebellion for democracy (or anything that would make the ruling Communist Party look bad). Japanese history books teach that their involvement in WWII was one of self-defense and omits the genocides and war crimes committed by them. If you think modern industrialized nations of the West don't do the same, think again (after all, it wasn't until very recently that the U.S.. stopped making films that re-wrote how its slave history "wasn't so bad" and how the enslaved people "liked" it ... with certain textbooks even still promoting this revised "history"). It's insidious.

For most of the past two millennia, the world's assumptions of the Celtic and Viking era Norse peoples were that of war-hungry barbarians, but that's only because their enemies (Rome and Christianity) won the long war and wrote the history books that make themselves look more civilized and their enemies more barbarous (as a way to justify their military ambitions). Worse still, no one questioned this history, and even pagan kingdoms of religious tolerance like Lithuania surviving well into

---

110   Jerzy Kloczowski, *A History of Polish Christianity*, trans. Malgorzata Sady
(Cambridge: University of Cambridge Press, 2000), 54–55.

and through most of the Middle Ages in the Baltic go completely ignored in modern world history.

So, your takeaway challenge here is to question the history of things you hold dear. The more fervently you value something, the more important it is for you to question it. This doesn't just include your own country's history; question your religious beliefs, your spiritual tradition, your cultural traditions, your family traditions, and most importantly, anything you just accept as "true" or "normal" because that is what you were raised to believe.

Take special note to learn from trustworthy sources too. A lot of the stuff online nowadays is only produced to generate ad revenue. (Blog writers and YouTube personalities who need to fill their weekly quota of articles and videos so as to pay the rent and keep their companies SEO compliant and trending on internet algorithms are often not going to do the research necessary for accurate information...their entire goal is just to get you to click through to their sites with your ad blocker off and get you to buy or sign up for something.) Of course, this is not to say that everything online is a distortion of the truth, as there are many reputable websites and personalities who earnestly do their due research, but when there's easy money to be made from promoting a lie and uneducated "opinions" are more attention-grabbing than factual truths, one must always be critical of the intention of the author.

Do the work. Discover the *real* history behind things in your life, and then assess changes as necessary. To fight your whole life for a cause that wasn't really a "cause" but rather a political or corporate machination of propaganda would be quite the wasted life, or worse, a life spent unknowingly fighting for the enemy.

Deities & Legends

BOUDICA

Boudica was the legendary Celtic queen who united various Celtic clans to take up arms and rise in revolt against Rome's armies. Despite her oft-told underdog defiance against the invading Roman juggernaut, the full details of her life and leadership aren't fully known, and a lot of it gets intertwined with local legend and folklore. Still, her generally agreed-upon history is that Boudica was married to the pro-Roman king of a Celtic tribe in Britannia who chose to be an ally of Rome in the hopes that the Romans would help destroy his rivals. Upon her husband's death, however, the Roman army cancelled their alliance and subsequently pillaged her lands, raped her daughters, and ruthlessly flogged her to near death.

This betrayal by the Romans and unforgiveable treatment of her, her family, and her people made her an avowed enemy of Rome looking for bloody vengeance. She amassed power by uniting various Celtic clans into a resistance against the Romans and by being elected the political and military leader of this Celtic union. Under her leadership, the British Celts won a string of military successes that pushed the invaders back toward the English Channel. Still, despite these initial victories, the Roman army would come out the ultimate victor after Boudica's forces suffered a major defeat in 60 CE. After this unrecoverable loss, the Romans fully subjugated the island (save for modern Scotland), though accounts differ as to the Celtic queen's own fate. Depending upon which sources you read (and which you believe), Boudica either died in transit to Rome where she was to be paraded through the streets as an exotic prisoner of war or she committed suicide via self-poisoning so as to prevent being taken prisoner and enslaved.[111]

Since her death, Boudica has been looked back upon as a great martial leader, feminist icon, and very capable fighter from atop the chariot with which she personally led her troops into battle. Even more inspiring, Roman accounts of her on the battlefield depicted her as a truly charismatic general whose rallying cries and inspirational *Braveheart*-esque speeches to her armies centered around reminding them that their freedom was on the line and that if a wealthy woman like her had everything

111   Tacitus, Book 14, *The Annals*, trans. Alfred John Church and William Jackson Brodribb, Internet Classics Archive, accessed May 2, 2020, http://classics.mit .edu/Tacitus/annals.html.

to lose by fighting against Rome, then men and those with far less to lose had no excuse not to take up arms and give it their all.[112]

THE MORRIGAN

Celtic goddess of war, battle, strife, death, regeneration, and the underworld, the Morrigan is known as a triple goddess, often being depicted as three women simultaneously: Babd (crow goddess of fear and confusion), Macha (sovereignty goddess of land, kingship, and horses), and Nemain (spirit goddess of battle-frenzy and havoc).

It was Gaelic Ireland wherein she became prominently associated with darkness, death, and warfare (but not in an evil way since darkness, death, and warfare weren't considered evil in and of themselves, just unavoidable aspects of life). On October 31 (Samhain/Halloween), she is believed to straddle both the physical and spiritual worlds, allowing contact between the lands of the living and the dead. In her affairs with humans, she is known for her ambivalence, sometimes helping them and sometimes harming them. Occasionally thought of as a Celtic equivalent to the Norse Valkyries, the Morrigan is more popularly known in modern times through the legends of King Arthur, wherein she is characterized as Morgan le Fay.[113]

ODIN

In Norse mythology, Odin is the supreme deity and one of the most multifaceted gods in Scandinavian myths and legends. As such, he is the patron god of quite a number of things, but he is probably best known for his patronage of wisdom, healing, sorcery, and war. A lot of stories about him tend to revolve around his pursuit of knowledge and all the things he is willing to do and sacrifice in order to learn more about everything and anything (including having one of his eyes plucked out and even submitting to

---

112   Matt Hollis, "Watling Street 60 AD—Boudica's Revolt," Kings and Generals, June 6, 2019, YouTube, 17:01, https://www.youtube.com/watch?v =5xxUc3T1_As.

113   Christopher Penczak, *Gay Witchcraft: Empowering the Tribe* (San Francisco: Red Wheel/Weiser, 2003), 49.

being the receiving partner in sexual intercourse, which Viking-era Norsemen regarded as the ultimate shame).

Odin's place in war was not that of a warrior on the front lines, but rather, he was more of an Athena-esque strategist. His immense wisdom allowed him to know the best moves to make, when to attack, how, and so on. Before going into battle, Norsemen would petition him for such combat knowledge as well as his personal favor (since his influence over the Valkyries allowed him to dictate who would survive the coming carnage). Moreover, Odin was the main god to whom warriors petitioned because he was in full favor of the kind of amorality that warfare often necessitates. Unlike other deities, he didn't look down on those who slaughtered, went berserk, and did whatever they had to do to win a war. To him, the ends always justify the means, as evidenced in his own personal pursuit of wisdom at any cost.[114]

THE VALKYRIES

The Valkyries were the handmaidens of Odin in Norse mythology and the preeminent psychopomps into the afterlife. They would descend on flying horses down into the carnage of a battlefield in full warrior regalia and personally escort dead soldiers' souls to either Valhalla or Fólkvagr where the dead would be able to feast, drink, and enjoy themselves heartily (both destinations being essentially the same, except the former was presided by Odin while the latter was presided by Freyja, a mighty goddess of war herself in addition to beauty, love, and sex).

In older accounts of the Valkyries (before Norse history was recorded through a more Christian lens), they took on a more active and sinister role in warfare. Not just passive escorts of the dead, they were previously believed to be able to decide who would live and who would die in battle, using dark sorcery to ensure the outcome. Still, the Valkyries were suscep-

---

114 Sturluson, *The Poetic Edda*, n.p.; Emma Groeneveld, "Odin," World History Encyclopedia, November 13, 2017, https://www.worldhistory.org/odin/.

tible to human emotions such as love, jealousy, and favoritism, allowing mortals to be able to change their fate by endearing themselves to certain Valkyries. Regardless, their decisions had to come with the consent of Odin, and tragic are the tales of Valkyries who slayed or saved humans without Odin's approval. From a historical perspective, they were based on stories of the earliest Norse warrior women who'd fight alongside the men.[115]

VELNIAS

In the native paganism of Lithuania, Velnias (sometimes spelled "Velinas") was an underworld deity who held dominion over and protected the souls of the dead. He was also quite the trickster who loved to play mischievous jokes on unsuspecting mortals. Despite his morbid associations and penchant for irksome chaos, Velnias was highly regarded as the militaristic savior of Lithuania during their wars against the crusading Teutonic Knights.

According to legend, it was Velnias who supernaturally enhanced the swords of the Lithuanian soldiers during the all-important and decisive Battle of Grunwald, a magical enchantment that was credited for the Crusaders' devastating defeat (a defeat that forced the Teutonic Knights to ultimately have to sign a peace treaty). Even before that, though, Velnias was regarded as the divinity responsible for gifting the Lithuanian people with knowledge of ironworking so that they could create weapons to defend themselves (secret knowledge Velnias stole from the blacksmith god Kalvelis).

Nowadays, Velnias is by and large associated with Satanism (his name being regionally synonymous with "Satan"). This was due to centuries of Christian missionaries capitalizing on his underworld aspects and singling

---

115   Daniel McCoy, "Valkyries," Norse Mythology for Smart People, accessed May 2, 2020, https://norse-mythology.org/gods-and-creatures/valkyries/; Riley Winters, "The Powerful Valkyries as Icons of Female Force and Fear," Ancient Origins, July 12, 2015, https://www.ancient-origins.net/myths-legends -europe/powerful-valkyries-icons-female-force-and-fear-003407.

him out as the "Satanic" deity when needing to find a Baltic pagan equivalent to the devil. Still, though, in the Lithuanian language, both the title for the recently deceased (*veliuonis*) and for "All Souls' Day" (*Velines*) are approximately named after him, the latter of which is regarded as one of the most important family holidays of the year.[116]

116   Darius James Ross, "Lithuania's Pagans Try to Turn Back the Clock," *The Baltic Times*, August 17, 2000, https://www.baltictimes.com/news/articles/1962/.

10
THE CHRISTIAN KINGDOMS

Cultural

Common Denominator

After the fall of Rome, much of Europe was up for grabs, and a series of back-and-forth warfare between the various native peoples commenced, each one wanting to fill the region's power vacuum and become the new superpower. However, it was the Frankish kingdom's Charlemagne who would win out and establish the foundations of Western Europe as we know it today, thanks in large part to his spiritual utilization of Christianity.

Charlemagne (a French portmanteau of "Charles the Great") came from a distinguished Christian family, and by the time he became king of the Franks, he had inherited a strong, well-administered empire that would encompass what is now France, Belgium, Switzerland, Luxemburg, the Netherlands, and parts of Germany. More so than his predecessors, he continued this family legacy of conquest with a much more religious focus.

The use of religion as a justification for war proved tactical (albeit he was also most likely sincere in his zealotry). You see, the usual problem that comes from ruling an empire composed of a patchwork of various conquered peoples is that there's no sense of unity, subsequently leaving the empire weak from internal factions and infighting. However, the one thing lots of these disparate Western European cultures had in common by the mid-eighth century CE when Charlemagne came to power was that many of them were now Christian (or at least had Christianity heavily mixed into their native spirituality). So, by capitalizing on this singular common denominator factor of religion between them all and forcefully portraying himself as a religious leader (as opposed to a regional or cultural leader of a specific ethno-cultural tribe as was more common in that era), Charlemagne tactically used his conquered subjects' faith against them to fabricate a shared identity that would keep them in line and maintain the status quo of their subservience to him.[117]

Papal Blessings

The singular act that forever married Christianity to militarism was when the Pope crowned Charlemagne as "Holy Roman Emperor" which spectacularly came about through a mix of sexism and survival. The thing to remember is that at this point in European history, the Pope was the biggest deal around. It didn't matter how powerful or how divinely mandated you claimed your legitimacy to whatever throne you sat upon to be, the Pope was still regarded as *the* divinely authorized ruler of the entire earth, outranking all kings and queens.

Of course, the Pope had no actual physical power or teeth to enforce his spiritual authority and relied mostly on militarily powerful Christian kingdoms to be his enforcers. Before Charlemagne came about, Christianity's

---

117   Richard E. Sullivan, "Charlemagne," Encyclopedia Britannica, updated January 24, 2021, https://www.britannica.com/biography/Charlemagne/Religious -reform.

de facto enforcer was the Byzantine Empire (aka: the surviving eastern half of the Roman Empire) over in modern-day Greece and Turkey. But something unprecedented happened in 797 CE: a woman named Irene Sarantapechaina became empress and ruler of the Byzantine Empire.

The Pope at the time, Leo III, absolutely did not want to acknowledge a woman as the lead defender of the Christian faith, and so in 799 CE when an Italian rebellion against the Pope needed to be squashed, Leo III broke precedent and reached out to Charlemagne to act as his muscle instead of Byzantine Irene. Being the opportunist he was, Charlemagne agreed, and was crowned as the "Holy Roman Emperor" as reward for putting down the rebellion (a passive-aggressive de-legitimization of Byzantine Empress Irene who was technically the *actual* holy successor to the Roman Empire). Now, with the Pope's official blessing, Charlemagne could legitimately claim military leadership over all people who adhered to Christianity. This legitimization of Western Europe to fight wars as God's soldiers would eventually come to a flashpoint centuries later during the Crusades.[118]

Onward, Christian Soldier

The Crusades were a strange and bloody mix of imperialism and resistance fighting between the Christian kingdoms of Europe and the Islamic Caliphates of the Middle East. Each side saw the other as foreign oppressors and saw themselves as defending their own spiritual turf. Add into the mix sanctimonious propaganda of doing God/Allah's will, and both sides just became that much more entrenched.

Its earliest beginnings were in the eighth century CE when Islamic empires conquered the Levant from the Byzantine Empire (the Levant being where Judaism, Christianity, and Islam all have *major* holy sites), but in the eleventh century, it started to seem like Islam would conquer the Byzantine Empire entirely and from there flood into Europe. So, Pope Urban II urged all Christians to not only stop the Muslim advance into

---

118 Monica Fleener, "The Significance of the Coronation of Charlemagne," (thesis, Western Oregon University Department of History, 2005): 1–29, https://wou.edu/history/files/2015/08/Monica-Fleener.pdf.

Eastern Europe, but also push them all the way back out of the Levant and recover the Levantine Holy Land while they were at it.

Now, these were the days of fire and brimstone in Catholicism (and before Christianity began really fragmenting from Catholicism into the numerous denominations of Protestantism), and unlike modern Catholic teaching, it was understood that you'd most likely go to hell after death unless you lived a particularly sin-free life. Thus, the spiritual incentive Pope Urban II offered to anyone who'd take up the fight was absolution, a complete and total forgiveness of all your past sins if you went on the Crusade (and thus, a free ticket into heaven).

For many people, they saw joining the military as their only shot for a happy afterlife. Still, there was also a much more earthly reason to join a Crusade: plundering the spoils of war was the only real way a feudalism commoner could rise beyond their station in life. And so, again, many people saw joining the military as their only shot at happiness in the hereafter and escaping backbreaking poverty.[119]

Rise of the Knights Templar

Over the centuries of back-and-forth holy wars for control of the Levant, some Catholic religious orders became so skilled in their military prowess that they frightened even the most powerful kings of Europe. Of all these orders, the Knights Templar are arguably the most infamous, and no one else experienced as spectacular heights and legendary falls from grace as these spiritual warriors.

They came into existence after the First Crusade ended in a Christian victory in 1099 CE. With the Levant back in their possession, the Catholic faithful began regular pilgrimages to the Holy Land, religiously inspired French warriors saw it as their duty to protect these pilgrims from bandits all along the routes to and from Jerusalem (because this was before banking, and you had to carry *all* your money with you on your person the entire trip). Over time, they became so skilled in fighting and rescuing

---

119 Department of Medieval Art and the Cloisters, "The Crusades (1095–1291)," New York Metropolitan Museum of Art, updated February 2014, https://www.metmuseum.org/toah/hd/crus/hd_crus.htm.

travelers in need anywhere along the pilgrimage routes throughout Europe and the Levant that they become somewhat of the medieval equivalent of a paramilitary AAA service.[120]

Just like nowadays, nothing succeeds like success, and the Knights Templar (as the spiritual warriors came to be known) became renowned throughout Europe for being so good at what they did. Nobles began bequeathing large amounts of land to them in lieu of going on sacred pilgrimages or Crusades themselves, and the Church declared them exempt from any and all taxes in all Christian kingdoms.[121]

This made them very, *very* wealthy, and they became wealthier still when they developed the Western world's first international banking system of deposits, withdrawals, credits, and loans (Tang Dynasty China was technically the first in the world, but their isolationism prevented that knowledge from spreading to the West). No longer did you have to carry all your money with you on the journey to Jerusalem; now you could deposit it at a Templar bank in or near your hometown, withdraw however much you needed at any major city along the way, and know that should you run into any problems anywhere, the most tough-as-nails religious military corps of fighting Catholic warriors would help you out.[122]

Knightfall

It all came crashing down in the mid-thirteenth century CE when the Muslims definitively conquered the Holy Land from Christian Europe once and for all. This meant no more international pilgrimages, which subsequently meant the Templars' banking, defense, and military services weren't really needed anymore. Even worse was that they were too financially successful for their own good.

---

120 Simon Worrall, "The Templars Got Rich Fighting for God—Then Lost It All," *National Geographic*, September 22, 2017, https://www.nationalgeographic .com/news/2017/09/knights-templar-crusades-dan-jones/.

121 Charles G. Addison, Esq., *The History of the Knights Templars, the Temple Church, and the Temple* (London: Longman, Brown, Green, and Longmans, 1842), https://www.gutenberg.org/files/38593/38593-h/38593-h.htm.

122 Tim Harford, "The Warrior Monks Who Invented Banking," BBC, January 30, 2017, https://www.bbc.com/news/business-38499883.

King Philip IV of France was drowning in debt to the Templars and found it easier to disband the Order rather than have to pay them back. He used the rumors surrounding the goings-on in their secret initiation ceremonies to accuse the Templars of practicing idolatry, sacrilege, homosexuality, evil sorcery, and other scandalous deeds during those closed-to-the-public rituals. It was all essentially the "fake news" of the day to misdirect the people away from Philip IV's own financial mismanagement of the treasury, and it worked. Based on these unsubstantiated and obvious lies, public opinion turned against the Templars, and even the pope officially disbanded their Order from the Church (thus cancelling all debts owed to them). The Knights Templar were no more, though their use of weaponizing Christianity for financial gain would live on.[123]

Christian Takeaway:
THE SIN OF OMISSION

One particular sin in the Catholic Church that is not often talked about (because it does not benefit those in power) is the sin of omission. Cutting through its theological interpretations, it's essentially all about not turning a blind eye toward injustice. Thus, in official Catholic doctrine, it is just as much of a sin to witness evil, injustice, or wrongdoing and not intervene to stop it as it is to commit it yourself.

Revolutionaries of the minority against a majority oppressor (most notably Martin Luther King, Jr. and Holocaust survivor Elie Wiesel) have appealed to the fence-sitting onlookers of their civil and human rights struggles through the use of this Catholic teaching to show how not taking a side is equivalent to siding with the oppressor. There is no neutrality; to sit on the sidelines or do nothing only allows evil and oppression to continue.

On a more everyday scale, this ranges from not speaking up for that woman being harassed on the bus, to not calling someone out on social media for their hurtful trolling or spreading of false information, to not vot-

123 Worrall, "The Templars Got Rich Fighting for God"; Martin Hickes, "Whatever Happened to the Knights Templar?" *The Guardian*, June 27, 2011, https://www.theguardian.com/uk/the-northerner/2011/jun/27/whatever -happened-to-the-knights-templar.

ing, and beyond. According to Catholic doctrine, just because the oppression and hate is not targeted at or affecting you personally does not give you spiritual reprieve from personal responsibility in helping to stop it.

So, for your takeaway challenge here, actively and vocally stand up for people and causes whose struggles, defeats, and victories do not affect you personally. Be the person who says, "Hey, man, that's not cool" when a friend starts making racist, sexist, or homophobic jokes or remarks. Be the person who takes the actual time and effort to perform a spell or say a prayer for social justice victories that won't affect you personally instead of the usual ones to benefit your own personal life in the form of health, wealth, and love. Be the one who steps in and does not passively ignore abuse against yourself or others. If you see something, say something. If you're capable of responding, respond. Ignoring the suffering of others is, after all, a sin.

Deities & Legends

ST. BARBARA

St. Barbara is a fascinatingly unique saint associated with the military whose story has become quite the legend. In fact, it's so legendary and filled with wild, hyperbolic magic that even the Catholic Church herself admits that a lot of it probably never happened. Nevertheless, she retains a devoted following and holds a special place as patron saint of artillerymen and miners (as well as all others who deal with gunpowder and explosives).[124]

The story goes that she was an extremely beautiful heiress living in the Roman Empire (in what is now Lebanon) during the third century CE. Because of her beauty, her pagan father locked her high in a tower (à la *Rapunzel*) to "protect" her from lusty men. However, Barbara's solitary meditations and time gazing out into the natural landscape from her vista viewpoint made her realize God's existence, and she converted to Christianity. This upset her father so much that he beat her and tried to burn

---

124   "St. Barbara," Encyclopedia Britannica, updated January 5, 2020, https://www.britannica.com/biography/Saint-Barbara.

her to death, but angels intervened and miraculously prevented any fire from harming her. Despite this, she was ultimately beheaded, though her executioners were struck down by thunderous lightning immediately after the deed was done.[125]

Because of her miraculous associations with fire and thunderous lightning, she became the patron saint of people who handle explosives. Spanish, French, and Italian armies would keep a statue of St. Barbara next to their storehouses of gunpowder in fortresses and on ships to spiritually safeguard against unintentional combustion, and she even became the official patroness of the Italian Navy.

In the U.S. today, The United States Army's Field Artillery Association and Air Defense Artillery Association hold the "Order of Saint Barbara" as an honorary society within their ranks. Additionally, according to one etymological origin legend, the pharmaceutical sedatives known as barbiturates were also allegedly named after her by their chemist inventor (Adolf von Baeyer) when he was celebrating his new discovery at an artillerymen's tavern on the feast day of St. Barbara (December 4).[126]

ST. GEORGE

Despite there being very little information on the life of St. George, he was once one of the most popular Catholic saints during the Middle Ages, especially during the era of the Crusades. He is officially the patron saint of England (whose red and white flag design is the medieval St. George's

---

125 "St. Barbara," Catholic Online, accessed May 4, 2020, https://www.catholic
.org/saints/saint.php?saint_id=166.

126 Jason Cutshaw, "Redstone Arsenal Celebrates St. Barbara Inductees," U.S.
Army, February 11, 2020, https://www.army.mil/article/232637/redstone
_arsenal_celebrates_st_barbara_inductees; Betsy Caprio, *The Woman Sealed
in the Tower: A Psychological Approach to Feminine Spirituality* (New York: Paulist
Press, 1982), n.p.; Henry Rzepa, Wyn Locke, Karl Harrison, and Paul May,
"Barbiturates," Molecules in Motion: An Active Chemical Exploratorium,
accessed May 4, 2020, http://www.ch.ic.ac.uk/rzepa/mim/drugs/html
/barbiturate_text.htm; Francisco López-Muñoz, Ronaldo Ucha-Udabe, and
Cecilio Alamo, "The History of Barbiturates a Century after Their Clinical
Introduction," *Neuropsychiatric Disease and Treatment* 1, no. 4 (December 2005):
329–343, https://www.ncbi.nlm.nih.gov/pmc/articles/PMC2424120/#b74.

Cross), and he had a large devotion among soldiers due to him probably having been a soldier himself in the Roman army during the late third century CE. And that's about all we somewhat verifiably know about him, though it is also highly likely that he was martyred for his faith as a Christian.

What St. George is most famous for, though (and why he was romanticized so much in the Middle Ages), is that one time when he saved a village by slaying an evil dragon who was harassing the townsfolk. This eventually became a popular tale told by wandering performance troupes and troubadours, and so St. George's knightly victory with the help of God against a dragon became so repetitively ingrained in the pop culture of the day that those who embarked on the Crusades prayed to him to possess such divinely aided military valor. There have also been many who claimed to have personally witnessed him assist their armies in battle while out on a Crusade. Thus, St. George became the idealization of a heroic Catholic soldier and is still celebrated on his feast day of April 23.[127]

ST. JOAN OF ARC

Arguably one of the most famous saints in the Catholic canon, her story has been the subject of countless books, movies, and video games due to its classic tale of an underestimated and painfully average young girl rising to greatness and glory in a man's world before ultimately being persecuted by the patriarchy (and the fact that it's a well-documented true story only furthers the faithful). In modern devotion, she's the patron saint of France, soldiers, women's Army Corps, and prisoners of war.

Her story is quite epic (and I *highly* suggest reading or watching the full story via your preferred medium), but the short version is that she was an illiterate peasant girl in fifteenth-century France during the Hundred Years' War in which France was currently losing badly to England. At thirteen, she received visions from saints who told her to lead the French resistance in expelling the English occupational forces. These celestial voices guided her to first go to the *dauphin* (the title for the heir-apparent

---

127 "St. George," Catholic Online, accessed May 4, 2020, https://www.catholic .org/saints/saint.p hp?saint_id=280.

to the French throne, France's equivalent to Britain's "Prince of Wales") to have him rightfully crowned as king (which could, by tradition, only occur in Reims, a city then currently under enemy occupation).

Against all odds, she successfully liberated Reims and then was given official command of a military force by the newly crowned king, which she then used to miraculously lift an ongoing siege at the strategic city of Orléans. She continued having major underdog upset victories like this until a failed attempt to retake Paris and other setbacks resulted in her eventual capture during her siege of Compiègne. Naturally, the English wanted to get rid of her since she was now the symbolic figurehead of the French resistance, so they set up a sham of a trial to try and find her guilty of witchcraft. However, much to the judicial court's astonishment, this uneducated young teen deftly never incriminated herself and flawlessly maneuvered around the prosecutor's complex legalese and wordplay traps.

So, instead, they claimed her guilty of crossdressing, both for the armor she wore on the battlefield and for the "male" clothes she wore in prison (which were the only clothes given to her and her only sliver of defense against being ogled and raped by her prison guards). At nineteen years old, she was burned at the stake.

Nowadays, she is seen as a symbol of French unity, pride, and resistance amongst all classes and sides of the political spectrum. The wealthy and conservatives respect her defense of the Catholic Church and her fighting on behalf of the French nobility. Meanwhile, the poor and progressives relate to her own origins of poverty and "everywoman" appeal as well as her defense of the weak and downtrodden against more powerful oppressors. Her feast day is May 30.[128]

---

128 "St. Joan of Arc," Catholic Online, accessed May 4, 2020, https://www
.catholic.org/saints/saint.php?saint_id=295; "Joan of Arc," Biography,
updated March 4, 2020, https://www.biography.com/military-figure
/joan-of-arc.

11
EUROPEAN MAGICAL COMMUNITY

Assembling Your Inner Council

From time to time, all of us need help. We need elder warriors whom we respect and admire to teach us what their more experienced lives have revealed to them. We all need this sage counsel from someone who has been where we are and has come through it victorious. For me, this counselor is B. Dave Walters. I'm deeply honored to say that I can count him as one of my oldest and dearest friends. Originally, I met him during a tough time in my life wherein I reached out to him as a stranger asking for help. Since then, I can firmly say that I am the success I am today thanks to his initial and continued counsel and wisdom.

So, whom else could I possibly ask to help give us a lesson on how to go about seeking spiritual counsel? It is probable, though, that you're already well familiar with who B. Dave Walters is. He is a fixture in the Dungeons & Dragons and Vampire: The Masquerade streaming communities; an actor, writer, and filmmaker who has numerous screenplays, novels, comic books, and nationally syndicated articles under his belt; *and* he's even the writer and director of the documentary film *Dear America, from a Black Guy* (as well as countless other endeavors that you can find more about via @BDaveWalters on all the social media).

Today, he's specifically here to tell you how seeking spiritual counsel helped him through a particularly low point in his own life and to teach you how to assemble your own spiritual council from whom to seek advice whenever you need them.

> *What would have become of Hercules, do you think, if there had*
> *been no lion, hydra, stag or boar—and no savage criminals to*
> *rid the world of? What would he have done in the absence of*
> *such challenges? Obviously he would have just rolled over in bed*
> *and gone back to sleep. So by snoring his life away in luxury and*
> *comfort he never would have developed into the mighty Hercules.*
> *—Epictetus*[129]

Around seven years ago, I hit a very low point.

I sat down in my meditation and entered into my Inner Temple. The room in question was a simple one with a candlelit stone table and three stools. Across from me sat "the Last Good Emperor" Marcus Aurelius and Seneca, the Stoic philosopher and statesman. I took a deep breath, and poured my heart out. All of it. My fears, the stress of trying to provide for my family, a recent repossession of my car that I'd managed to recover, and the impending threat of eviction looming over my head. And in the midst of that, a swift and crushing heartbreak had pushed me perilously close to what I feared might finally be my breaking point.

In my room I sat there with tears streaming down my face as I silently confided in my Stoic mentors in a way I had never expressed out loud.

---

129 Epictetus, *Discourses and Selected Writings* (New York: Penguin, 2008), n.d.

Everything inside of me, out on the table. And once I finished, in my Inner Temple I sat there looking at the two of them, and I saw them as clearly as if I could reach out and touch them.

They turned and looked at each other; Seneca just shrugged, and Marcus said ... "And?"

In that simple moment, I was freed. I found myself laughing out loud sitting there in the darkness in my real world meditation space. The sky wasn't falling, and I would be fine.

I had owned my own insurance agency for years, but the economic collapse of 2008 had taken a toll, and I'd returned to the workforce. The biggest blessing that arrived during this time was I discovered the Meditations by Marcus Aurelius, a book that changed my life. I've always been a resilient person by nature, but the discovery of Stoicism opened my eyes to the fact that the life approach I'd arrived at instinctually was reflective of one of the grandest philosophical traditions of all time. The simple, cool objectivity of Stoicism meshed seamlessly with my own background in Buddhist non-attachment to create a lifeline to keep me afloat in the midst of a sea of chaos.

But, by 2013 it had all caught up to me, so I turned to one of my greatest and most useful tools, which I would like to share with you now: Assembling your Inner Council.

I am of the opinion that something inside of us is connected to an infinite pool of information, a pool that can be readily accessed with a little practice.

Step 1: Enter into your meditation. Don't stress too hard about getting it "right," just open your mind to the intention. You might see things with your inner eyes, hear with your inner ears, or just experience a non-specific knowing. The most important thing to keep in mind is not to take it too seriously. Don't stress about what's real and what's "just" your imagination. Let it flow without judgment.

Step 2: Decide who you want to connect with. It can be anyone living, dead, or mythical. I myself have gods, heroes, angels, historical figures, and the Almighty available to me in my Inner Temple.

*Step 3: Decide where they'd be when you want to meet them,
and go there in your meditation. First impressions matter!
You want to start off your relationship by treating them with
respect like you would if you met them in the "real" world.*

*Step 4: Invite them back to your place! What does your Inner Temple
look like? It can be as big or small as you like, as complex or simplistic
as feels right to you. Again, there is no wrong way to do it.*

*Step 5: Talk with them. Interact with them as much or as little as
you like, about anything that's on your mind. Finish by asking
them to join your Inner Council so you can call upon them again
in the future, and return to your normal state of consciousness.*

*And that's it! If it seems simple, it's because it is! Here is how you'll
know that you've gotten it: The members of your Inner Council will be able
to surprise you. I've run into all sorts of things over the years; Zeus refused
to participate unless he could sit at the head of the table (not a problem,
my table is round). The ArchAngels and some deities just don't like being
around each other, like two similarly charged magnets that repel each
other.*

*Make no mistake though: This simple process will allow you to connect
with a fundamental force of nature, an infinite wellspring of knowledge
and well-being that will comfort and protect you in the best of times, and
the worst.*

—B. Dave Walters

BRUISES, BRIGID & A BETTER LIFE

Childhood and trauma are two things that really shape our character
and psyche for much of our life. So what happens when you have a traumatic childhood? How do you battle against the enemies that are your
own family? How do you find the internal valor and courage to live your
own life despite and different from everything you were taught and experienced growing up? Well, those are the very questions behind why I've
asked our next guest warrior to come and talk with us.

His name is Dr. Daye Condon, and when I first met him a few years ago when he was the tech lead for a book tour I was doing in Northern California, we quickly became friends. His commitment to a kilt and unabashed openness in his devotion to Celtic deities is just the kind of self-assured person I love spending time with. I initially had no idea about his traumatic past, though as our friendship continued, he began trusting me with more of his own personal history.

And that's why I asked him to come here today and share with you his story of how he survived and overcame a traumatic past through the help of a Celtic warrior goddess to become the PhD in Pagan Studies Comparative Theology and co-owner of a metaphysical boutique in California's Central Valley that he is today. With over thirty years of experience in personal Celtic magic, the Celtic gods have seen him through some intense things. This is his story.

When I was young, I grew up in a very abusive home. I've had many bones broken from beatings and been told that I should never have been born and that my parents wished me dead. The only thing in my life that could bring me joy was spending time with my Grandmother, who was teaching me the old myths, legends, and stories about the Celts and Druids.

When I turned 11, the abuse had become so bad that I attempted suicide, but even failed in that. One night after a bad experience of being beaten, I snuck out of the house to my hiding place out by the riverbank. And while thinking about whether I should attempt suicide again or run away, I started crying uncontrollably. I then yelled very roughly:

"Brigid, Great Warrior, Goddess of the Hearth. Why am I so hated and unloved by everyone? What did I do to earn this pain? I was told you loved and protected us all!"

Then I started chanting something my Grandmother would often say when she was angry or hurt:

"No Fire Shall Burn Me, No Water Shall Drown Me, No Air Shall Knock Me Over, No Earth Shall Swallow Me for the Moon and the Sun are with Me. I am the Child of the Great Mother Danu and She and her Children are always watching over me."

I continued to cry and chant this over and over until I cried myself to sleep. In my dream, I saw a woman with long flaming red hair and brilliant white skin. Her voice was so sweet and gentle. The first thing I remember her saying was:

"What took you so long? I have been here waiting for you to call to us."

She spoke to me about many things in that dream. In the end, she told me that although she was the one who answered my call, she would not be the one to watch over and guide me. She told me to watch for the Old Woman that watches from the shadows.

When I woke up the next morning laying on the riverbank, most of my bruises had already yellowed or completely healed. Sitting there watching me from under a tree was an old Lady, who asked me my name and why I was there. Still traumatized, I just blurted out everything that had happened in my life. She smiled at me and told me that the tides were turning, that today everything I knew to be true would change and I was not alone anymore. I asked her how she knew, and she just laughed, hugged me, and sent me home.

As I was walking away, I turned to say thank you and ask her name, but she was gone. When I walked into the house, my Grandmother was there. She was screaming at my family who had been hurting me and told them that she was taking me to my father's sister who was estranged from the family, and that if they tried to stop her she would bring the wrath of all creation on them. She saw me, smiled, and said:

"I see it has finally happened. I am so very proud of you. It's time to learn to be who you were meant to be."

She then drove me to my aunt's, and I never felt that pain of abuse again. Many times, in my life since, I have called out to the Tuatha De Danann (the Celtic Deities) for strength and aid. The Old Woman that I saw on the bank of the river comes to my dreams often and we talk of many things. With their continued support, I am able to be a warrior in my own life story.

—*Dr. Daye Condon*

DISMANTLING THE TAPESTRY
OF OPPRESSION

Oppression doesn't just happen in an instant. It's not a finished product that appears out of nowhere. No, like everything, the tapestry of oppression is woven together over time thread by thread, and though the finished product of systemic hate and injustice can seem imposing and too complex to dismantle, that's only the case if you try to remove it all in one fell swoop. But if you simply pull at the threads, the loose ends, the parts of the tapestry that are already fraying, then, with time, the whole thing can unravel just as piecemeal as it was woven.

To help jumpstart us into dismantling the systemic oppression that still surrounds us in the twenty-first century, I've invited my friend Siri Plouff, an adept practitioner of Scandinavian magic who also runs the online Nordic magic shop called Northern Lights Witch (www.NorthernLightsWitch .com). Oh, and get ready, because they're going to bring in the big guns; we're enlisting the aid of the Valkyries for this one. So, read well and prepare your tools as Siri instructs. Tonight, we ride with the Valkyries to cut the oppressive ties that bind.

Valkyries, the fierce femmes of Norse mythology, lend their voices to justice. For activists, the Valkyries can provide a specific figure to embody and call on for aid. They are connected to Skuld, *the* Norn *deity for the "future," or "what should be." There is always a choice. They are also connected to healers—the* Eir *or the doctor goddess, allowing us to heal from battle and build the world we wish to see. They are evocative, and the tales of the Valkyries have fascinated people for centuries.*

Njál's Saga describes a ritual that twelve Valkyries weave, connecting them back to the Norns. Six of the twelve are named, which is either because of an incomplete manuscript or a purposeful exclusion. So there are six with names and six supporters, and they weave together a fabric of victory from the entrails of their enemies, with the skulls as weights. Njál's Saga *gives the words they sing.*

They tie together the fates of those they oppose, and then tear it down and each carries it into battle with her. The songs that they sang together speak of the death of the self-righteous rulers, as well as the protection of others, and at the end each brings with them a pennant to the battles in the North and South to claim warriors.

I've adapted this ritual to a modern context, to help us embody the righteous energy of the Valkyries. The tearing apart of the loom is a beautiful way of looking at systemic oppression, and then dismantling that oppression. The entrails woven together show the intertwined fate of white supremacists, misogynists, homophobia, transphobia, and all those who oppose collective liberation. Here is an outline of the ritual:

Materials needed:

- Red yarn or rope, cut into 12 long strands
- 12 Stones (in place of actual skulls)
- Paint—black, red, or white (whichever of these colors works best for you)

Step 1: Dedicate each of the twelve threads to an oppressor, whether that is a system or a personal abuser. You can also repeat different oppressors, or list the same one twelve times.

Step 2: Paint the name of the oppressor upon each stone and then tie each with a length of rope.

Step 3: Weave together the threads, chanting their doom. Write this chant to work for each of the twelve threads you have identified:

I call out, I transform, I am the Valkyrie
Weaving wyrd and threads of fate
The loom drips with blood;
Viscera of enemies, weighted with skulls of the slain
I weave swiftly, weave wisdom and justice,
I weave for the people, for liberation,
I weave the undoing of [insert oppressor here]
Release from this world injustice
Grant us speed and victory,
And hands to heal this land and our people.

Step 4: When the weaving is done, tear it apart. Rip it, cut it,
bite it, destroy it. Embody the rage you feel as you attack
the weaving. When you are done, you may want to leave the
tattered remains of your weaving on a revolutionary altar.
You may also scatter it, burn the threads, or carry them in a
satchel as you go about your own revolutionary work.

—Siri Plouff

ATTITUDE HEALING

Most of us will never have to put our faith, resolve, and valor to test on a battlefield. The theatres of war are now witnessed through television and computer screens from the comfort of our own homes, with only a small percentage of us having to actually experience its terrors and fears first-hand. There are, however, many battlefields in life, and one of the most common ones takes place in the theatre of our own body. Diagnoses, test results, and foreign invaders into our physical self can be just as frightening and deadly as any enemy on the battlefield.

When thinking of a person who could speak of being a warrior in such a theatre of war, my own mother was the first person that came to mind. I'll admit that I am probably biased to her story because I was a front-seat spectator through the scary time of it all, but *because* I was there to witness her real-time fear, coping, and focus on faith through the life-and-death uncertainty of it all, I *know* it is a story that can help many others. After all, my mother isn't the only mother who had been diagnosed with cancer, and she won't be the last. This is the story of one Catholic woman's fight against the great unseen enemy and her healing attitude that helped to vanquish it.

It was December 31, 2014, when I received the call from my doctor that the
lump I found in my breast was indeed a tumor and I would have to follow
up with a surgeon for further testing for Cancer. Yes, he said the big "C"
word. Was I scared? Was I angry? Was I worried? Yes to all three! It was
at that moment when I hung up the phone that I knew I had a difficult road
ahead of me and I knew exactly how I was going to handle it all. Being a

Catholic, I had my Faith to hold on to but I also was a true optimist and from that moment on would remain positive and not allow any negativity into my thoughts.

I had Faith that my God would see me through this and that I would be around for many more years because leaving my husband, children, and family was not an option. I believe in prayer and miracles but I also believe you have to take matters into your own hands and help yourself through the tough times if you want to get the desired end result, and in this case the end result was to LIVE!

So I prayed for healing every day, welcomed prayers and good vibes from family and friends and eliminated anything in my daily routine that would have a negative connotation to it and could bring about negative thoughts. I did not have breast cancer; instead, I had a "boob boo." My husband and I came up with that clever play on words. I referred to my chemo meds as my "magic potion." Rather than focusing on all the harm it does to your body while killing all the bad cells, I focused on the fact that that same medicine was going to be the magic potion that would shrink that tumor to a tiny particle that would then be removed during my double-mastectomy.

When it came time for radiation treatments I just simply "went to get some rays at the tanning salon." As time went by, I came to realize that those around me, both family and friends, had adopted my positive attitude and continued to use the verbiage I used when speaking of my "boob boo" diagnosis.

Aside from personally dealing with my diagnosis, as a dance teacher, I had to find a way to explain to all my young dance students why I would not be able to teach them for a while. I wanted to be honest with them putting it in terms that they would understand at their young age but also and most importantly wanted them to be witness to someone who was diagnosed with the "C" word and would live to prove that it was possible to overcome. I truly believed I would be a survivor and wanted them to see that through prayer and positivity someone they loved could beat the odds and live to tell their story.

Most of my students attend Catholic schools and I knew they would understand the need to pray for me and my recovery but I also wanted to instill in them the need to remain positive and believe that I would soon return to resume dance classes with them. I wanted to use my diagnosis as a teaching tool. I wanted to show them, that while trusting in God, how important it is to also keep a positive attitude and know that they had the power within them to overcome any difficult situation.

Through all the tests, surgeries, and treatments, I never once thought I was going to die because I was both prayerful and optimistic that my Faith and attitude would prevail. In my opinion, although I believe that with God all things are possible, I also believe that you have to help yourself to make the impossible happen. The two go hand in hand. You can't just pray for something and wait for it to happen. You have to do your part in reaching the outcome you want while holding on to your Faith that God will be at your side helping you along the way. Through my journey I hope all those I loved and who loved me would learn that relying on their Faith as well as relying on their own strengths are the most powerful weapons one can take into any type of battle.

—Celia McVey

PART 4

INDIA & SOUTHEAST ASIA

Greater in battle than the man who would
conquer a thousand-thousand men, is he
who would conquer just one—himself.
SIDDHARTHA GAUTAMA (THE BUDDHA)

12

INDIA

Cultural

HINDU INDIA

To be a warrior in ancient India, you had to be born into it. You may be a natural-born military genius or have the athletic prowess to wield a weapon better than anyone else around, but if you weren't *born* into the warrior caste, then you almost certainly weren't going to be given the chance to be a warrior. This was mainly because of the high level of honor and respect that warriors held in traditional Hindu society, and therefore only an upper, more "privileged" caste could be eligible for such a prestigious career.

Caste Iron

This religious caste system in India was a multitiered class system that determined pretty much all your life limitations from whom you could marry to which jobs you could have to where and with whom you could even socialize. Whichever caste your father belonged to when you were born (because Hindu society has historically been a patriarchal one) determined your caste for the rest of your life, and religion was used as the justification to keep this system in place.[130]

Underpinning much of this historic rationalization of class discrimination is the religious Hindu belief in reincarnation and that you are destined to reincarnate into the physical world over and over until you reach a spiritually philosophical understanding of the true nature of the Universe beyond the falsehoods of *Maya* (cosmic illusions). However, if you died before being able to transcend past all the Maya, then it was your actions in this lifetime that determined your lot in your next lifetime.

Essentially, at its most generalized core, if you were benevolent and dedicated to spiritual development during this life and in past lives, you got a chance to reincarnate into a better station in your next life, but if you were malicious and lazy, then you were reincarnated into a worse station in your next life. Thus, it was an unspoken understanding that a poor person in a lower caste *deserved* their wretched lot in this life because they were a bad person in previous lives, and a wealthy upper-caste person *deserved* such comfy luxury because they were a good person in previous lives.[131]

Stained Class

At the very top of this socioreligious hierarchy was the Brahmin caste made up of priests, teachers, and religious officials. The second tier was the

130 "Caste Discrimination: A Global Concern," Human Rights Watch, September 2001, https://www.hrw.org/reports/2001/globalcaste/caste0801-03.htm.

131 "Beliefs of Hinduism," Khan Academy, accessed May 11, 2020, https://www .khanacademy.org/humanities/ap-art-history/south-east-se-asia/india-art/a /beliefs-of-hinduism.

Kshatriya caste made up of the warriors, rulers, and government administrators. Third was the Vaishya caste made up of businesspeople who create
and facilitate the selling of goods such as farmers, merchants, and artisans.
Last was the Shudra caste who were basically the manual laborers who
were forced to do all the grunt work and backbreaking menial jobs no one
wanted.

However, below this bottom level was the (now outlawed yet still very
much socioeconomically enforced) Dalit caste (aka: the "untouchables")
who were relegated to all the duties that were regarded as spiritually pollut-
ing (such as the cleaning and handling of corpses), promoting the belief that
if you even touched them, their impurity would spiritually infect you.[132]

BUDDHIST INDIA

Into this already-centuries-old Hindu caste system, the Buddha was
born (debated to be sometime between the mid-600s BCE to the early-
400s BCE). It was his absolute disgust for the sociocultural inequality that
he saw all around him that inspired him to break away from Hinduism and
try to find another, more equitable way in which humans could escape the
endless cycle of death and rebirth.

Rebel with a Cause

Though Buddhism is now a small minority religion in India, the Buddha's rebellious beginnings in his homeland can still be seen today in just
how many lower-caste Indians are converting to Buddhism as an overt

---

132 "How India's Caste System Works," EuroNews, February 23, 2016, https://
www.euronews.com/2016/02/23/delhi-water-protests-expose-india-s-ever
-present-caste-system; Phillip Martin, "Even with a Harvard Pedigree, Caste
Follows 'Like a Shadow,'" The World, March 5, 2019, https://www.pri.org
/stories/2019-03-05/even-harvard-pedigree-caste-follows-shadow; "What Is
India's Caste System?" BBC, June 19, 2019, https://www.bbc.com/news
/world-asia-india-35650616.

political protest of self-emancipation. Thus, in modern India, Buddhism is often seen as the religion of the poor, working class, and oppressed.[133]

However, unlike the majority of his modern Indian followers, the Buddha did not come from the ranks of the common man; he was born into a life of luxury as a prince in the aristocratic warrior caste. In fact, most of his early life revolved around his opulent pursuit of life's basic pleasures, completely oblivious to the suffering of others due to the well-insulated upper-class bubble in which he lived. The changing point, however, was when he took an unauthorized detour from a highly staged parade so as to learn what life was *really* like in the kingdom that he'd one day rule.

On this detour, he saw, for the first time in his life, just how bad most people had it outside the palace. He saw wretched poverty, untreated disease, withered old age, and most shockingly, death. These were the things he could never un-see, and it haunted him so much that he left his wife and son and cushy life in the elite warrior caste to, instead, wander around the countryside in abject poverty trying to find spiritual answers to humankind's suffering because he could not agree with ancient Hinduism's "you're poor and sick because you were a bad person in a previous life" mentality.[134]

Savior Self

Ultimately, the harsh reality of life on the road as a lower-class, non-elite member of society caused the Buddha to acquiesce in his belief that a life of extreme self-denial would make it easier to attain enlightenment than a life of extreme self-indulgence. He also gave up his belief in being personally able to save all of humanity from the sufferings and worries of life, realizing that hard times and discomfort were just unavoidable experiences of life as a human and that the only thing that can save you is yourself. His philosophies taught that by accepting life as it is (not filtered

---

133 Krithika Varagur, "Converting to Buddhism as a Form of Political Protest," *The Atlantic*, April 11, 2018, https://www.theatlantic.com/international/archive /2018/04/dalit-buddhism-conversion-india-modi/557570/.

134 Andre Ferdinand Herold, *The Life of Buddha*, trans. Paul C. Blum, Sacred Texts, 1927, http://www.sacred-texts.com/bud/lob/index.htm.

through the distortions of our wants, desires, and preferences), by avoiding extremes of excess and deprivation in all aspects of life, and by being kind and empathetic toward all other living beings, you could become enlightened and stop reincarnating into a world where you'd inevitably suffer and die. No leader or guru could do this for you; though they could point the way, the onus was entirely on the individual.

In a way, it was similar to Hinduism (which makes sense because he was born and raised Hindu for his formative years, similar to Jesus being born and raised Jewish), but one of the major differences from Hinduism was that his guidelines for spiritual enlightenment (known as the Noble Eightfold Path) were the same for *everyone* across the board. In contrast, traditional Hinduism taught that the path to salvation was different for each caste and that the poor and disenfranchised would need to take a different route than the wealthy and powerful. By leveling the playing field and vocally rejecting the existing caste system and religious justifications for it, the Buddha found himself with a large following of (surprise, surprise) the poor, sick, outcasts, and oppressed lower classes within Indian society.[135]

From Cruelty to Kindness

Buddhism remained a fringe religion in India for the next few centuries until the Hindu warrior king Ashoka came to power in 268 BCE, proactively spreading Buddhism's message of peace within his empire and catalyzing its dissemination throughout the rest of Asia. This is ironic because Ashoka was one of the most brutal rulers in Indian history who conquered via merciless annihilation of his neighbors and came to power by murdering his own family members. Granted, a lot of the wicked acts committed by him in his life before he became a Buddhist have been overdramatized (so as to make his conversion to Buddhism seem more poignant and

---

135   Célestin Bouglé, *Essays on the Caste System*, trans. D. F. Pocock (Cambridge: Cambridge University Press, 1971), n.p.

impactful); nevertheless, his commands as a military leader were, indeed, historically quite cruel by any standard.[136]

Like any empire, Ashoka's needed to constantly conquer new land so as to receive more tax revenue so as to be able to govern and militarily control previously conquered lands (the vicious cycle of empire building), but something very unprecedented happened when he conquered the city-state of Kalinga on India's east coast. After his victory, he felt *immense* regret and shame for the sheer volume of human lives taken, families destroyed, and devastation caused by him in this particularly brutal campaign. From this, he converted to the then-fringe religion of Buddhism and set forth to spend the rest of his life trying to redeem himself and atone for all the horrors he knowingly caused.

It's hard to overemphasize just how much of a big deal this was. The ruler of the military-revering ancient Hindu world was now a part of the peace-loving, minority fringe religion of Buddhism (it'd be somewhat comparable to something like President Nixon suddenly becoming a devout hippie while in office because he felt bad about what he was doing to Vietnam). Immediately Ashoka swore off military conquest and instead believed that a ruler's main priority should be the safety, health, and happiness of his subjects. And despite being a *severe* Buddhist, he promoted the tolerance of all religions and used tax revenue to develop infrastructure and an early welfare system that looked after the basic human needs of all, with an emphasis on those who needed the most help: the poor.[137]

Despite his heavy promulgation and political backing of it, though, Buddhism's prominence in India didn't last long after Ashoka's immediate rule. Still, although Buddhism would never again become as prominent

---

136   Jacob N. Kinnard, *The Emergence of Buddhism: Classical Traditions in Contemporary Perspective* (Minneapolis, MN: Augsburg Fortress, 2010), 82–86.

137   Pankaj Mishra, "Ashoka the Great," *Boston Globe*, December 5, 2004, http://archive.boston.com/news/globe/ideas/articles/2004/12/05/ashoka_the_great/; Kristin Baird Rattini, "Who Was Ashoka?" *National Geographic*, April 1, 2019, https://www.nationalgeographic.com/culture/people/reference/ashoka/.

of a spiritual force in India as it was during Ashoka's reign, it managed to survive, grow, and thrive among the peoples east of its homeland.[138]

Indian Takeaway:
CHECK YOUR PRIVILEGE

Historically and mythologically, Buddhism traces its origins to a wealthy, trust-fund-esque, spoiled aristocrat who spent a good portion of his life blithely oblivious to the struggles and injustice that the 99 percent of society around him experienced. More pointedly, its origins trace back to the moment this pampered, self-indulgent prince took a step back to check his privilege and reassess that the world did not revolve around him and that his personal experience was not the experience for the vast majority of others.

This is important to us now just as much as it was back in BCE India. Yes, everyone's life is hard, and we're all striving for things and struggling against other things amid our own personal internal battles. However, we often get so caught up in the reality of our own problems that we forget that a lot of people have it a lot worse out there than we do.

I mean, just the fact that you are reading this book right now shows that you not only have access, free time, and wealth enough to spend on a luxury item not necessary for your survival, but that you also have the education to *read* it. Additionally, regardless of if you got this from a library or bookstore, ordered it online, or downloaded it illegally, you also have *access* to the services and technology that made that possible. Whether you agree with me or not, you *are* privileged if only for all the circumstances behind you reading this book right now.

As a warrior, it's imperative that we put the world into such objective perspective. "Privilege" is not a terrible thing, not something to fear having because of the negative connotations the word often carries. No, "privilege" is power, and with it, you can uplift the oppressed, donate more generously, and muscle the spotlight onto the people and causes who need

---

138   Kanai Lal Hazra, *The Rise and Decline of Buddhism in India* (New Delhi: Munshiram Manoharlal Publishers Pvt. Ltd., 1995), n.p.

to be shown. However, if you refuse to acknowledge your own privilege, then you are disallowing your own power and being a disservice to those who need your power.

So, your takeaway challenge here is to really dive in deep and check your own privilege, or rather, identify in which areas of life you possess privilege (because you *do* possess it in one place or another). Once you identify it, utilize it. If you are blessed with financial security, make a donation. If you have connections, maneuver the spotlight where it needs to shine. If you have a following on social media, spread awareness. If you have magical knowledge that came from access to elusive or expensive teachers, books, or tools, share that knowledge with others who don't have such privileged access by tutoring, mentoring, or sharing your knowledge with the masses by starting a free blog or podcast. There are innumerable ways to do this, but unless you acknowledge and accept your privilege, you'll keep yourself powerless and all those who are relying upon you and your power.

Deities & Legends

GANDHI

If no other name in this book has been familiar so far, Mohandas Gandhi is absolutely someone you've at least *heard* about. He was a Hindu lawyer and political activist who led India in nonviolent resistance for their independence against Great Britain, which, in turn, inspired nonviolent civil rights movements all over the world, particularly that of Martin Luther King, Jr. in the United States and Nelson Mandela in South Africa. Because of the gravity of his place in history as the grandfather of nonviolent revolution, we'll spend a little extra time looking into his story.

Nonetheless, it should be made clear, as with all humans who are catapulted into iconic legends on a pedestal, he was not perfect (no one is). Educated in Victorian-era Britain, he had a lot of closed-minded faults: such as being extremely racist toward Black people in his early life, sleeping next to his underage grandniece to specifically test his vow of celibacy later in his life, and his severe homophobia and attempts to erase queerness from Hindu history throughout his life (the latter of which you can read more about in one of my other books, *Queer Magic: LGBT+ Spirituality and Culture from Around the World*), and if that wasn't enough, he would be hated by his own son as a bad father both during his life and after his death.[139]

On the flip side, however, *because* he had a "proper" Victorian education in Britain, he was intimately familiar with the West and how their politics and culture operated, and he utilized that knowledge against them successfully. And while his whole life is fascinating, there are plenty of places to find more info on that; for our time here, we'll focus on both how his Hindu-Jainist-inspired campaign of nonviolence won India its freedom and the religious divides that were amplified by Indian independence.

Everything really went into motion in 1919 after the British used machine guns to fire into a crowd of around fifteen to twenty thousand unarmed people. These people were protesters that had assembled to decry the extension of austere wartime laws (such as the imprisonment of Indians without trial) after WWI had ended and there was no more war. This gave Gandhi the realization that there would be no compromising with the British and called for a massive boycott of all British goods. He knew that the British were militarily stronger, so the best thing to do was hit them in the wallet. By him advocating that the people of India start to make their own clothes and support Indian-made goods, the revolution had begun.[140]

---

139   Randy P. Conner, David Hatfield Sparks, and Mariya Sparks, *Cassell's Encyclopedia of Queer Myth, Symbol, and Spirit* (London: Cassell & Co., 1997), n.p.; Lauren Frayer, "Gandhi Is Deeply Revered, But His Attitudes On Race And Sex Are Under Scrutiny," NPR, October. 2, 2019, https://www.npr.org /2019/10/02/766083651/gandhi-is-deeply-revered-but-his-attitudes-on-race -and-sex-are-under-scrutiny; Sarfraz Manzoor, "Father to a Nation, Stranger to His Son," *The Guardian*, August 9, 2007, https://www.theguardian.com/film /2007/aug/10/india.

140   "Mahatma Gandhi," Biography, August 20, 2019, https://www.biography.com /activist/mahatma-gandhi; Mihir Bose, "Amritsar, 100 Years On, Remains an Atrocity Britain Cannot Be Allowed to Forget," The Guardian, April 12, 2019, https://www.theguardian.com/commentisfree/2019/apr/12/britain-amritsar -massacre-centenary-1919-india.

His faith mixture of Hinduism's focus on taking action in the here and now and Jainism's pacifist nonviolence steered his leadership. So, when the British imposed a heavy tax on salt (a staple good for survival in India) and outlawed the loophole of Indians being able to make salt themselves, Gandhi led a protest march to the sea to illegally manufacture salt in direct defiance of the law. Again, the British responded with extreme violence. This time, however, the excessiveness of Britain's violence started to make their colonial rulership over India become unpopular with British citizens back at home who regarded their armies murdering nonresisting, impoverished Indians as shameful and below everything Britannia stood for in the eyes of the world.[141]

After WWII ended, it was no longer economical or popularly supported for war-ravaged Britain to maintain control over an India in constant economic revolt. Even with independence guaranteed, though, Gandhi had to deal with deep, internal, murderous divisions between Hindus and Muslims (the two largest religious groups in India). Gandhi managed to garner a temporary armistice between them after going on a hunger strike that almost killed him. Despite his efforts, though, his lifelong work for a sovereign India made from the peaceful union of Hindus and Muslims failed to manifest. The defunct British colony was split into two separate countries to divide the religions since Hindus and Muslims of the time could not peacefully coexist together: India for Hindus and Pakistan for Muslims (and later Bangladesh for Muslims east of India after more cultural fighting and genocides).[142]

The other major internal religious problem was the Hindu caste system. Gandhi wanted it gone but disagreed with his advisors on how to do it. Gandhi believed it to be a spiritual issue (and thus off-limits for secular legislation), arguing no need to make laws abolishing it because human-

---

141   Whitney Sanford, "What Gandhi Can Teach Today's Protesters," The
       Conversation, October 1, 2017, https://theconversation.com/what-gandhi
       -can-teach-todays-protesters-83404.
142   Haimanti Roy, "The Road to India's Partition," The Conversation, August 14,
       2017, https://theconversation.com/the-road-to-indias-partition-82432.

kind will just naturally come to understand how it is morally wrong and want nothing to do with it someday soon in the future. His advisors and staff, however, believed it to be not a religious but a socioeconomic issue, arguing that laws needed to be made *now* against it because the upper castes would never have a change of heart and give up any portion of their power willingly.

Ultimately, Gandhi's assassination in 1948 (by a Hindu religious extremist who hated him for his tolerance of Muslims) allowed his advisors to win out in 1950 and legally abolish discrimination based on one's caste. Still, although it cannot be legally enforced, the caste system remains socially enforced to the present day.[143]

INDRA

In Hinduism, Indra is the king of the gods who enforces his rule through his command over thunder, lightning, rain, and rivers (thought to originate from the same prehistoric prototype deity from which Zeus, Odin, and other Indo-European ruling sky gods also originated). In particular, though, sacred Hindu texts and poems praise him substantially as a war deity and as the idealization of the kind of masculine strength that men should strive to possess.

Depicted as a regal, mustachioed warrior atop a white elephant, he was born into the universe literally ready to fight and with a propensity for violence. Both kings and soldiers believed that in order to be successful in a battle, they needed Indra to be on their side. However, he was known to have a weakness: he absolutely could not stand anyone ridiculing his

---

143 Manali S. Deshpande, "History of the Indian Caste System and Its Impact on India Today," California Polytechnic State University Department of Social Sciences, 2010, https://digitalcommons.calpoly.edu/cgi/viewcontent.cgi ?referer=https://www.google.co.in/&httpsredir=1&article=1043&context =socssp; "This Day in History: Gandhi Assassinated," History, updated January 27, 2021, https://www.history.com/this-day-in-history/gandhi -assassinated.

virility or masculinity (as typical of a "macho" man who overcompensates his insecurities with aggression).[144]

Indra also appears in some mystical sects of Buddhism but often under the name "Shakra" and with a much less hawkish temperament. Buddhists regard him more as a well-intentioned tester who challenges your resolve by having you confront something scary in order to see if you're disciplined enough in your Buddhist training to see through the illusion.[145]

KARTIKEYA

Kartikeya (who has *many* other names) is a very interesting Hindu deity because not only is he the official god of war, but he is also the generalissimo of the armies of the gods and the embodiment of perfection. Visually, he's distinctive for riding atop a peacock (national bird of India and Hindu symbol of the overcoming of harmful habits and sensual desires) and for having six faces around his head (representative of his ability to see all around him to counter any "surprise" attacks against him).[146]

In modern times, his worship is mostly concentrated in South India among the Tamil people who refer to him more popularly as Murugan. Here, Murugan's devotees gained the notorious reputation for the severity of pain displayed in their public worship of this martial deity, most infamously through the skewering of their tongues, cheeks, and skin with up to 108 metal spears (Murugan's iconic weapon).[147]

144 Jarrod L. Whitaker, *Strong Arms and Drinking Strength: Masculinity, Violence, and the Body in Ancient India* (New York: Oxford University Press, 2011), n.p.

145 "Shakra," *Soka Gakkai Nichiren Buddhism Library*, accessed May 12, 2020, https://www.nichirenlibrary.org/en/dic/Content/S/106.

146 Subhamoy Das, "Lord Kartikeya," Learn Religions, updated May 7, 2019, https://www.learnreligions.com/lord-kartikya-1770301.

147 A. Shrikumar, "Tracing the Roots of the Tamil God," *The Hindu*, updated January 22, 2015, https://www.thehindu.com/features/metroplus/society /tracing-the-roots-of-the-tamil-god/article6808508.ece; Greg Rodgers, "Thaipusam Festival: Ritualistic Face and Body Piercing," Learn Religions, updated June 19, 2020, https://www.learnreligions.com/what-is -thaipusam-1458358.

13
SOUTHEAST ASIA

Cultural

THE KHMER EMPIRE

Originating during the early ninth century CE in what is now Cambodia, the Khmer (kuh-MEHR) grew to dominate much of Southeast Asia for the next six hundred years, though nowadays, they are probably most remembered as the civilization that built Angkor Wat, the massive Hindu temple complex (whose silhouette is emblazoned on the modern Cambodian flag).

Monarch Mediums

Here, in the jungles of Southeast Asia, the Theravada denomination of Buddhism is the most prevalent. Unlike more communal-focused and scripture-heavy denominations (Mahayana and Vajrayana, respectively), Theravada is more focused on using personal gnosis and self-reliance to train one's mind to see beyond the ephemeral illusions of this world. Enlightenment cannot be learned through teachers or studies, only realized, coming in an instant or not at all, and it is an inward individual journey everyone must make on their own.

Before we get deep into Theravada, however, we need to talk about the predominately Hindu Khmer Empire. Despite all its unprecedented success in the region, the biggest problem the Khmer Empire had all throughout its reign was its internal wars of revolution—not by the poor and downtrodden, though, but by the wealthy and powerful themselves. You see, the Khmer kings didn't really have a whole lot of resistance from the lower classes because they cleverly crowned themselves a "chakravartin" (universal ruler) in a special Hindu ceremony. This essentially made them divine and were seen as the gods' representatives on earth.

Moreover, a main duty of the Khmer god-king was to constantly perform rituals to communicate with the ancestors so that he could keep getting them to protect his people from the wrath of the gods and from malevolent spiritual forces. With the king as their only medium to do this, the common people (who were caught at the bottom of a rigid social hierarchy) were less committed to taking down the king, the only person shielding them from supernatural evil. Thus, thanks to this religious reliance upon the king as their only spiritual protector, the king retained ultimate, unquestioned power ... until, of course, he didn't.[148]

---

[148] "Khmer Empire," Encyclopedia.com, updated May 1, 2020, https://www
.encyclopedia.com/history/encyclopedias-almanacs-transcripts-and-maps
/khmer-empire.

After the Faith Is Gone

Nothing lasts forever, and around the beginning of the fourteenth century CE the Khmer Empire imploded, thanks in part to the people's conversion from Hinduism to Theravada Buddhism. Remember, the people's Hindu faith is what gave the king his cult of personality. Whether they liked him or not, they grudgingly needed him to rule them so he could spiritually protect them. After about five hundred years of this, Theravada Buddhism started to become more popular, and the Buddhist concept of *you*, the individual, being the only thing responsible for your own salvation suddenly made the king's cult of personality and protective duties against otherworldly enemies obsolete.

Inspired by Theravada Buddhism's focus on self-empowerment and its ideas of egalitarianism, the king's royal identity as divine ruler began to diminish, in turn weakening his authority over his subjects. Thus, when massive ecological crises subsequently coincided with Thai and Mongol invasions, the now-Buddhist king no longer had a cult of personality, religious justification for rulership, or unified internal support, and just like that, the Khmer Empire was no more.[149]

THE KINGDOM OF SIAM

After the fall of the Khmer, the Thai people rose as the next regional power, and their kingdom of Siam did the impossible: they maintained native independence and never became a colony of any European power. They ruled a *heavily* Buddhist kingdom, but they also paradoxically managed to have an aristocratic upper class and semi-divine absolute monarch supported by the supposedly egalitarian religious outlook of Theravada Buddhism.

149   Leonard C. Overton and David P. Chandler, "Cambodia," Encyclopedia Britannica, updated March 10, 2021, https://www.britannica.com/place /Cambodia/The-decline-of-Angkor.

The King and We

How did the king of Siam pull this off? Well, it all has to do with the spiritual semantics of karma. Theravada Buddhism was adopted as the state religion right off the bat as a way to disassociate the new kingdom from their former Hindu Khmer overlords. The ruling powers of this Siamese kingdom, however, did keep the idea of a divine king, but they just adapted it to Buddhism.[150]

The king of Siam was believed to be predestined to rule based on karma from past lives, and since karma is never wrong, understands the bigger picture, and knows better than limited human mortal minds can comprehend, the common folk assumed that the ruling hereditary monarchy is in power because that is what's cosmically best for the universe at this moment in time. The caveat being that the king has to rule effectively (not kindly or fairly, mind you... just effectively). Karma only justified his inheritance of the throne, not his everlasting position on it.[151]

Siam eventually evolved into modern-day Thailand and still maintains a justified-by-karma king with whom democratic Buddhist revolutionaries are often at odds (though his powers are limited because it's technically a constitutional monarchy). Nevertheless, intense militarism continues to uphold him as a semi-divine ruler (as exemplified by how it's illegal to step on paper money because the bills contain images of the sacred king, and also how it's illegal to speak ill of the royal family since that's a form of punishable-by-law blasphemy).[152]

150 U.S. Department of State, "History of the Jewel," PBS, accessed May 16, 2020, https://www.pbs.org/edens/thailand/history.htm.

151 Clare Veal, "The Feudal Photograph of a Democratic Dhammaraja: Secularism and Sacrality in Thai Royal Imagery," *Digital Philology: A Journal of Medieval Cultures* 8, no. 1 (Spring 2019): 66–85, https://doi.org/10.1353/dph .2019.0015.

152 Phil Sylvester, "12 Laws in Thailand: How to Stay Out of Jail," World Nomads, February 1, 2020, https://www.worldnomads.com/travel-safety /southeast-asia/thailand/a-travellers-guide-to-thailands-laws.

WARTIME VIETNAM

No exploration of revolution and social justice in Southeast Asia is complete without at least mentioning Vietnam and its underdog victory against the military machine of the United States. Now, entire volumes of books, numerous documentary series, lots of Academy Award-winning films, and generation-defining songs have been made that cover this conflict in intimate academic and artistic detail. For our purposes here, we'll just take a quick glimpse into how the faith and spirituality (or lack thereof) of North and South Vietnam's leaders played a big part in how things ultimately turned out.

Unfortunate Sons

Unlike other nations of Southeast Asia, Vietnam was heavily influenced by the more community-focused Mahayana Buddhism than the self-focused Theravada. In time, Mahayana mixed with Vietnam's native folk beliefs to become the communal spiritual identity of the people. However, once France began colonizing the region in the latter half of the 1800s, Catholicism was *heavily* promoted and shown favoritism by the new ruling class of French colonists. This created a lasting bad image of Catholicism as the outsider religion of the oppressor over the majority of the common people who were mostly Buddhist. So, when the U.S. backed Ngô Đình Diệm as the leader of South Vietnam (an out-of-touch, upper-class, Vietnamese *Catholic*), many of the common people saw this as a continuation of oppressive colonial rule, just masquerading behind a native face and name.

To make matters worse, Diệm's sister-in-law (and the de facto First Lady) "Madame Nhu" went on a puritanical religious morality crusade outlawing a whole number of things including dancing, contraceptives, divorce, abortion, sex outside of marriage, padded bras, and even playing certain sports such as wrestling and boxing. Then Diệm himself began actively persecuting Buddhists, leading to the infamous scenes of Buddhist monks setting themselves on fire as protest against Diệm's religious oppression (suicide protests that Madame Nhu further fueled by publicly mocking them).[153]

You can see how this kind of overzealous spiritual leadership by Diệm and his out-of-touch, ultra-Catholic family didn't help to inspire the Buddhist-majority South Vietnamese people or actively unite them against an enemy when they needed it most. Just the opposite: it promoted civil unrest, exacerbated discord, and led to his own army assassinating him. Still, the U.S. backed this leader because he was "Western," compliant, and would be cooperative to their economic interests in the region once they'd win the war.

In contrast, the leader of communist North Vietnam (Ho Chi Minh) was an avowed atheist and, for strategic purposes, much more tolerant toward religious diversity in comparison to Diêm. Ho Chi Minh even went so far as to declare an edict that his government would uphold the freedom of religion for all citizens without favoritism. So, when spiritual push came to shove, this leader with no religious affiliations and no outward favoritism tended to be seen as the lesser religious evil in comparison to a leader who was a personal devotee of the colonial oppressor's faith and went out of his way to specifically persecute the country's majority faith. After the active murdering of Buddhists and lack of sympathy for social justice protestors by the South Vietnamese powers that be, South Vietnam lost international public support and numbers of its people began to

---

153 Robert Templer, "Madame Nhu Obituary," *The Guardian*, April 26, 2011, https://www.theguardian.com/world/2011/apr/26/madame-nhu-obituary; "This Day in History: Buddhist immolates himself in protest," History.com, July 28, 2019, https://www.history.com/this-day-in-history/buddhist -immolates-himself-in-protest.

see an atheist communist future as a lesser evil in comparison to Diệm's Western-backed foreign theocracy.[154]

Southeast Asian Takeaway:
COMMUNITY INVOLVEMENT

The road to hell is paved with good intentions, and if you've ever gone out of your way to help someone or do something good only to have it blow up in your face or make things worse, then you know exactly what this timeless maxim is talking about. It's not bad to want to help people. It's not bad to get involved and make a change. But if the results of your wanting to help and getting involved end up creating more problems, then who cares about your intentions because the people whom you're trying to help would've been better off without your help.

As we crusade for justice and make the world a better place, we have to, every step of the way, make sure that "justice" and "better place" is true for those we're trying to help, not just ourselves. The U.S. military fiasco in Vietnam is an example of this. The people of South Vietnam absolutely *did not* want to be taken over by their communist compatriots in the north, and so when the Western world powers stepped in to help them and uphold "justice" and a "better future" for the South Vietnamese, they just made things worse because they were installing *their own* models of "justice" and a "better future" that benefitted *themselves* rather than what the people *actually* wanted.

So, for your takeaway challenge here, examine how you are (if at all) incorporating the community's input and involving the people you are trying to help. Before throwing money immediately toward the most popular national charity for that cause, do your research to see if there are any

---

154   William J. Duiker, *Ho Chi Minh* (New York: Hyperion, 2000), 367, 523; "President Hô Chí Minh and Belief and Religion," Socialist Republic of Vietnam Government Committee for Religious Affairs, August 12, 2013, http://religion.vn/Plus.aspx/en/News/71/0/1010068/0/4646/President_Ho _Chi_Minh_and_Belief_and_Religion; "Ngo Dinh Diem," Encyclopedia Britannica, updated January 7, 2021, https://www.britannica.com/biography /Ngo-Dinh-Diem.

local nonprofits run by community members themselves on the ground level who are more intimately aware of the kinds of changes that need to happen in their own community. Rather than reactively finding a way to awkwardly insert underrepresented people into your movies, stories, and creative endeavors as a "solidarity" PR stunt of tokenism, why not ask a person from that actual underrepresented community to help flesh out and play the character, or even take it a step further and assist that community in finding funding and opportunities to create representations of themselves in their own projects.

Rather than say a prayer for or enact a ritual to bring about a beneficial manifestation that you believe will be of most help, take a step back and see what the *community* is actually wanting to manifest for themselves, not what *you* think they want. For example, a calming spell to soothe the spirits of angry protestors is *not* what they want, even if all the protesting is making you worried and anxious. They want their voices heard and are using their anger in a positive way. So, why not say a prayer and do spellwork to actually help their cause, not temper their aggression into "peaceful" lethargy?

Remember, a true warrior does not fight for themselves—they fight for those who need their protection. So make sure you're fighting for a world that the people you're trying to help actually want, not a world you think is best for them. When in doubt, always ask yourself: "The people I'm trying to help…are they here at the table with a voice in the decision-making?"

Deities & Legends

PHRA ANGKHAN

In Thai Buddhist belief, each day of the week is ruled over by a different deity; Tuesday is the day of Phra Angkhan, god of war and conflict. Usually depicted astride a water buffalo, he is associated with the planet Mars and has many martial qualities associated with him such as being both hot-headed and particularly fierce in battle. Beyond his warrior aspect, though, he is also associated with hard work and exemplifies the phrase of putting "blood, sweat, and tears" toward a goal.[155]

THE TRƯNG SISTERS

The Trưng sisters are known as Vietnamese national heroines for leading the revolutionary movement against China's first occupation of Vietnam and having briefly established a female-ruled kingdom. Their legacy of rebellion and resisting foreign invasion is still nationally revered to this day, and though they were ultimately unsuccessful, their inspiration instilled in the Vietnamese people the defiant optimism that helped them to eventually succeed in overthrowing Chinese occupation hundreds of years later.

According to the histories and legends, the two Trưng sisters (Trưng Trắc and Trưng Nhị) were born to a well-to-do family in Chinese-occupied northern Vietnam during the early first century CE. Despite the foreign rule and the heavy Confucian influence in Vietnam, it was a unique time in Vietnamese history when attitudes toward women were more liberal than what they had traditionally been or would be in the future. This allowed the Trưng sisters to receive a well-rounded education and be allowed to become avid practitioners of the martial arts.

Trưng Trắc (the elder sister) was widowed soon after her marriage because her influential husband was assassinated for plotting the overthrow of their Chinese overlords. So, in response, she and her younger sister rallied the Vietnamese upper class to take up arms against the Chinese, and they themselves led the attacks, successfully capturing over sixty strategic Chinese citadels (with their Vietnamese armies being commanded mostly under female generals). With the Chinese on the back foot, the Trưng sisters declared a new independent and autonomous kingdom run by women (since women

155 "Mysticism in the Garden of the Gods," Thai Tourism Guide, September 25, 2012, https://blogthaitourismguide.wordpress.com/2012/09/25/mysticism-in-the-garden-of-the-gods/; "The Garden of the Gods," Muangboran Museum, 2018, https://www.muangboranmuseum.com/en/landmark/the-garden-of-the-gods/.

did most of the work during the revolution). This kingdom lasted only three years, though, as the Chinese soon returned *en force*.

The weakness of the Trung sisters was that their revolution was composed almost entirely of the upper class which, though successful, is never sustainable without the lower-classes' majority support. Yes, rule by the upper class is common around the world, but it can only be maintained if the lower-class majority can be convinced that it is in their best interest to have the upper class rule over them. This was not the case for the kingdom created by the Trung sisters, and so without the needed support of the lower classes, they were defeated by the returning Chinese. Rather than be captured, the sisters were said to have committed suicide by drowning themselves in a river. After their death, Vietnam would not be fully independent again until about nine hundred years later in the tenth century CE.[156]

VISHNU

Vishnu is one of the main gods in the Hindu pantheon and though mostly associated with India, he was *the* supreme deity of the heavily Hindu Khmer Empire. Officially, he is the god of protection, sacrifice, safety, peace, and the good of society. The massive temple complex of Angkor Wat was dedicated to him, and he became associated with the warrior kings of the Khmer.[157]

Vishnu is usually depicted as a blue-skinned human with four arms, riding atop the legendary eagle *Garuda*. He is said to have incarnated many times in this world as epic heroes and sage teachers, and in some sects, his avatars of *Rama* and *Krishna* are more popular than Vishnu himself (some Hindus also consider the Buddha to also be an avatar of Vishnu). Regard-

156 Lyn Reese, "The Trung Sisters," Women in World History, accessed May 18, 2020, http://www.womeninworldhistory.com/heroine10.html; "Trung Sisters," Encyclopedia Britannica, updated March 1, 2016, https://www.britannica.com/topic/Trung-Sisters.

157 Encyclopedia Britannica, "Hinduism," *Britannica Encyclopedia of World Religions* (Edinburgh: Encyclopedia Britannica, 2006).

less, it is believed that Vishnu's main objective in earthly affairs is to maintain the upkeep of the world and protect it from supernatural harm.[158]

Vishnu, out of all the Hindu gods, is often considered the ideal leader. He is the center balance between both creation and destruction who is able to see the value in his enemies and the weaknesses in his allies. Moreover, he is neither too serious nor too flippant. He understands the need to balance both work and play, and he can be engaged yet not attached (allowing him to adapt and always make the best leadership decisions without pride or ego).[159]

158 "Vishnu," BBC, updated August 24, 2009, https://www.bbc.co.uk/religion
      /religions/hinduism/deities/vishnu.shtml.
159 Subhamoy Das, "An Introduction to Lord Vishnu, Hinduism's Peace-Loving
      Deity," Learn Religions, updated May 15, 2019, https://www.learnreligions
      .com/an-introduction-to-lord-vishnu-1770304.

14

INDIAN & SOUTHEAST ASIAN MAGICAL COMMUNITY

YOGIC REJUVENATION

To help with the self-care aspect of being a warrior, I've invited Giovanni Vázquez, Jr., the yoga instructor from the University of Nevada, Las Vegas, to meet us here and lead a yoga exercise to help rejuvenate our minds and bodies and keep us in top spiritual and physical shape for the war effort.

While living in Las Vegas, I met Giovanni (or Gino, as his students call him) back when I was looking to take my first-ever yoga class. With all the flash-in-the-pan niche yoga teachers out there, I wanted to learn from a yogi who taught from a Hindu-authentic perspective, and so when I read his course description and instructor bio on the UNLV public roster, I was thrilled to see that he didn't dilute the religious essence of yoga by having it be "themed" or any other twenty-first-century appropriation of this sacred Hindu ritual so as to cash in on "fad exoticism." His course emphasized the profundity of understanding one's self and discovering universal truth based on authentic Hindu perspectives, and I wasn't disappointed.

So, I knew no better yogi than Gino to come and give us a quick, refueling yoga session. He has since moved from Vegas, but his practice and teaching of traditional yoga certainly will never end. So, if you like this remote beginner/intro exercise, feel free to foster a deeper development of your yoga practice by reaching out to a local yogi near you.

In times of conflict and uncertainty, I turn to yoga to help keep me sane. You may not have 90 minutes to practice a completely full-out yoga session, but here's one routine that anyone can do that is short, rejuvenating, and effective. Other than stretches and postures, yoga is focused on breath, which is the bodily hack to linking mind and body together and creating a spiritual sense of clarity.

Begin by setting up the environment to remove distractions. Phone on silent, computer asleep, TV off. Feel safe in this space you're creating for your wellness. Lie your body down with your back on the floor, then with the arms to the side and parallel next to the body, flip the palms up and allow the body to rest. Take a moment to feel and adjust accordingly until you feel noticeably more at ease.

Next, slowly lift one leg at a time and slowly place it back down. Follow this with the arms, shoulder blades, and head before starting over again with the legs. No need to rush, just explore being in your temple and your range of movement. If your lower back feels uncomfortable, bend your legs at the knees and place your feet on the floor softly.

This should not feel strenuous. It should feel slow, easy, and gentle. However far your range of motion is, that is alright. Do not focus too much on the movement of your limbs, instead allow your mind to wander. The reason behind this is that your body is in kinetic meditation.

Once you notice your body is continuing the kinetic meditation without your conscious mind telling it to, stop and fully relax once more. Notice your mind as it is. Is it turbulent or clear? Do not judge your thoughts, just take note of what is rising to the surface. If they are uncomfortable, let them float on by like clouds without trying to hurry them out. If they are enjoyable, let them also pass by without trying to grasp them to stay.

Notice how you're breathing. Is it high in the chest? Is it to one side? Is it in the belly? Inhale, pause, and allow your body to exhale with a loud, breathy "HAAAA" sound. The focus here is to let go of any thoughts that are lingering in your mind. As tension builds inside during moments of stress, this breathing exercise teaches us that we can dissolve tension in our body by intentionally clearing out our lungs. Do this 3 times.

Next, place your hands on the belly, just below the belly button. Allow your fingers to connect with your skin and your thumbs to sit on the belly button. Feel the sensation as you inhale. Visualize the inhale originating from that space deep in your abdomen, just below the belly button. Inhaling the belly up, cause the ribs to then expand and the chest to lift for a full breath at lung capacity. Pause and allow the body to feel this new energy inside you. Exhale in reverse, first lowering the chest, then compressing your ribs, and then shrinking your belly so that it is soft once more. Do this at least 3 times.

Afterward, with your mind and body filled with new breath and purged of old breath, cultivate the awareness to choose what to do with this new energy you have summoned into your physical temple. Choose what thoughts deserve your focus. The outside world is always in chaotic motion that you can never fully control, but you can control what is in your mind. So, the next time you feel overwhelmed with stress and everything is just too much, repeat this soft yoga meditation to allow your sacred breath to clean your mind and body. It won't change THE world, but it will change YOUR world.

To close, bring your hands together at heart level, bow your head, and express gratitude for the first new thought that comes into your new mind. Namaste.

—Giovanni Vázquez, Jr.

BEING IN-BETWEEN

Being a warrior is never a straightforward affair. The romanticized idea of a warrior is one who is fully and supremely sure of themselves, otherwise how could they be so strong and fight for the betterment of others, right? Wrong. Warriors are humans, and each human is never perfectly sure or always supremely confident in themselves at all times. One such area of internal uncertainty is in self-identity, especially when one's identity has the familial, cultural, ethnic, and traditional expectations of a self that you don't necessarily agree with or fit into.

For such a frank discussion on the internal cultural battle of being a warrior, I've asked my friend from college, Vi Le, to come and give us some of her experienced advice. Nowadays she works in Special Education for the public school system in Oakland, California, but in university, I initially met her because we were both in an extracurricular dance troupe together. We bonded through our mutual understanding of what it's like to have competing, expectational cultural pressures based on identity.

I, a straight-outta-Dublin-looking Latino/Irish mix who was often too "white" for many Latinx and too "Latinx" for many whites. She, a proud daughter of two Vietnamese refugees who was too "American" for Vietnamese society and too "Asian" for Americans. From her life stories of balancing and battling this uncomfortable cultural no-man's-land, I was inspired to better unapologetically navigate my own life in my own cultural no-man's-land. So, for all you mixed-race, culturally incongruent, and ethnically-pulled-in-different-directions warriors and allies of such warriors, here's a special bit of counsel just for you.

In the Vietnamese language there's really no term for "you" or "Mr./Mrs."
If you want to address a stranger, you use familial terms based on age: anh/
chị *(big brother/ big sister),* chú/cô *(uncle/aunt), or* ông/bà *(grandpa/
grandma). If you want to be more casual, you simply call them* bạn *(friend).*
It's so subtle but also really beautiful; it's community and connectedness.

Born and raised in the U.S., I've always struggled to feel connected to
my culture. I always felt pulled in two different directions.

It's hard to feel connected when the majority of people around you don't look like family, and the ones that do don't accept you. I've developed so much social anxiety around interacting with other Vietnamese people, especially older ones. They're either shocked that I know any Vietnamese at all or they ask me why my Vietnamese isn't better. Translation: the bar is set so low that I feel embarrassed for trying to connect or so high that I couldn't possibly reach it. Either way, I'm labeled as "other." The worst, though, is the rejection from my own family. "You're not really Vietnamese." "She's American, that's just how they are." These are just some of the phrases I grew up hearing. To the shame of my parents, I can't read or write beyond an early elementary school level in my native language. I'll never be the ideal "Vietnamese" child.

Living in the U.S., I'm only ever seen as "Asian" (whatever that means). To the surprise of no one, I excelled at math. I was a "model student" because I learned at a young age to be quiet and not speak out of turn. My skin color means I'm hard working and non-threatening. Despite that, I'm told "to go home" and that "this is America," as if I wasn't born here. As if my parents didn't sacrifice everything to give me and my siblings a brighter future after fleeing war-torn Vietnam. Growing up I watched my mother work tirelessly as a nail stylist, as a small business owner, to serve people who didn't respect her. I was taught in history class about how America valiantly and strategically exited from "foreign affairs" they didn't need to be involved in, while my father at home can't let go of the resentment he holds toward his American brothers-in-arms for abandoning him when he needed them the most while he mourns the loss of his home and country.

But I choose to find strength in this duality, in being in-between. I get to choose which pieces I make part of my identity. From my Vietnamese side I embrace the history, traditions, and beautiful language while rejecting the intolerance, misogyny, and ageism. From my American side I embrace the diversity, open-mindedness, and opportunities while rejecting the racism, self-righteousness, and selfishness.

I'm currently working toward a Master's in Speech Language Pathology, a field that is 92 percent white. I want to make sure we can better the

*lives of everyone receiving these critical services, regardless of their race,
gender, orientation, or any other historically detrimental factor. I work
in the public school system. When children come to school, I want them to
learn from people who look like them, who have had similar experiences.
I also want them to learn from people who are drastically different from
them. My job is to help them find their voice and express themselves but it
is also to teach them to listen to and celebrate others. I couldn't do all this
without both of my cultures.*

—*Vi Le*

THE FILIPINO EXORCIST

To round out our warrior education here in India and Southeast Asia,
I thought it important to get representation from a cultural perspective
into which we hadn't previously delved: the Philippines. So, I've invited
my Filipino friend Ryan Omega to come and share with you the harrow-
ing account of that one time he took on the mantle of spiritual warrior
to literally exorcise a demon from this realm by utilizing the magic of his
Catholic-infused folk-Filipino upbringing.

Now, I've gotta say, the very first time I met Ryan at that late-night
witchy goth club off of Hollywood Boulevard, I could just *sense* this was
a man of magical prowess, and our daylight conversations and hang-
outs since then have only furthered my faith in his experienced ability to
connect to the unseen. Lots of people *say* they have this connection, but
Ryan's the real deal.

You, however, may actually already be familiar with Ryan since (in addition to having a lifelong involvement in the occult, paranormal, and spiritual
world) he's a popular livestream and podcast host, producer, director, and
game designer. He also has a hit RPG/LARP podcast and Twitch channel
("Life. Action. Roleplay!"). So, if you're like me and find Ryan's real-life
exorcist tale exciting, then you can follow him and find out more excitement
via his Twitter (@RyanOMGa) and his Instagram (@RyanOmega).

*One night, I got a call from my friend, Kate, who lived in Burbank and
knew of my abilities, asking me to respond to some unspecified "negative"*

energy left by a roommate who just moved out. This sounded like a simple clean-up of negative energy. However, they mentioned that sage didn't seem to neutralize the energy and that caught my attention and raised my alertness.

On arrival, I felt the presence of an incredibly negative, suffocating energy. I went into the room; it definitely had dark energy but also that room seemed to be darker than the rest of the house, even with the lights fully on. It took an hour to clean the negative energy; I had to energetically sandblast the negative energy to clear it. But then afterward, when we opened the windows, suddenly everyone inside the room was choking and couldn't breathe. The room became visually darker again.

In response, I went outside to my car and retrieved my exorcism kit consisting of candles, my grandmother's rosary blessed by the Vatican, and my grandfather's item of faith: a Knights of Columbus sword. Returning to the house, I detected that the negative energy was actually outside the room, not in it, and so I went to the patio just outside the room's window.

I started burning a couple candles from my kit to better sense the energy. The candles' fire gave small illumination but also casted shadows that looked inky, and these shadows started moving on their own even when the candlelight stayed perfectly still. The shadows moved like tentacles and they led to a storage shed. The initial impression I got was that this entity inside the shed was syphoning energy through these appendages.

I made contact with the entity and asked what he was doing. He claimed that he didn't know but that he also didn't want to be there. I gave him the benefit of the doubt and asked where he wanted to go, to which he said that he wanted to go back to Hell. Despite the darkness, the figure's skin looked like burned leather and seemed to be wearing rags.

I created a portal to the fiery place, drawing doors between dimensions, and asked for permission to send someone there, letting them know he originally came from there. They explained that he was punished, which is why he was trapped on earth. I explained that he didn't belong here either, he was harming people and needed to be returned. They acquiesced to taking him back.

I then told the demon that he only had a couple of minutes to travel through the portal before it closed. The demon eyed me suspiciously as it backed towards the portal. All the while, I held my grandfather's sword out in front of me to protect myself. The entire time, he kept his eyes on me. By now, Kate had joined us and was right behind me, so I was protecting Kate as much as myself.

My eyes darted away for a moment, catching a moving shadow, and the demon extended his arm to successfully swipe his claw through my chest. Even though there was no physical injury, the aura around my chest looked tattered. Energy was leaking out of me as if I was bleeding. This got me angry enough to shove the demon into the fiery portal using the aura of my grandfather's sword. As he was falling backward into the portal, there was no sound. I then sealed the portal to make sure he didn't come back.

We inspected the house once more, and there was no longer any signature of negative energy around. But for a few days after the incident, I went into a depression. I didn't understand why, not until I realized that the demon's attack left an infection in my aura.

That next Sunday, I accompanied my relatives to a Catholic Mass, and while I'm not a religious man, I stood in line to receive Communion. However, once I got to the priest, I crossed my arms as a sign that I wanted a blessing instead of the Communion wafer (in Catholic belief the actual transubstantiated body of Christ). The priest asked me what he should pray for. I decided to tell him the truth, as bizarre as it was. Whether he believed me or not was not important; he gave me his blessing, and I left healed.

—Ryan Omega

PART 5

EAST ASIA

*Thus it is that in war the victorious strategist
only seeks battle after the victory has been
won, whereas he who is destined to defeat
first fights and afterwards looks for victory.*
SUN TZU, THE ART OF WAR

15
CHINA

Cultural

DYNASTIC CHINA

China has a long history of warfare and conflict, of legendary heroes and torturous atrocities, of military innovations helpful and harmful. Then again, when you're one of the rare cultures to have existed in continuity from the dawn of civilization to the modern era, you're going to have experienced a whole lot of everything. This was the civilization that gave us gunpowder, landmines, hand grenades, semiautomatic repeating crossbows, and other game-changing weapons of war. China has made more than its fair share of contributions to the ways in which the world goes to war, but its native spiritual traditions arose as a way to discourage and mitigate the need to go to war.

A Tale of Two Faiths

Around 771 BCE, the era known as the "Spring and Autumn Period" commenced in China, and though the name makes it sound like a tranquil and placid time, it was anything but. This era was defined by the crumbling of the Zhou dynasty that had become too self-indulgently decadent and out of touch with the common people. Eventually, once the Zhou fell, things just got worse as countless warlords fought amongst themselves for two and a half centuries to fill the power vacuum in what is now called the "Warring States Period." During all this turmoil, however, two major spiritual traditions were directly born in response to these societal collapses and ceaseless wars, Taoism and Confucianism, but they each sought to eradicate humanity's propensity for war in two very different ways.

The founders of Taoism and Confucianism were Lao Tzu and Confucius, respectively (though technically Lao Tzu didn't "found" Taoism, but rather was just the first and most influential person to theorize and write about it...that is, assuming he even existed at all since there is much dispute on that too). They were born, grew up, and lived in, arguably, this most chaotic time in Chinese history. Believing there had to be a better way for humans to coexist with one another without the need to constantly kill each other, they both looked to human nature as an example of perfect, harmonious peace for society to emulate. That's about where the similarities end, though. The fundamental difference between the two faiths is the way in which they define humanity's true "nature."

Hands-Off Approach

Taoism tends to see human nature as inherently neutral in terms of morality. We contain a balance of both virtue and vice within us, and if we flow through life finding joy in the current moment without being worried by specific expectations of *how* our life will unfold, then, like a river, we will eventually get to where we want to go just by not resisting the flow of life. The Universe/nature knows best, and if we just let people be themselves and be allowed to pursue their own interests without a lot of top-down micromanagement, then there would be no need for war since everyone would be doing their own thing, pursuing their own happiness, and competition would be pointless since hierarchies and expectations are nonexistent.

The "unnatural" problems come when we humans meddle with nature and try to manipulate things to come out a specific way (such as wanting a *specific* lover or needing a person to behave in a *specific* manner for us to be happy, or needing a *specific* circumstance to never change so as to feel "safe"), which then leads to the use of deceit, force, and violence to ensure those specific results come about. Taoism encourages us to just relax and trust that though we may not get *specifically* what we want, we'll ultimately get what we need and will be satisfied in the end, regardless. Thus, coercion and force to attain anything would be unnecessary.[160]

Hands-On Approach

Confucianism, however, tends to see human nature as good and well-intentioned but inherently corruptible and self-serving. If left to our own devices, we will do the moral thing because we are good people, but our morality is skewed by our emotional preferences (as exemplified by putting our family and friends' needs over the needs of strangers, even if those strangers' needs are more immediate and deserving). Thus, we are not inclined to do the objectively moral thing, but rather the subjectively moral thing within our self-created parameters of favoritism.

Hence, obviously there are incessant wars because each person is "out to get theirs" since everyone is inherently looking out for their own and for the good of their self-selected circle of people close to them rather than for the good of the community at large ("my family comes first," "my friends come first," "my country comes first," "my religion comes first," etc.). A society cannot peacefully exist like this with everyone doing their own thing according to their own flawed moral compass and helping only

160 Derek Lin, trans., *Tao Te Ching: Annotated & Explained*, by Laozi (Woodstock, VT: SkyLight Paths Publishing, 2006), n.p.

a selected few based off of emotional ties as opposed to off of *true* merit or need.

Thus, Confucianism advocates that a severely rigid hierarchy and central authority needs to exist to keep everyone in line and not allow our human nature to drive undue favoritism. If everyone knew their place in a society based on honor and merit (as opposed to capricious emotions and social connections) and dutifully served the people above them while helping those below them, then peace would prevail and there'd be no need to fight each other because everyone will have their needs met in an objectively balanced and fair way.

Thus, an all-powerful emperor needs to be in charge, and so long as he is working for the betterment of all those under him and all those under him obey him, harmony is maintained. Only when a ruler is corrupt, a lower-rank person steps out of line, or rewards are granted based off of anything other than merit does the stability of society start to crack.[161]

Legally Speaking

Despite both Taoism and Confucianism being born from societal collapses and seeking to end centuries of destructive warfare, it would be a third Chinese philosophy that would actually end the Warring States Period and bring about ordered peace in the land. This new school of thought was called "Legalism" (which is essentially Confucianism taken to its most conservative extreme), and its philosophical (becoming a religion unto itself) worship of cold logic changed everything.

In a nutshell, Legalism was all about using a logical, methodical approach to problem-solving while eliminating emotion and personal preference from *all* decision-making because humans could not be trusted to make the right decisions due to their inherent selfishness and biased emotions. Unlike Confucianism, Legalism was of the opinion that people were not inherently good and that their morality was wholly shaped by the legal limits placed upon them (e.g., the only thing preventing you from

161   Chang Wang and Nathan H. Madson, *Inside China's Legal System* (Oxford: Chandos Publishing, 2013), n.p.

hurting or killing someone you don't like is the fact that you know you'll be punished for it, not because you think hurting or killing that person is "wrong"... or not committing a crime only out of fear of being caught and punished, not because you think the crime itself is "wrong"). The result was a religiously upheld cold, indifferent, ultra-bureaucratic system of government and militarism reinforced through a particularly harsh legal system and divinely backed police state.[162]

The adoption of Legalism, however, served as a double-edged sword. This cold, indifferent bureaucracy wherein emotion and preference were no longer factors at play in important decision-making did, indeed, ensure that advancement in government and in the military was now solely based on merit and performance as opposed to having the right breeding or net-working. So, when the warlord of the state of Qin adopted Legalism as his governing pseudo-religious philosophy of choice, his administrators, advisors, and leaders (in government and military) became the best in the land, and with better leaders, generals, and soldiers (all promoted only through merit), the Qin conquered all their rivals and established the first imperial dynasty of a united China in 221 BCE.

Yet, poetically, the other edge of the sword was that Qin's religious adherence to the austerity of Legalism caused the brutally repressed common people to overthrow the dynasty only fifteen years after its founding. Throughout the successive dynasties of China, the ruling emperors would uphold, promote, and administer their empires based on various mixes of Taoist, Confucian, Legalist, and Buddhist philosophies (depending on which best aligned with their own religious outlooks and political agendas). In 1912, the last imperial dynasty fell (Qing Dynasty), and the country descended into civil war until it was forcefully unified under the

162   Emily Mark, "Legalism," World History Encyclopedia, January 31, 2016,
       https://www.worldhistory.org/Legalism/.

leadership of a corrupt, genocidal, Buddhist-raised Christian military dictator named Chiang Kai-shek.[163]

REVOLUTIONARY CHINA

Like we did during our trek through Vietnam, it is impossible (and somewhat irresponsible) to ignore the successful communist revolution that occurred in China out of fears of it being "controversial." Regardless of your already-formed opinions against or in favor of what happened in China during the late 1940s, the fact that a small rabble of progressive, atheism-accepting peasants overthrew a conservative military dictatorship that was backed by the most powerful Western economies in the world at that time is profound and has had long-reaching effects right to the present. (Plus, to not want to talk about certain world-changing historical events just because they're controversial serves no one.)

Red Star Rising

Nowadays, China is still a communist state, but only superficially. Arguably, they are the *most* capitalist nation on earth (with bare-minimum workers' rights, nonexistent environmental protections, a severe concentration of wealth in the top 1 percent of society, a legal system *heavily* favoring corporations over people, economic colonization over poorer nations' resources, and the list continues). However, their main difference from the West is that they're a totalitarian oligarchy (as opposed to a Western democratic oligarchy) parading under the pretense of "communism" because of the positive associations that word has in mainland Chinese society (a lot like how many political organizations in the U.S. are given names that infer the exact opposite of their intentions: e.g., the nonprofit "Citizens United," which

---

163 "Shang Yang," Encyclopedia.com, updated May 23, 2018, https://www
.encyclopedia.com/people/social-sciences-and-law/sociology-biographies
/shang-yang; Yang Shang, *The Book of Lord Shang: A Classic of the Chinese School of
Law*, trans. J. J. L. Duyvendak (Clark, NJ: The Lawbook Exchange, Ltd., 2003),
n.p.; "Legalism," Encyclopædia Britannica, updated February 12, 2019, https://
www.britannica.com/topic/Legalism.

advocates for the interests of corporations in government as opposed to the interests of actual human citizens).[164]

Still, like any political system that makes a hard right turn after its leftist leaders embrace the perks of power and continues to go horribly off-rail as time marches on, communism in China started out (like everything … including the road to hell) with good intentions and was popularly supported by the poorest of the poor and the most oppressed in society. So, before we move on to the rest of East Asia, we'll take a brief look into those early days and see not only how this revolution was so progressive in a social justice sense, but also how its iconic leader, Mao Zedong, utilized his iconoclastic atheism to garner widespread public support.

Power to the People's Republic

For most of Chinese history, the common folk were trapped in Confucianism's rigid social hierarchy with little to no possibility for upward social mobility (though they could always fall further downward). This deeply engrained Confucianism in government policy left little chance for the masses to improve their lot in life, and so whenever a war broke out, the poor and oppressed fought because they forcibly *had to*, not because it would personally affect them or because they would personally benefit from a victory.

Mao Zedong, however, made it a pillar of his twentieth-century war strategy to empower the common people and inspire them to see how fighting in the revolution benefited them directly. To do this, he made a lot of social justice reforms within his military ranks that benefitted the most disenfranchised people, thereby lifting their spirits to *want* to fight in the revolution so that, upon victory, these reforms could become permanent and more widespread.

Since Mao was an avowed atheist, he was not beholden to any cultural traditions that relied on religious or spiritual justifications for keeping the

---

164 Vincent Kolo, "China's Capitalist Counter-Revolution," Socialism Today, December 2007–January 2008, http://socialismtoday.org/archive/114/china .html.

status quo intact and the oppressed under aristocratic heel, and thus he was more philosophically free to enact more progressive reforms than previous leaders with religious convictions would allow (especially in contrast to his *very* Christian rival, Chiang Kai-shek).

In addition to declaring women as equals to men in every way (which controversially flew directly in the face of millennia-old, deeply held traditional Confucian teachings), Mao Zedong also declared that women were deserving of property and inheritance rights and full political and medical sovereignty over their own bodies (a radical thing back in 1940s China... or 1940s anywhere for that matter). On a more grand scale, he also declared that all people deserved a basic education, prohibited arranged marriages, criminalized sexual relations with and marriage to children, granted all people (aged eighteen and up) regardless of class, race, or sex the right to vote, and more (even directly calling out China's historical patriarchy as a "great rope" that needed to be cut to free women from bondage).[165]

It should be mentioned that there were definitely some regressions too (Mao having a tendency to reverse and then reinstate some of his edicts depending upon how problematic they were becoming to his cult of personality), but overall, the poor and downtrodden saw that their life could change for the better in the exact ways they had always wanted it to if this atheist-led revolution was successful. If the revolution failed, then their lives would return back to that of religiously rationalized servitude and inequality, losing all the social justice gains that they had attained while in atheist Mao's army. Thus, by making social justice reforms a pillar of his political platform and promulgating secularism in government over religious-

---

165 Mao Tse-Tung, *Quotations from Chairman Mao Tse-Tung*, trans. D. Weinberg (New York: BN Publishing, 2007), n.p.; Rebecca Cairns and Jennifer Llewellyn, "CCP Social Reforms," Alpha History, September 23, 2019, https://alphahistory.com/chineserevolution/ccp-social-reforms/; Yuhui Li, "Women's Movement and Change of Women's Status in China," *Journal of International Women's Studies* 1, no. 1, 3 (January 2000): 30–40, https://vc.bridgew.edu/cgi/viewcontent.cgi?article=1626&context=jiws; Chang Sun, "The Changes of Mao Zedong Thoughts on Women's Liberation after the Founding of People's Republic of China," China University of Geosciences, Beijing, 2013, 922–926, https://dx.doi.org/10.2991/asshm-13.2013.171.

inspired rule, Mao continuously added new, very feverous troops to his ranks, even after big military losses.[166]

By October 1949, Mao's ragtag communist army of the oppressed and disenfranchised had expulsed the ruling conservative military dictatorship and its aristocratic benefactors off China's mainland (from where they escaped to Taiwan), and many of Mao's progressive reforms did, indeed, stay in place just as promised. However, absolute power corrupts absolutely, and by the mid-1970s, famines, failed attempts at industrialization, fanatical vigilantism by self-created armies of indoctrinated youths, and other corruptive problems plagued the Chinese Communist Party's supposed utopian workers' paradise. Today, China remains one of the greatest military powers and largest atheist and totalitarian states in the entire world. Its idealistic, progressive beginnings as a hopeful band of the poor and oppressed fighting for social justice against a conservative, religious dictatorship now only exists in the pages of history books like this one here (if it's allowed to be taught at all).

Chinese Takeaway:
THE WAY OF NO WAY

Despite modern warfare being a highly mechanized and remote affair, soldiers around the world are still routinely trained in the martial arts just in case close combat becomes necessary. As warriors ourselves, it is wise to learn from the masters, and one of the greatest martial arts masters of the modern era is unarguably Bruce Lee. His self-described fighting style of "Using no way as way; having no limitation as limitation" is, indeed, one of the (if not *the*) most effective styles for us both in physical combat and in the spiritual battles of daily life.

As Bruce Lee saw it, all fighting traditions were too limiting and were only effective in the vacuum of specific rules and regulations that both

---

166 Maj. Shawn Russell, "Mao Zedong's 'On Guerrilla Warfare' and Joseph Kabila's Lost Opportunity," *Small Wars Journal*, July 10, 2012, https://smallwarsjournal .com/jrnl/art/mao-zedong%E2%80%99s-on-guerrilla-warfare-and-joseph -kabila%E2%80%99s-lost-opportunity; Mao Tse-Tung, *On Guerrilla Warfare*, trans. Samuel B. Griffith (New York: BN Publishing, 2007), n.p.

sides needed to follow, thus not applicable in the real world (e.g.: don't expect a champion boxer to hold up as well in a real street fight wherein kicks, weapons, grapples, and other tactics forbidden in the ring are all fair game). Like an attacker in the real world, life also doesn't come at you in a specific, regulated, predictable way. Life comes at you any which way it can, and though you may be masterfully trained for life to come at you in a certain way, your masterful adherence to that one way leaves yourself woefully unprepared for the myriad other ways life can and does come at you.

Deeply inspired by Taoism, Bruce Lee's *Jeet Kune Do* philosophy on the martial arts and life in general is a tradition whose bedrock foundation is on having no tradition. Rather, it seeks to incorporate all traditions and styles without preference, and if you read his books on the martial arts or look at any of his self-choreographed films, you'll see this in action. In the course of a single fight sequence, he'll switch from a British boxing jab, to a Japanese judo throw, to a French savate kick, to a Chinese Wing Chun counter strike, to down-and-dirty street-fighting bites to the leg and kicks to the groin.

To Bruce Lee, if you weren't prideful about "tradition" and were open to all styles, then you could be ready for and respond to any attack that came your way (a lesson probably best exemplified in his great, unfinished film *Game of Death*). Similarly, if we cling too tightly to our own cultural and spiritual traditions, we hold ourselves in too rigid of a position to be able to interact with the world accordingly (since life will throw everything at you without respect for your cultural traditions or spiritual taboos). We are to "be like water" whose amorphous softness and disregard for a fixed shape makes it invulnerable to attacks while simultaneously allowing it to be erosive and destructive like a river or a tidal wave if need be.

So, for your takeaway challenge here, loosen up on being so fixated on all traditions of which you consider yourself a member. Look to how other people around the world are fighting the good fight and see if such strategies could enhance your own activism. Rather than only use the magical rituals and styles of your initiated tradition, seek out alternate ways of doing the same spell from other traditions and become more diverse in your ability to manipulate natural forces of the universe. Instead of always engaging in protests and civil rights movements in the same manner you've always done (because it's familiar), learn about other ways you can get involved and add those alternative avenues into your activism arsenal. Be like water and exchange your prideful rigidity toward traditions for the endless expanse of flexible possibilities that is no tradition. Free your mind and begin incorporating the "way of no way."

Deities & Legends

GUAN YU

In Chinese folk versions of Taosim and Buddhism, Guan Yu (alternatively known as "Guandi") is a martial deity who counts both criminal and law enforcement personnel among his most devoted (especially in Hong Kong). He's exceptionally interesting because he was a real person who lived during the chaotic wars of China's brief "Three Kingdoms" era (early to mid-third century CE) and became such a renowned general that he was immortalized in epic fictional books a thousand years later. These books became the classical canon of Chinese literature, which helped his legend to grow, culminating in his deification as the god of war in Chinese folk beliefs.

What we know about his human life is that he was a brilliant general, and although he was defeated and captured by Cao Cao (pronounced "Tsao Tsao," another *ultra-renowned* general during the same era), Cao Cao did not follow the tradition of executing him. Rather, he saw the military genius in Guan Yu and recruited him into his own army. Guan Yu served him dutifully for a time, but ultimately defected. Eventually, though, he was betrayed by his own allies (which his enemy Cao Cao explicitly warned him would happen) and was executed.[167]

As legends grew about him (both from his actual life and fictionalized cameo in the legendary *Romance of the Three Kingdoms* literary epic), his supernatural abilities became ingrained in the cultural zeitgeist, and people

---

167 Owen Jarus, "Guan Yu Biography: Revered Chinese Warrior," Live Science, February 25, 2014, https://www.livescience.com/43681-guan-yu.html.

began regarding him as the iconic model of courage, loyalty, and martial skill. Nowadays, these same virtues are held in high esteem by both organized crime and police forces throughout China, all of whom often petition Guan Yu to aid them in their conflicting endeavors.[168]

SHAOLIN WARRIOR MONKS

The Buddhist monks of the Shaolin Monastery (popularly known as the "Shaolin Temple") are famous the world over for originating Shaolin kung fu (alternatively spelled gung/gong fu). Their history is intertwined with legend and fiction, rumors and romanticism, but the interlacing thread that connects it all is the almost supernatural prowess with which these peace-devoted monks have defeated (and still can defeat) opponents in physical combat.

According to the generally adhered-to story (which is a mix of facts and fantasy) the Shaolin Monastery was established by a Buddhist missionary from southern India in the late fifth century CE. However, it wasn't until another Buddhist Indian missionary called Bodhidharma came to the monastery a few decades later that fighting became a staple of the religious order (though some argue that Shaolin martial arts predate his arrival). Bodhidharma preached a version of Buddhism called "Chan" (more popularly known by its Japanese name "Zen") that mixed Buddhist discipline for enlightenment and self-improvement with Taoist focus on the necessity of universal balance and on looking to nature's example for how to achieve harmony.[169]

168   Athena Chan, "Why Guan Yu—Warrior God Known as Duke Guan—Is Worshipped in Hong Kong and Asia by Police, Gangsters ... and Businessmen Alike," *South China Morning Post*, July 6, 2019, https://www.scmp.com/news /hong-kong/society/article/3017346/revered-police-gangsters-and -businessmen-warrior-deity-duke; Ruru Zhou, "Guan Yu," China Highlights, updated March 18, 2021, https://www.chinahighlights.com/travelguide/china -history/guan-yu.htm.

169   Bodhidharma, *The Zen Teaching of Bodhidharma*, trans. Red Pine (New York: North Point Press, 1987), ix–xvii.

Upon his arrival, Bodhidharma found the Shaolin monks (and nuns, who often get left out of Shaolin history) to be too unnaturally out of balance, having lost touch with the real world from being too heavily involved in the pursuit of the spiritual one. Yes, they were wise and learned in the sutras, but they were physically frail and unhealthy. So, Bodhidharma taught them kung fu as an exercise regimen to strengthen their body in harmony with their mind so they could be as physically strong as they were intellectually smart, a return to natural balance as a complete being. As the monastery grew, so did its assets and landed estate, and so the monks (many of whom were former soldiers) began using their kung fu exercises in actual combat to defend the monastery from continuous thieves and bandits.[170]

Their cementation into superstardom came in the early seventh century CE when they agreed to use their fighting abilities to help assist General Li Shimin in his revolutionary overthrow of the Sui Dynasty and establishment of the new Tang Dynasty. By aiding the revolution militarily, the Shaolin Monastery garnered imperial favoritism and funding during the Tang Dynasty. Subsequent dynasties would follow suit and try to recruit Shaolin monks (and former monks) in various battles to expand their empires and put down internal revolts.[171]

In the early to mid-twentieth century, the monastic order would suffer much repression by both the republican and communist Chinese regimes, but by the latter half of the twentieth century (with China's hard switch toward all-but-in-name capitalism and the growing international fandom

170 Debra Kelly, "The Truth About the Legendary Shaolin Monk Warriors," Grunge, April 2, 2020, https://www.grunge.com/198843/the-truth-about-the -legendary-shaolin-monk-warriors/; Sara Naumann, "A Brief History of the Shaolin Temple," TripSavvy, January 21, 2019, https://www.tripsavvy.com /brief-history-shaolin-temple-1495708.

171 Emma Lu, "When Shaolin Monks Came to Aid the Tang Emperor," Vision Times, February 26, 2020, https://visiontimes.com/2020/02/26/when -shaolin-monks-came-to-aid-the-tang-emperor2.html.

of kung fu films) the Shaolin Monastery became a profitable tourist attraction while still remaining a functioning monastery.

Nowadays, the order runs a vast commercial empire based off of its Shaolin "brand," which is met with much controversy as *very* materialistic and against Chan Buddhist teachings, though its current head abbot Shi Yongxin (who has an MBA degree) argues that he is just keeping with the times and that the commercialization of Shaolin is helping to spread the monastery's teachings to a global audience.[172]

SUN TZU

The famous author of one of the (if not *the*) most influential books on military strategy, *The Art of War* (still studied in military academies the world over), Sun Tzu was a legendary military general during the Spring and Autumn Period of sixth century BCE China who pioneered warfare techniques and soldier discipline trainings that were millennia ahead of his time. Though some historians debate whether or not he actually existed, his accredited *The Art of War* is a real book that was widely read and implemented in China from the Warring States Period onward.[173]

According to legend, Sun Tzu got his start in military leadership when a feudal warlord challenged him to train his royal harem of concubines into a lethal fighting force. Accepting the challenge, Sun Tzu divided the warlord's women into two groups, placing the top two ranking courtesans as the group leaders. At first, none of the women took him seriously and laughed at it all. Sun Tzu's immediate reaction was that, as their top leader giving the orders, he was at fault for not explaining his orders

172 Barbara O'Brien, "Warrior Monks of Shaolin," Learn Religions, March 8, 2017, https://www.learnreligions.com/warrior-monks-of-shaolin-4123247; Christopher Beam, "The Rise and Fall of Shaolin's CEO Monk," Bloomberg Businessweek, December 28, 2015, https://www.bloomberg.com/news/features/2015-12-28/the-rise-and-fall-of-shaolin-s-ceo-monk.

173 Gen. David Petraeus, "'The Art of War': As Relevant Now as When It Was Written," *The Irish Times*, March 26, 2018, https://www.irishtimes.com/culture/books/the-art-of-war-as-relevant-now-as-when-it-was-written-1.3440724.

clearly enough (communication being effective only insofar as the audience understands the message). When he tried to train them again, this time with more self-awareness on clarity, the two group leaders simply laughed at him again. They were both immediately executed, and from then on out, the rest of the courtesans obeyed diligently and became a highly drilled military unit. This greatly impressed the warlord, and he made Sun Tzu general of his armies for accomplishing such a feat.[174]

Not much else is really known about Sun Tzu, himself, but he is credited with being supremely successful in various battles and having compiled his philosophies on warfare in *The Art of War*. In this famous book, he utilized the teachings of Taoist philosophy to revolutionize the way leaders should approach and conduct war. Some of his insights include: the importance of recognizing opportunities as opposed to creating them, adapting to the physical terrain, only engaging in economically cost-effective battles, the use of spies and intelligence gathering before launching an attack, the importance of troop morale, the need to abort a pre-planned strategy if it is not working and adjust to what's going on, and even how the chain of culpability for failure starts from the top down (i.e., leaders are responsible for the failure of their subordinates).[175]

Aside from direct strategy, the book is also philosophical in nature, emphasizing the importance of what goes on *before* the battle as more important than during it. Direct conflict should be avoided unless absolutely necessary, but when it does happen, the side with the more disciplined soldiers, the more gathered intelligence, the more self-awareness, and the more belief in their ability to win will come out victorious.

---

174   Alicia McDermott, "Sun Tzu: Famous Chinese Strategist and Philosopher," Ancient Origins, October 9, 2018, https://www.ancient-origins.net/history -famous-people/sun-tzu-0010817.

175   "The Art of War," National Geographic, August 31, 2020, https://www .nationalgeographic.org/encyclopedia/art-war/; Sun Tzu, *The Art of War*, trans. Lionel Giles (Ballingslöv: Chiron Academic Press, 2015).

The book's Taoism-heavy wisdom has been read and admired by leaders and game-changers from Napoleon and Mao Zedong to Colin Powell and Tupac Shakur. However, because of its universal insight into the human psychology of conflict in general, Sun Tzu's teachings have also been adapted and appropriated by CEOs for corporate warfare, coaches for sports teams, and even lonely singles wanting to improve the art of seduction on the battlefield of finding love.[176]

176   "The Art of War," History, updated August 21, 2018, https://www.history
       .com/topics/ancient-china/the-art-of-war.

16

THE MONGOL EMPIRE

Cultural

Environmental Silver Linings

Mongolia has become synonymous with conquest. Though in modern times it's a landlocked country with a small GDP and even smaller population, these barren steppes are where one of the greatest, most world-altering, and largest contiguous land empires originated. Led by their great khans, bickering tribes of nomads managed to unite and conquer almost all of Asia and the Middle East *and* managed to hold control over the most religiously and culturally diverse empire the world had seen.

However, due to the unprecedented human devastation that was left in their wake, they also helped to massively reduce carbon levels in the environment. Their total destruction of urban centers provided the conditions necessary for places to grow wild once again with native flora and fauna, a return to its natural state without human interference or manipulation. So, while they may have been devastating to humanity, the Mongols proved to be a big boon to Mother Nature and the ecological health of the globe.[177]

Nothing Sacred

One of the biggest advantages the nomadic peoples of the Eurasian Steppe had going for them in warfare was their shamanic religion. They had an animistic belief in the sanctity of the natural world and of the spiritual realm of the ancestors. To them, just being out in nature was sacred. Every river, lake, mountain, and expanse of land held spiritual power and energy. Everything was sacred, and in that way, also nothing was sacred (because the value of something as *sacred* doesn't have as much impact if *everything in the world* is sacred, just like being seven feet tall wouldn't be special if *everyone* was seven feet tall).

To them, the Divine did not exist in ornate temples nor in lavish mosques or monasteries. The gods existed all around them at all times, and so when these nomads came raiding into town, they did not withhold their violence from religious men, women, or shrines, nor did they hold anyone or any one place as more "sacred" or inherently more "valuable" than anyone or anyplace else. They killed children, used their enemy's friends and family members as human shields, and even dressed prisoners of war in Mongol clothing so as to have their enemies mistakenly kill their own people for them. There were no ethics or rules to warfare.[178]

Nothing and no one was safe since everything and everyone was equally sacred, and this was a marked advantage in war because while their enemies were working with a self-imposed handicap by taking the "high road" of religiously ethical rules of engagement, the steppe nomads had no such restrictions and therefore had more options and tactics available to them.

177   Jon Henley, "Why Genghis Khan Was Good for the Planet," *The Guardian*, January 26, 2011, https://www.theguardian.com/theguardian/2011/jan/26 /genghis-khan-eco-warrior.

178   Mark Cartwright, "Mongol Warfare," World History Encyclopedia, October 10, 2019, https://www.worldhistory.org/Mongol_Warfare/.

(It'd be like banning chemical weapons because of how effective they are in killing people; the armies that adhere to that ban because it's "not ethical" and "immoral" are limited in how they can fight, while those who don't care and go ahead and use chemical weapons are at a severe tactical advantage in any battle and in winning the war itself.)

Nomad's Land

By 1206 CE, a man named Temüjin (who, despite being born an aristocrat, grew up in crushing poverty) had become the leader of a steppe confederation of various Mongol tribes held together by his sheer force of will and was given the title "Genghis Khan" (which roughly translates to "Universal Ruler"). Soon after, he set his sights on expanding his realm beyond the arid steppes and toward the more fertile lands to the west. However, Genghis was a very different leader than any steppe tribe had had before; rather than shoot-first-ask-questions-later aggression, he preferred to not use his military might if he could help it.

He preferred to practice psychological warfare to scare an enemy into surrender instead of having to fight them into submission. If they chose surrender, he would leave the entire populace and city unharmed. If they chose to fight, every living person would be killed, no exceptions (save one horribly maimed person to spread news of his victory and intimidate other peoples into not fighting).[179]

Genghis Khan's empire eventually stretched from Eastern Europe and Mesopotamia all the way to the Korean peninsula and eastern shores of China. With such a large territory under a single, united rule, an era of peace endured. Yes, there were many rebellions, but all these cultures, civilizations, and religions were no longer fighting with one another and were now forced by their Mongol overlords to interact with each other in

179   Owen Jarus, "Genghis Khan, Founder of Mongol Empire: Facts & Biography," Live Science, February 10, 2014, https://www.livescience.com/43260-genghis -khan.html; "This Day in History: Genghis Khan Dies," History, updated August 17, 2020, https://www.history.com/this-day-in-history/genghis-khan -dies; Léonie Chao-Fong, "The Conquerors of Asia: Who Were the Mongols?" History Hit, January 15, 2020, https://www.historyhit.com/the-conquerors -of-asia-who-were-the-mongols/.

a civilized, nonviolent manner. For all the ice water running through his veins, Genghis knew that if he wanted to keep what he had conquered, the people needed to be happy, and so as a ruler, he is ironically also remembered as an unprecedented champion of religious and ethnic freedom.

Pax Mongolica

Back in his childhood, Genghis had seen firsthand how internal fighting could keep a great people small and weak. So, he was determined to not show favoritism among the *many* religions and cultures over which he ruled so that the people would have one less reason to keep fighting against his rule and against each other as they had historically been doing before he conquered them. All religions and cultural traditions were tolerated as equals in the Mongol Empire, and every person within the empire could worship and live however they pleased.

Additionally, high positions in government and military were awarded based on merit alone, not one's race or ethnic background. All cultures were valuable (well, except those that chose not to submit and were thereafter annihilated), and the best minds from each culture were encouraged to continue their research and share findings with one another. Moreover, intolerance was not tolerated, and any single religion or culture that began to persecute others with fanatical zeal was *immediately* and *mercilessly* put down.[180]

In terms of faith and philosophy, the history books directly written about Genghis Khan's advocacy of religious and legal tolerance of all faiths went on to directly inspire the founding fathers of the United States, in particular Thomas Jefferson, George Washington, and Benjamin Franklin. Based directly on the example of religious freedom in Genghis's multicultural empire, so, too, did the U.S. founders attempt to establish a similar tolerance in their own fledgling nation of culturally different colonies that each had conflicting goals and interests. Tolerance was seen as the best way to

---

180 "Genghis Khan," Biography, updated August 30, 2019, https://www
.biography.com/dictator/genghis-khan; Jack Weatherford, "Genghis Khan—
Hero of Religious Freedom?" OZY, October 31, 2016, https://www.ozy.com
/news-and-politics/genghis-khan-hero-of-religious-freedom/72553/.

keep such disjointed people united in a single nation as Genghis Khan had once done in his diverse empire.[181]

Still, nothing lasts forever, and all things must pass. In vies for succession, Genghis's descendants would divide the empire into competing factions just like their squabbling ancestors. This regular descent into civil war whenever the chief ruler died eventually destroyed the Mongol Empire from the inside out, all this only about one hundred and fifty years from Genghis first coming to power in these barren, arid steppes.[182]

Mongolian Takeaway:
TAKING IT TO THE LIMIT

How far are you willing to go to win the war? How much would you give, do, and sacrifice to ensure that the world would be a better place for those who are oppressed, for the environment, for animals, for what you call "justice"? Are there any lines that you will not cross? If victory could be guaranteed at the cost of doing something you consider "wrong" or immoral, then would it be worth the cost? Would the ends justify the means?

These are tough and controversial questions, but in times of struggle and in times of war, these are the kinds of decisions each of us will have to make. For the great khans of the Mongol Empire, one major contributing factor to their success was their willingness to go all in to win a war. Morals and ethics be damned; they knew that in a war, winning is everything. Genghis Khan established an unprecedented empire of religious tolerance, cultural diversity, and ethnic equality...but only after he set those ideals aside to do whatever it took to be victorious in war.

This is not just some medieval "temporary amorality" either. Admired and well-respected leaders throughout the world, including revered U.S. presidents, have often set their morals and ethics aside to do immoral and unethical things during wartime to ensure that they would win.

---

181   Jack Weatherford, *Genghis Khan and the Quest for God: How the World's Greatest Conqueror Gave Us Religious Freedom* (New York: Penguin Random House, 2016), n.p.

182   Anne F. Broadbridge, "The Rise and Fall of the Mongol Empire," TED-Ed, August. 29, 2019, YouTube, 5:00, https://www.youtube.com/watch?v=wUVvTqvjUaM.

Abraham Lincoln suspended the writ of habeas corpus (the law that prevents the government from imprisoning an individual indefinitely without showing cause) so that anyone who protested against or was deemed counterproductive to Union army military operations could be silenced without him having to go through the legal system (the Supreme Court declared such a suspension illegal, though Lincoln refused to cooperate with the Supreme Court's ruling and kept doing it anyway).[183]

Woodrow Wilson (U.S. president during WWI) demanded that Congress give him absolute authority to control the press and postal system so as to silence all free speech opposition to the war effort (resulting in Congress granting him most such powers). Hell, even WWII hero Franklin Roosevelt suspended the human rights of U.S. citizens of Japanese descent so as to round them up into concentration camps out of (unfounded) fear they might be spies or agents of the enemy. All of these actions were taken as "necessary" evils to win a war and ensure victory (or so the presidents believed and justified to themselves and to the public). In their own minds, winning the war effort was worth such objectively immoral actions because the cost of losing the war was far too great.[184]

So, for your takeaway challenge here, do a deep meditation to honestly assess your own morals and ethics and know where your limits (if any) are. If it is in your spiritual tradition, get in touch with deceased, ancestral leaders and heroes of the past whom you admire, and ask their advice on how far they were willing to go (and then follow up with research to see where their personal morals and ethics historically took a back seat to the needs of the "greater good").

I cannot say that there is "no right or wrong answer" to this since we all have our own moral codes and opinions on whether or not the ends justify the means. So, in each of our hearts, there is *absolutely* a right and a

---

183   "President Lincoln Suspends the Writ of Habeas Corpus During the Civil War," History, updated May 24, 2021, https://www.history.com/this-day-in-history /president-lincoln-suspends-the-writ-of-habeas-corpus-during-the-civil-war.

184   David Greenberg, Margaret MacMillan, et al., "Stretching Executive Power in Wartime," *The New York Times*, May 27, 2007, https://campaigningforhistory .blogs.nytimes.com/2007/05/27/stretching-executive-power-in-wartime/.

wrong answer. Are my limits yours? Are your limits your enemies'? Your friends' and allies' limits? Your spiritual teachers' limits? The mind games in any revolutionary endeavor are confusing enough already; learn to know yourself and your limits before the battle influences you rather than your own sacred, inner truth.

Deities & Legends

SÜLDE TNGRI

Modern-day Mongolia is heavily Vajrayana Buddhist (the same denomination Westerners know better as "Tibetan" Buddhism, the one with the Dalai Lama), but their shamanic ancestors used to believe in many heavenly beings called *"tngri"* (pronounced "TEN-gree," and all tngri are seen as aspects of the one god *Tngri*, with a capital "T"). Each tngri held dominion over various physical aspects of the natural world as well as over abstract concepts. The tngri who specialized in personal protection in battle by acting as supernatural bodyguards were called *sülde tngri* (somewhat similar to a guardian angel but more vicious and proactive).

Despite each Mongol warrior having their own personal sülde tngri watching over them in battle, individuals could also petition the help of other people's sülde tngri. Naturally, the more successful a warrior was in battle, the more popular their sülde tngri became in being petitioned for help. After Genghis Khan made his indelible mark in the Mongol world, his sülde tngri became the one to whom *everyone* petitioned and whom everyone wanted protecting them (even in preference over their own personal one). Over time, Genghis's sülde tngri became highly worshipped as a deity in its own right, even outside of battle. Thus, Sülde Tngri (with a capital "S" and "T," originally Genghis Khan's personal spiritual protector) became the de facto deity of warriors and war in the shamanic Mongol pantheon.[185]

---

185 Walther Heissig, *The Religions of Mongolia*, trans. Geoffrey Samuel (Berkeley: University of California Press, 1970), 84–90, https://archive.org/details/bub _gb_OzDMbpw7EecC/page/n99/mode/2up.

TNGRI (THE SUPREME SKY GOD)

Tngri (with a capital "T") was the one supreme god in the shamanic worldview of the medieval Mongols (not to be confused with lowercase "t" tngri, who were seen as individual and autonomous sub-aspects of this one god in the world…akin to the Catholic belief of both Jesus and the Holy Spirit being simultaneously independent entities yet also aspects of the one God, known collectively as the "Holy Trinity"). This supreme deity was believed to be omnipresent yet unknowable, above the natural laws of the universe, and beyond human comprehension, though according to various legends, it was assumed that He lived in the sky.

Some scholars credit the Mongol great khans' devotion to Tngri as a major reason for their empire's unprecedented religious tolerance. As the medieval Mongols admittedly saw it, they couldn't know for certain that other religions weren't already worshipping Tngri since Tngri was so unknowable and beyond the limits of human understanding. The Mongols, themselves, couldn't even be certain if *they* were even worshipping Him in the way He prefers since He is so incomprehensible. So, to them, it was possible that the gods of other religions could, perhaps, just be different aspects of Tngri.

Moreover, in Mongol spiritual worldview, humans were believed to be inherently weak in spirit and imperfect, and since only Tngri is perfect in all things at all times, humans were regarded as having no business passing judgment on others since to be human is to be imperfect. A succinct maxim for the compassion of Tngri would be "don't judge somebody just because they sin differently than you."[186]

---

186   M. R. Reese, "The Ancient Practice of Tengriism, Shamanism and Ancient Worship of the Sky Gods," Ancient Origins, December 2, 2014, https://www .ancient-origins.net/myths-legends-asia/ancient-practice-tengriism -shamanism-and-ancient-worship-sky-gods-002387; Rafael Bezertinov, "Deities," *Tengrianizm: Religion of Türks and Mongols*, trans. Norm Kisamov (Lubbock: Texas Tech University Press, 2000), 71–95. http://www.hunmagyar .org/turan/tatar/turk.html.

17

JAPAN

Cultural

CLASSICAL & FEUDAL JAPAN

Medieval Japan has become the stuff of legend. With countless films, video games, manga and anime series, and more all shaping our modern understanding of what Japan's feudal age was like, the true history of this oft-romanticized era often gets muddled with the imagined fantastic. However, before Japan dove headlong into the warrior culture of samurai, ronin, and romanticized militarism, early Japan was anything but. This was the classical Heian era of Japan (794–1185 CE), infamous for the imperial court's obsession with art, luxury, pomp, and appearances.

Vanity Unfair

Self-isolated in their decadent bubble of excess at the capital of Heian-kyō (later renamed Kyoto), the kinds of offenses that were seen as most egregious among the ruling elite were things like wearing the wrong color shading in the inner lining of your kimono or writing a poem to someone that someone else was shunning because that person's sister-in-law had made a pass at someone else's boyfriend. (It was very much a *Real Housewives* and *Melrose Place* level of aristocratic pettiness and "champagne problems" that engulfed the lives of the central government.)

This kind of severity of gentility and preoccupation with superficiality meant that those who did the aristocracy's dirty work of keeping the common folk subdued (the military) were regarded as spiritually impure. Yes, it was a special sort of cherry-picking religious hypocrisy in which the Heian court existed. They were devoutly Buddhist and, on the one hand, overtly detested the fighting, war, and militarism that ran counter to the Buddha's pacifist teachings, yet they were also *exceedingly* engrossed in the materialism of luxury and sensual excess, all of which also ran counter to the Buddha's teachings of temperance and self-moderation in all things. It's never wise to throw stones when living in a glass house, and it would be this justified-by-religion derision toward warriors that would help cause the Heian court to shatter.[187]

Because the Heian aristocracy wanted nothing to do with the supposed "spiritual impurity" of the military, they delegated the task of raising and maintaining armies to the clan nobles outside the capital. The idea was that if each clan noble kept the peace in their own provincial territory, then not only would the Heian courtiers not have to be personally involved with (and thus not spiritually tainted by) the military but also no peasant

187 Shikibu Murasaki, *The Tale of Genji*, trans. Edward G. Seidensticker (New York: Alfred A. Knopf, 2006); Sei Shōnagon, *The Pillow Book of Sei Shōnagon*, trans. and ed. Ivan Morris (New York: Columbia University Press, 1991); Michael Hoffman, "Understanding Heian Nobles' Snobbishness," *The Japan Times*, April 16, 2016, https://www.japantimes.co.jp/news/2016/04/16/national/history/understanding-heian-nobles-snobbishness/#.XtXBeTl7mM8.

rebellion could grow big enough to challenge the status quo. Ironically, though, this just caused a different kind of problem. With the provincial clans being allowed to have their own private armies and a blithely aloof central government disinterested in what those armies were doing, regional wars broke out among the various provincial clans in numerous vies for power.

Nevertheless, the ensuing chaos of Japan's centuries-long feudal era would, ironically, be its most socially mobile time. With numerous peasant revolts, warlords coming in and out of power, and a toothless central government, there was no stability to ensure that each stratus of society stay in their lane, and so through acts of armed rebellion, a Japanese peasant could, for the first and last time until many centuries later, rise above their station and create a better life for themselves and for those in their village. The era of the samurai had begun.[188]

The Sound of One Sword Slashing

In our modern, twenty-first-century world, much of the West (Japan, itself, as well ... but more on that in a bit) tends to romanticize the samurai of feudal-era Japan as the consummate warrior-philosopher. Extremely skilled in how to kill a person yet also extremely adept in exploring the spiritually existential Zen questions of the soul, these soldiers are idolized in history and in pop culture as the idealization of self-control, stoic restraint, spiritual reflection, and martial ability. But was this really the case? Yeah ... but only to an extent.

It's important to understand that "samurai" was a hereditary title exclusive to warriors of a "noble" bloodline. Anyone could be conscripted to be a soldier in a medieval Japanese army, but to be a samurai, you had to have been born into a samurai family (which were all members of the aristocracy,

---

188 Marius B. Jansen et al., "Japan: The Heian period (794–1185)," Encyclopedia Britannica, https://www.britannica.com/place/Japan/The-Heian-period-794 -1185 (accessed June 1, 2020); "Heian Period (794-1185)," Metropolitan Museum of Art Department of Asian Art, October 2002, https://www .metmuseum.org/toah/hd/heia/hd_heia.htm; David Desser et al., *Seven Samurai: Origins and Influences*, New York: Criterion Collection, 2006.

though their degrees of wealth varied) and maintain a verifiable pedigree for which a lord could trace your lineage (very similar to being a "knight" in medieval Europe). Being of the upper class, samurai therefore had a lot more leisure time and economic security to pursue artistic endeavors, master the ways of the warrior, and participate in spiritual pursuits and religious ceremonies, all of which helped establish the basic underpinnings of the samurai mythos as a warrior-philosopher. And while there did, indeed, exist samurai who exemplified the spiritual epitome of warrior virtue and prowess (most notably Miyamoto Musashi), they were the rare exceptions.[189]

Samurai were hired killers first and foremost, and naturally, the better you were at doing your job, the better pay and rank of honor you could expect, so self-improvement in combat ability was more often honed because it was just good business than it was a personal ideal for which to strive. The religious-philosopher part came about as a way to improve this combat ability, but not necessarily for spiritual insight in and of itself. You see, the samurai were largely drawn to Zen Buddhism (the Japanese adaptation of Chinese Chan Buddhism as practiced by the Shaolin monks). They favored Zen over their native Shinto or other branches of Buddhism because it focused heavily on self-reliance and the importance of being strong both mentally and physically.

As a byproduct of practicing Zen meditations and mental focus techniques, a samurai was better able to keep his stoic calm amid the chaos of battle and fight more ferociously due to having control over his instinctive fear of death. Zen's focus on the ephemerality of all things also helped samurai make sense of the world, theirs being one of endless violence and short lifespans. All the other deep philosophical stuff was mostly just a means to the end of being able to better kill people and being okay with dying young. Ultimately, Zen was favored by the samurai not because it helped them better follow the Buddha's teachings, but because it was the most practical

189   Desser et al., *Seven Samurai: Origins and Influences.*

religious outlook that coincided with and aided in their line of work as hired killers employed in a profession with a high mortality rate.[190]

SHOGUNATE JAPAN

After the fall of the self-indulgent Heian court in the twelfth century CE, Japan's warrior class experienced its golden age. These ensuing centuries were rife with civil wars and endless conflicts, perfect for the samurai who were in high demand, but once all of Japan was unified under a single shogun in 1600 CE, peace came to the islands, leaving no need for so many active-duty soldiers anymore. Now, under the new Confucianism-inspired Tokugawa Shogunate, the aristocratic samurai had to adapt to a world that didn't need them anymore.

The Future Ain't What It Used to Be

The samurai in this era of peace were a far cry from the battle-hardy samurai of Japan's feudal era. Now, they were soft, out-of-shape office bureaucrats and white-collar civil servants who filed documents and counted figures (and those were the lucky ones as *many* of them were just chronically unemployed). The ability and psychological need of samurai to openly carry their weapons (not unlike modern open-carry enthusiasts) helped them outwardly compensate for feeling severely emasculated by the times, having gone from "mighty warriors" to "replaceable paper pushers."

As the years went by, it became illegal for anyone except a samurai to carry a sword, and so the sword was all the samurai had left to outwardly show the world that they were still masculine and powerful. That is exactly why so much mythic and spiritual prominence was forcibly placed on the samurai sword (*katana*) during this peaceful time in Japanese history.

---

190 Barbara O'Brien, "Samurai Zen: The Role of Zen in Japan's Samurai Culture," Learn Religions, updated January 13, 2018, https://www.learnreligions.com /role-of-zen-in-samurai-culture-449944.

Compensational Steel

It's true that the sword had always been the symbolic "soul" of the samurai, but now by artificially elevating it to stratospheric heights of transcendent spiritual and mythic importance, the samurai were kept satisfied by being provided a psycho-philosophical outlet to feed their ego of still being connected to their masculine glory days as virile warriors despite, in actuality, being doughy, white-collar, mid-tier office workers. (If you've read the book or seen the film *Fight Club*, you know exactly the kind of showy overcompensation for fragile masculinity that I'm talking about.)

And, of course, the samurai class itself was all too on board to hype up their own mythic and spiritual status to regain their image as manly warriors (even though many of them couldn't fight to save their lives). Religious texts and books on the philosophy of the warrior, the Zen techniques of weaponry, and other self-aggrandizing topics began to be published by the learned samurai class themselves to add manufactured meaning to their now routine, cushy, emasculated, impotent lives.

However, the lie eventually became the truth. As the past became more of a distant memory, the samurai class inundated pop culture with their writings, musings, and revised histories about themselves. This manufactured, self-romanticized image of the samurai as the perfect philosopher-warrior and spiritually enlightened soldier became all the public could remember. Like in any other culture, history is written by the winners, and since the samurai warrior caste of Japan became its upper-class winners, they wrote their own enduring histories of themselves.[191]

---

191   Lawrence Winkler, *Samurai Road* (Cheyenne, WY: Bellatrix Books, 2015), n.p.;
       "Life During the Edo Period," Ancient Civilizations Online Textbook, accessed
       June 3, 2020, https://www.ushistory.org/civ/10e.asp; "Samurai," Encyclopedia
       Britannica, updated March 2020, https://www.britannica.com/topic/samurai;
       James Earl Hataway, Jr., "Zen and the Samurai: Rethinking Ties Between Zen
       and the Warrior," (master's thesis, University of Tennessee Knoxville, May
       2006), https://trace.tennessee.edu/cgi/viewcontent.cgi?referer=https://www
       .google.com/&httpsredir=1&article=6006&context=utk_gradthes; "Samurai,"
       New World Encyclopedia, accessed June 3, 2020, https://www
       .newworldencyclopedia.org/entry/samurai#Tokugawa_Shogunate.

Japanese Takeaway:
THE SHEATHED SWORD

In the legendary Akira Kurosawa film *Sanjuro*, the main character of the gruff rolling stone *ronin* played by Toshirō Mifune agrees to help a group of idealistic warrior youths to right wrongs and restore justice through his expertise at sword fighting, racking up an impressive body count along the way. Yet despite there being no evil or injustice that he cannot slay or best in combat, the character growth lesson he learns throughout the film is that of the sheathed sword.

This is most pointedly brought to his attention when, after being criticized by an aging aristocratic woman for being too unnecessarily violent in his rescuing of her, she goes on to lecture him about how the best swords are those that spend a majority of their time in their sheaths. A sword that is in constant use, always out of its sheath, and coming into violent contact with other objects gets damaged more easily and dulls more quickly. Mifune's character begrudgingly understands the parallel and realizes that just like his sword, he, too, will become burned out, fragile, and useless in battle if he is constantly looking for and engaging in unnecessary and avoidable fights.

This lesson on weapon maintenance is important for warriors like us. Oftentimes, we are so endeared to a cause and so passionate about justice that we wear ourselves out, stretch ourselves too thin, and ultimately make ourselves less effective than we could be in the good fight. More than just taking a self-care rest to freshen up for the next fight, the deeper lesson of the sheathed sword is to be more selective on when and where to apply ourselves. If we tackle and strike at every wrong in the world, we will break (physically, mentally, or both).

Additionally, it is unhealthy to always be looking for a fight. Whatever you look for in this world, you will find it. Those of us who are always on the lookout for another cause to defend and another injustice against which to take up arms, no matter how minute, will always find one, and the constant fighting will quickly render our swords and ourselves ineffective for the more important, dire fights. Also, if we look too hard for the next fight, we will find problems that don't really exist and start seeing enemies in our allies, all as warped excuses to go on another crusade and be able to wield our sword of justice once again.

So, for your takeaway challenge here, learn to be more temperate in your activism. You cannot save everyone, you cannot solve all the world's problems, and you will never be able to reach a point where there will be no more battles to fight. But you *can* be more selective on *which* battles to fight, on *which* people you can reasonably save, and on *how much* realistic time and energy you have so as not to become too jaded or burn yourself out to exhaustion.

The same applies for your spiritual activism too. You can wear yourself out just as easily by resorting to spellwork over every minor inconvenience you encounter or by being too fixated on and frequent in your cursing and hexing of others. Before long, you'll find a new rationale to enact "justice" everywhere and new enemies in everyone, and what a dark, miserable way of seeing the world that is. Never forget that the swords most effective at cutting down enemies and slaying the wicked are those that spend a majority of their time in their sheaths.

Deities & Legends

BUSHIDO

Bushido is the legendary warrior code of the samurai, often lauded by Western cultures as the native Japanese equivalent to the "code of chivalry" among the knights of medieval Europe since both codes focus on serving a feudal lord through the upholding of specific, religious virtues. These samurai virtues are rectitude, courage, benevolence, politeness, sincerity, honor, loyalty, and character. Perhaps more controversially, though, (just like the code of chivalry), bushido is more of a historical reimagining of warrior honor than actual reality.[192]

---

192 Tim Clark, "The Bushido Code: The Eight Virtues of the Samurai," Art of Manliness, updated June 16, 2020, https://www.artofmanliness.com/articles/the-bushido-code-the-eight-virtues-of-the-samurai/.

As we previously explored, after the civil wars ended and Japan was unified by the Tokugawa Shogunate, the samurai became emasculated shadows of their former glory who deeply needed to find a way to outwardly exude the honor, virility, and "manliness" that they felt they had lost during the centuries of peace that permeated the Tokugawa era. It was during this time that bushido first became codified and written down. Previously during the golden age of the samurai of feudal Japan, bushido was just informal suggestions that were held to be ideal yet rarely practiced (because all those self-imposed rules and codes of conduct weren't practical in actual warfare or combat situations where your life was on the line during an era of constant, chaotic violence).

Bushido as a unified concept, however, wouldn't come into popular consciousness among the Japanese until the twentieth century when the nationalistic (and increasingly fascist) government saw it as a means to brainwash its citizens into a sense of racial and cultural superiority as well as to glorify the military into an almost religious entity. The goal was imperial expansion, and a citizenry who worshipped the military and placed their nation's soldiers on an infallible pedestal would be more likely to not only join and support the military in all their questionable endeavors, but also be shunned for daring to say anything bad or critical about the military. Through reverence for the propagandized overly romanticized "historical" warrior code, dissent for war was suppressed and fascism was allowed to flourish.[193]

HACHIMAN

The Shinto deity of warriors and war, Hachiman is the deified kami (spirit divinity) of Japan's fifteenth emperor during the fifth century CE: Ōjin, whose history is now intertwined with legend. In fact, out of all the

---

193   Leo Braudy, *From Chivalry to Terrorism: War and the Changing Nature of Masculinity* (New York: Vintage, 2005), n.p.; Rich Duffy, "Bushido: Way of Total Bullshit," Tofugu, December 8, 2014, https://www.tofugu.com/japan/bushido/; Damian Flanagan, "Bushido: The Samurai Code Goes to War," *The Japan Times*, July 23, 2016, https://www.japantimes.co.jp/culture/2016/07/23/books/bushido -samurai-code-goes-war/#.Xtxl4KZ7mM8.

Shinto deities, Hachiman is arguably one of the most popular if having around 20,000 out of the 80,000 or so Shinto shrines in Japan being dedicated to him is anything to go by (though the exact numbers vary since many shrines are not officially registered).

It wasn't always this way, though. Originally in ancient Japan, Hachiman was the deity of agriculture and fishing. However, by the eighth century CE when Buddhism became the religion *du jour* of the upper classes, Hachiman became regarded as a *bodhisattva* (an enlightened being somewhat similar to a "saint" in Catholicism).

During the twelfth century CE, the Minamoto clan (who held Hachiman as their patron deity) overthrew the Heian government and established military rule over Japan. They heightened Hachiman's militaristic side to coincide with their own family legacy and legitimacy to rule through conquest and war. By the time the Minamoto lost their power and endless civil wars ensued, Hachiman had become indelibly engrained in the public consciousness as the supreme warrior divinity. During the following centuries of continuous fighting and warfare that defined Japan's feudal era, Hachiman became ever more popular, whether because you needed his aid as a warrior samurai or because you needed his protection from warrior samurai.[194]

SŌHEI

In feudal Japan, the sōhei were Buddhist warrior monks who could best be described as a mix between the Shaolin monks of China and the Knights Templar of Crusader Europe. Like the Shaolin monks, they were monastics who became adept at physical violence and the martial arts due to the need to protect themselves and their rich, landed estates, and like the Knights Templar, they were a far-flung, organized network of spiritual soldiers with garrisoned bases throughout the land.

Their origins date back to the Heian era of classical Japan when the pleasure-seeking and hypocritically Buddhist imperial courtiers began assign-

194   Tsurugaoka Hachimangu, "Hachiman faith," Tsurugaoka Hachimangu, accessed June 6, 2020, http://www.tsurugaoka-hachimangu.jp/hachiman_ faith/ (site discontinued); "Hachiman: Shinto Deity," Encyclopedia Britannica, updated August 19, 2019, https://www.britannica.com/topic/Hachiman.

ing unqualified, equally hypocritical lackeys as abbots of major Buddhist temples and monasteries. The disconcerted monks at these locations, for decades, descended upon the capital of Heian-kyō in massive protests but to no avail. It became clear that the powers that be would only listen to force, and so some temples banded together and formed their own fighting regiments, which proved more effective at getting the government to listen and acquiesce.

This caused major controversy among the Japanese people (monks *and* laypersons). Many saw these monks and their use of violence as completely against what the Buddha taught, and as monks, they were supposed to be the role models for all Buddhists seeking enlightenment. Many others, however, saw the violence as completely in line with the Buddha's teachings because it was righteous violence in the fight for justice and came only as a result of all other nonviolent avenues having been exhausted.

As the years went on and Japan descended into its violent feudal era, the sōhei of various temples became involved in the chaotic fighting, aligning themselves with various sides for various conflicts. They became organized mercenaries for whomever they saw as spiritually "in the right" of a conflict (or whoever was the highest bidder). Their power was psychological just as much as it was physical since enemy soldiers would fear the spiritual curses placed upon them by these holy men just as much as their intimidating reputation on the battlefield. Eventually, most of the sōhei ended up allying themselves against the warlord Oda Nobunaga, a mistake in hindsight since Oda was winning the war of unifying Japan. Oda's successors eventually did unify Japan and subsequently eradicated the warrior monks for having fought against them on the losing side of history.[195]

---

195   Martin Repp, "The Problem of 'Evil' in Pure Land Buddhism," in *Probing the Depths of Evil and Good: Multireligious Views and Case Studies*, ed. Jerald D. Gort, Henry Jansen, and Hendrik M. Vroom (Amsterdam: Rodopi, 2007), n.p.; Herbert Kikoy, "Sohei: The Warrior Monks of Medieval Japan," War History Online, July 28, 2018, https://www.warhistoryonline.com/instant-articles /sohei-the-warrior-monks.html; Leo Stone, "Sohei: Buddhist Warrior Monks of Medieval Japan," Kings and Generals, October 15, 2020, YouTube, 21:15, https://www.youtube.com/watch?v=KHedbN-rL2Q.

18

EAST ASIAN MAGICAL COMMUNITY

CANDLE OF BANISHMENT

To start our East Asian magical community lessons with a bang, I thought we should touch upon something a bit controversial, yet very necessary for us warriors to know: how to manifest vengeance upon our enemies quickly and without a lot of ado. Time is precious, and it is the most valuable finite resource each and every one of us has. We have a world to change, an environment to restore, oppressed to uplift, and tyrants to overthrow…we don't have time for other people's problematic behaviors to bog us down from these grander fights.

Inevitably, though, there will always be "lesser" annoyances in our life. So, how can we quickly banish these annoying or bothersome people who are bogging us down yet aren't major enough to merit a full-scale crusade that would monopolize our time and attention away from more important things? Well, that's the question on which I've asked my friend Ryan to come here and give us some advice.

As you'll see by the nature of this banishing spell, Ryan has asked that I refrain from exposing his surname (and no, he's not the "Ryan" we met back in the Philippines). This Ryan I've known since my time at university, and, without divulging too much personal info, I can say that he is a Chinese practitioner of different magical styles and has a very practical approach to living life. He's one of the most straightforward people I've ever met, and he's absolutely not one to suffer fools. Here, he'll give you a candle spell he used when one such fool became a problem at his workplace.

> My name is Ryan, and simply put I don't have a lot of time to deal with people's bullshit. In my magical and divinatory practice, I don't believe in sugarcoating things and I am there to provide the most straightforward approach to situations. My magical focus incorporates a variety of traditions from my personal cultural background and incorporating magic from my teachers in eclectic backgrounds.
>
> In my life, I am very focused on my personal survival. I know that sounds very mundane or very unenlightened, very "material" for lack of a better word. What I would like people to know is that I come from a very low socio-economic level, which is why my personal survival and especially my job is something I take seriously. This ritual came from a situation where a newly hired managerial figure took it upon themself to try and sabotage my work, tried to move me to a different location that was slower, and overall made it a difficult work environment.
>
> While the ritual was meant to help protect myself against them, it was also a way of sending them on their merry way out of my workspace, which definitely worked effectively.
>
> You will need the following items:
> - A free-standing pillar candle (red on top, black on the bottom)
>   (If you are unable to procure one, a glass-encased candle with this color combination will suffice.)

- *Red Pepper flakes (sending people away and to cause harm)*
- *Black Pepper powder (protection)*
- *Crab Shell powder (sending negative energy back to the source)*
- *Alum powder (silencing gossip)*
- *Clove powder (silencing gossip)*
- *Lemongrass essential oil (clearing negative energy)*
- *Bergamot essential oil (empowerment and control)*
- *Bowl*
- *Heat-proof plate*
- *Knife*
- *Sharp needle or pick*
- *Clean working surface*

Preferably this should be done during the waning moon phase, but if you can't wait, you can also do this on a Saturday.

In a bowl, mix the Red Pepper, Black Pepper, Crab Shell, Alum, and Clove. As you add each herb, pray over them with intention, something along the lines of "may [name of target] be gone from my life through your gifts" or something heartfelt. If you don't want to use Crab Shell because you can't find it or you feel uncomfortable using it, then don't use it.

Take the candle and, with the knife, cut the top portion so it is flat. Turn the candle upside down and carve a new tip from the black end that can be lit. Be sure to expose some of the wick from the black portion to make it easier to light.

With a needle or pick, write the name of the individual onto the candle lengthwise. Coat the candle in a few drops of the Lemongrass and Bergamot essential oils. Be sure to wash your hands after this portion.

On a clean working surface, sprinkle the powder mixture in a line. Roll the candle through the line of powder to try and get the powder to stick onto it as best you can. Whatever herbs don't stick, move them onto your heat-proof dish.

Carefully melt the bottom of the candle and stick it onto the heat-proof plate. If you have the luxury of burning the candle at your workspace, then that would be great. If not, burn this either on your altar or on top of your toilet's water tank.

Prior to burning this candle, softly knock three times on the altar and pray over it that your troubles be sent back to where they came from and those with intent to harm you are chased away. Light this candle and burn to completion. If you are unable or uncomfortable with leaving a candle unattended, be sure to pinch out the candle rather than blowing it out.

Once the candle has been completely burned, take some of the residual wax and sprinkle it around the place where your target will walk through, like their work desk or locker to ensure they touch or walk through the mess. In my case, I was able to burn the candle at work and this particular person took it upon themself to touch the remnant of the candle and dispose of it themself. Unsurprisingly, this person ran into a bit of bad luck and eventually quit due to some shenanigans.

—*Ryan*

INVESTING IN SELF-CARE

To balance out the aggressive banishment spell we just learned, I've asked another friend of mine to come and teach us something more peaceful and rejuvenating, yet no less important for any warrior to know: self-care. My friend Dr. Adam Miramon was the specific person I asked to teach this to us because not only is he a queer activist warrior specializing in healing, he also holds a Doctorate of Acupuncture and Chinese Medicine.

If you're from the Washington, D.C., area, you might already be familiar with Dr. Miramon as a local Sister of Perpetual Indulgence, as the head of the *Healer's Guild for the Order of the Elemental Mysteries*, or as the owner of the healing practices *Transformational Acupuncture* and *Uptown Acupuncture*. In fact, he's also a personality in the virtual teaching realm via the online series *On Point: A Dive into Acupuncture* (of which he is the producer, writer, director, and star). For all these reasons, there was no better warrior-healer I could think of to give us vital counsel in how healing is an investment in one's self, specifically through the avenue of traditional Chinese medicine and acupuncture.

If you have ever flown on a plane, you have heard flight attendants say, "Put your oxygen mask on before assisting others." The same holds true for self-care. One conversation I have with all of my patients within my acupuncture practice is to gauge their overall stress level and the activities they practice for stress management. Self-care is a ritual or practice to reduce your stress and nourish your mind, body, and spirit. These three parts are often interrelated within the theories of Traditional Chinese Medicine. As a doctor and licensed professional, I am always stressing the importance of self-care and stress management with my patients.

The concept of qi (齐), *pronounced "chee," is the foundation of Taoist practice and Chinese medicine. A quick search for the definition of "qi" can produce results such as an ethereal substance, breath, vital substance, energy, etc. These definitions have little meaning without a basic understanding of Chinese philosophy and medicine. One literal translation of the Chinese character* 齐 (qi) *is "air" or "breath." However, qi is more than just a person's breath—it is their vitality. Therefore, a good working definition in the context of Chinese medicine is "life force." This concept has roots in other cultures as well such as* prana *in Hindu philosophy,* mana *in Polynesian mythology, and* pneuma *in Greek mythology.*

The organ that receives qi is the fei (肺) *or lung. Our bodies have three lungs—our skin and two in the upper chest. Breathing is a vital component in the creation and stability of qi. Healthy qi equates to improved resilience during times of adversity. What activities build qi and, in effect, build resilience? The exercises I recommend most often are meditation, yoga,* Tai chi (太極), *and* Qigong (气功).

Each of these exercise forms requires engaging the breath, engaging the fei, and, in effect, building and strengthening qi. Meditation is a practice of reflection, mindfulness, or focus while utilizing a breathing technique. Yoga is a set of physical, mental, and spiritual practices that involve both engagement of the physical body and breath. Tai chi and Qigong are internal martial arts that involve breathing, meditation, and gentle movements. All of these practices have considerable physical, mental, and emotional benefits.

As a queer activist, there are many times when self-care has been critical for my mental, physical, and emotional health. One of the most challenging areas of my life has been, and continues to be, my relationship with my biological family. Most family members are socially conservative and continue to vote for politicians, laws, and policies that seek to dehumanize and demonize people like me. My interactions with these family members over the years have swung between avoidance and banishment, and both extremes are unhealthy. How do I care for myself knowing my family will not change? I approached these family members like a bad investment.

Rather than continue to invest time, energy, sweat, and tears—all could be considered forms of qi—into conversations that always end the same, I chose to stop having these conversations to preserve my mental and emotional health. When a statement, comment, or conversation pops up that violates my moral and ethical code, I respond with "There is a lot to unpack with that statement, maybe you should talk to your therapist." Changing the way we interact with people within our lives can be a form of healing and self-care. Self-care is an investment, but most importantly, it is an investment in yourself.

—Dr. Adam Miramon, DACM, LAc

A WARRIOR IN THE GARDEN

For our final guest warrior before we resume our global trek and venture back down to the Southern Hemisphere, I've asked my friend and spiritual mentor, B. Dave Walters, to come back and give us a bit more warrior advice. We last met B. Dave back in ancient Rome when he counseled us on how he found strength in communing with the Stoic philosophers and on how we can form our own internal spiritual council. Now, however, he's here to teach us something a bit more brutal, a bit more physical, and quite a bit more martial.

You see, in addition to being the African-American comic book creator, writer, director, and TTRPG celebrity that he is now, B. Dave also has black belts in both Shaolin Kung Fu and Tai Chi. Not only that, but he actually used his martial arts prowess on a nightly basis back when he used to be a bodyguard for a *very* famous heavy metal rock band (yes, you are familiar with them … no, I will not name them). So, he's verifiably a living, breathing philosopher-warrior himself, and he's returned to talk about what it's like being a martial arts master in the twenty-first century.

> *"I judge you unfortunate because you have never lived through*
> *misfortune. You have passed through life without an opponent—*
> *no one can ever know what you are capable of, not even you."*
> *—Seneca*[196]

It is with a heavy heart that I must inform you: The chivalric era is over.

You will almost certainly never be in a sword fight. The odds are incredibly slim that you'll ever be called upon to defend yourself, despite what fear-mongering right-wing media might tell you.

So what purpose do the martial arts have in the twenty-first century?

The same purpose they've always occupied since the founding of the Shaolin Temple in 497 AD: To temper the mind, and strengthen the body. At our core, our reptile brain only comprehends two sources of danger: Either we don't have enough to eat, or something is trying to eat us. In a very real biological sense our bodies react the same way to a heated exchange at work as to a charging grizzly bear. Diligent martial arts practice can help you learn to control your mind, and more importantly your emotions so that you respond rather than react to what life throws at you.

My own journey into the martial arts started when I was in college and became a superfan of the rap group the Wu-Tang Clan. My love of the music led me to branch out to the old Shaw Brothers Kung Fu movies where many of the samples in my favorite rap songs had come from. One day I was walking across campus, and I heard a voice say to me as clear as day, "You should train in Kung Fu." I immediately thought to myself, "I can't right now because of school and work, but I will as soon as I graduate." It took me a few more years, but I graduated in May '01 and by June

---

196   Ryan Holiday and Stephen Hanselman, *The Daily Stoic: 366 Meditations on Wisdom, Perseverance, and the Art of Living* (New York: Penguin, 2016), 166.

I had signed up for classes in Shaolin Kung Fu and Tai Chi, and went on to earn black belt rankings in both.

Two important points bear mentioning here: Black belts are a Japanese ranking system, and most Chinese arts have no such thing, other than to categorize students for Western understanding. Second, in Japanese the rank of black belt is called "Shodan," which literally means "beginning degree." It's a common misconception to believe earning a black belt means you've "finished" a martial art, when in truth it actually means you've learned enough of the basics to really begin the endless journey.

One way my training helped me is I used to hate small spaces, being pinned down or constrained in any way. Because when I was young my sister would sit on my chest and pin me down and act like she was going to spit on me, and I absolutely hated it. This fear plagued me all my life until I started training in grappling, and being put in uncomfortable situations came with the territory. I distinctly remember thinking to myself, "I'm not going to die. I can panic and get put into an arm bar submission or stay calm and figure this out," and I did. I have taken that mentality with me every day since to challenges like acting on screen, speaking in front of crowds of thousands or boardrooms of three—the much harder challenge, by the way. When the tension and nerves start to bubble up and my brain wants to go into fight or flight, I can stay calm and centered, because I know how to fight.

There is a saying: "The best time to start jiu jitsu is 10 years ago. The second best time is today." There is no way to properly express the mental, physical, and emotional benefits of martial arts training. Your confidence will increase as your fear decreases; a natural outgrowth of knowing you can handle whatever anyone throws at you. As you see your body change and you begin to do things that used to be out of your reach, you'll have tangible proof that you can do anything you set your mind to.

Martial arts styles are as diverse as types of dancing; no one kind is a fit for everyone. Start by looking up videos online and see what looks like fun to try, and start at home. When you're ready, visit a class and if something doesn't quite feel right move on to the next one. The right teacher and training partners will feel like the family you never had and fill in a gap you never knew existed.

And on the off chance you are ever called upon to defend yourself or a loved one, I leave you with one last thought: It's better to be a warrior in a garden, than a gardener in a war. Good luck on the endless journey, and I can't wait to spar with you!

—B. Dave Walters

PART 6

OCEANIA

*The way to lose any earthly kingdom is to
be inflexible, intolerant, and prejudicial.
Another way is to be too flexible, tolerant
of too many wrongs, and without
judgment at all. It is a razor's edge. It
is the width of a blade of pili grass.*
QUEEN LILIʻUOKALANI
(LAST SOVEREIGN MONARCH
OF THE KINGDOM OF HAWAIʻI)

19
ABORIGINAL AUSTRALIA

Cultural

Dreams vs. Religion

Similar to what we'll see when we arrive in the Americas, Australia has an infamous history of encroaching European colonialism going to war so brutally against the land's native peoples that the native peoples have since lost sovereign control over their homelands. Unique among British colonies, Australia was settled more as a faraway place to ship criminals than as a place of economic exploitation, which it later became. Of course, before Europeans came, this island continent thrived with numerous tribes of First Nations peoples (commonly grouped together under the name "Aboriginals" akin to the descriptor of "Native Americans" being a catchall adjective for all native peoples of North America, regardless of tribal affiliation).

Like any people (humans being what we are), inter-tribal fights and skirmishes are known to have happened among the Aboriginal peoples of Australia long before Europeans came to the continent. However, all these indigenous fights were neither seen nor the same as wars of conquest and religion, and so when the British started to really settle this new southern landmass, Britain's Protestant Christianity and the Aboriginal concept of "The Dreamtime" clashed in an oppressive struggle that still goes on today.

Aeon in Flux

To understand Aboriginal Australia, we've got to understand their unique, all-encompassing, holistically spiritual outlook on the world called "The Dreamtime" (itself being a catchall term for an abstract concept for which various tribes have various words and definitions). At its essence, it's a metaphysical understanding of time, existence, and reality wherein all those concepts are seen as malleable and in constant flux. This, of course, is radically different from how most Western cultures regard time, existence, and reality as definite and linear as well as from how many Eastern cultures regard them as illusory and cyclical.

Granted, with so many different native tribes in Australia, it's hard to get a consensus on what Dreamtime exactly is and is not (because each ethnic and cultural tribe has their own differing histories and legends on the subject), but in a very overgeneralized sense (while staying in the shallow end of the quantum physics rabbit hole that is Dreamtime), it's largely centered on how the most ancient ancestors of Aboriginal Australians created all of existence at the very beginning of time, referred to as The Dreamtime.

This Dreamtime, however, is not a fixed point in the past; it is an endless continuum that encompasses past, present, and future all into a single, ongoing moment (often referred to as "The Dreaming"). So, in a way, the moment of all creation at the beginning of time is technically the same moment right now, which is also the same moment as every moment in history and every moment that ever will be. Mind you, it's not that the past and future don't exist and that we're all living in the New Age "now," it's that the past, the "now," and the future are all existing simultaneously, overlapping, separate yet coinciding together. The word "everywhen" is probably as succinct as you can get when talking about The Dreaming.[197]

This simultaneous compression and eternal expansion of time makes the concepts of "reality" and the separation between the "physical" and "spiritual" realms very tricky to discuss in absolutes. The barriers between dreaming and wakefulness are blurred since being asleep and being awake are happening at the same moment, and the barriers between the physical world and the spiritual afterlife are blurred because all "dead" people are technically still alive right now since we are all in that same singular, endless moment of existence (thus also meaning that we dually exist in a "dead" state too, because the eternal future after our deaths is also happening right now).

Moreover, because all of existence was created together, all of existence is linked together as being all from each other like a big family (somewhat similar to the scientific cosmology of all things being one thing since all things were originally one until the Big Bang). This means all of nature (including humans) are inherently sacred and interconnected even if they do not seem to be by the physical senses. Naturally, though, this spiritually unique way of seeing the world eventually clashed with Britain's linear Protestant Christianity of temporal absolutes, a fixed separation between physical life and the afterlife, and man's divine dominion over nature.[198]

197 Christine Judith Nicholls, "'Dreamtime' and 'The Dreaming'—An introduction," The Conversation, January 22, 2014, https://theconversation.com/dreamtime -and-the-dreaming-an-introduction-20833.

198 Muswellbrook Shire Council, "The Dreaming," Working With Indigenous Australians, updated June 2020, http://www.workingwithindigenous australians.info/content/Culture_2_The_Dreaming.html; "The Dreamtime," Aboriginal Art Association of Australia, accessed June 7, 2020, https://www .aboriginalart.com.au/culture/dreamtime3.html.

Guerrillas in the Midst

When the British started to truly colonize Australia in 1788, they brought along a hierarchical and static religious worldview wherein God placed (white, male) humans superior to all the rest of nature. This sense of human superiority over nature proved to be a self-imposed stumbling block for them when dealing with the Aboriginal peoples because the Aboriginals were masters of guerrilla warfare. Aboriginal respect for and reverence of nature (stemming from the concept of united sacredness within The Dreaming) allowed them to see their environment as an ally in the war effort, rather than just a bunch of non-sentient obstacles as the British did.

It should be noted, though, that "guerrilla warfare" as we traditionally define it doesn't really capture the true essence of their combat style; it's just the closest bit of succinct vocabulary one can say to give a good idea of combat style without having to venture down the rabbit hole of military semantics. The most accurate (but clunky) way of describing it as preferred by the intelligentsia of academia would be to say that the Aboriginal Australians fought "low-intensity, irregular, disruptive, small-scale engagements utilizing natural hideaways and blurring the division between civilian and combatant."[199]

Despite that sounding pretty much like the definition of guerrilla warfare, the reason it can't *officially* be called "guerrilla warfare" in its most technical sense is because the Aboriginal tribes didn't fight as a united whole from a central command for any political ends. (I know, I know…"po-TAY-toh, po-TAH-toh," but you know how intense some people get with semantics.)[200]

The thing is, while the British were logging and leveling the natural land to make room for cities, pasturage, and farms, the Aboriginals kept it

---

199 Wilton Eckley, "Guerrilla Warfare," in *Magill's Guide to Military History*, ed. John Powell (Pasadena, CA: Salem Press, 2001), n.p.

200 Ray Kerkhove, "Tribal Alliances with Broader Agendas?: Aboriginal Resistance in Southern Queensland's 'Black War,'" *Cosmopolitan Civil Societies Journal* 6, no. 3, 2014, http://dx.doi.org/10.5130/ccs.v6i3.4218.

how it was, thus always allowing them to have the more defensible position. From these positions, various tribes held councils with one another and developed sophisticated signaling to communicate around language barriers, and together, these tribal forces from different cultures would descend from their defensible positions in sacred nature and coordinate hit-and-run strikes that would not necessarily shed as much blood as possible, but rather do as much economic damage as possible. They understood that they didn't have to attack better-armed colonists directly in order to repulse them, instead attacking their land motivations for being there in the first place.[201]

Whitefellas

Still, it's important to keep in mind that this wasn't an all-out war of a united Aboriginal front versus a united colonist front. This "war" took place throughout Australia on countless smaller scales of multiple skirmishes and massacres of native peoples (both in an "official" capacity and in a decentralized manner of homesteaders forming militia mobs to do what they pleased since they were too far in the bush for the law to affect or punish them).

Remember, to the Crown, Aboriginals were not really "people," and so to mobilize a war against them would be (in their eyes) the same as mobilizing a war against all the kangaroos on the continent. They were only seen as animals to be tamed and used as forced labor or shot dead if they proved uncompliant (though time has shown who the *real* "animals" were).

The biggest killer, however, wasn't the *kartiya* (an Aboriginal word from Northern Australia for white people that approximates to "whitefella"); it was disease. Both unknowingly, and then later purposefully, the colonists spread diseases to the native peoples who had no developed immunity.

201   Ray Kerkhove, "A Different Mode of War—Aboriginal 'Guerilla Tactics'
        in Defining the 'Black War' of South-Eastern Queensland 1843–1845,"
        Sovereign Union—First Nations Asserting Sovereignty, 2014, http://
        nationalunitygovernment.org/content/different-mode-war-aboriginal
        -guerilla-tactics-defining-black-war-south-eastern-queensland.

As their numbers plummeted, not only did it cancel out their defensive advantage from holding the natural terrain as sacred, but it also made them unable to continue effectively striking at the whitefellas' economic incentives to stay in Australia.[202]

Losing Their Religion

Once the official, government-sanctioned massacres against the Aboriginal Australians finally stopped in the year 1928, much of the damage had already been done. Lost generations of Aboriginal children were taken from their families and given a European "Christian" schooling and upbringing. As time marched on, the native peoples lost much of their oral history and traditional spirituality, so much so that in an uncomfortable irony due to centuries of forced conversions, about 73 percent of Aboriginal Australians identified as Christian in 2009, compared to 63 percent of nonindigenous Australians. (That's not to say some don't practice a synergy of Christianity and traditional spiritual beliefs, but yes, nowadays Aboriginal Australians are more likely to be Christian than the country's white, non-native majority of Australians with actual Christian ancestry).[203]

What's the status today, though? Surely if the Aboriginal peoples of Australia are (for the most part) majority Christian like their white counterparts and the federal government made an official apology in 2008 for atrocities done to indigenous peoples, things must be better, no? No. As

202 Ronald M. Berndt and Robert Tonkinson, "Australian Aboriginal peoples," Encyclopedia Britannica, updated April 19, 2018, https://www.britannica .com/topic/Australian-Aboriginal; Lorena Allam, and Nick Evershed, "The Killing Times: The Massacres of Aboriginal People Australia Must Confront," *The Guardian*, March 3, 2019, https://www.theguardian.com/australia-news /2019/mar/04/the-killing-times-the-massacres-of-aboriginal-people-australia -must-confront.

203 Toni O'Loughlin, "Recognition for Aboriginal Christians," *The Guardian*, July 28, 2009, https://www.theguardian.com/commentisfree/belief/2009/jul/28 /uniting-church-aboriginal-australia.

of June 8, 2020, it's estimated that about 75 percent of Australians hold an internal, implicit bias against the native peoples of their own country.[204]

This is not a happy note from which we'll move on to the next leg of our global trek, but it's important to feel uncomfortable about awful realities. A problem like racism, even non-showy latent racism, has to be acknowledged as a problem if it's ever going to be overcome (whether here in Australia or anywhere else in the world). To ignore it or dress it up and sugarcoat it so as to make us feel more comfortable only allows the problem to persist. It's beneficial to feel uncomfortable; it means you *know* deep down that there's something wrong here. Knowing there is something wrong, it is now your duty to do something about it because you can no longer say you didn't know.

Aboriginal Australian Takeaway:
THE SACREDNESS OF SPACE

In their fight for survival and against the oppression of colonization, the Aboriginal First Nations peoples of Australia possessed an important advantage: spiritual allyship with the land. This spiritual allyship went beyond the usual advantage of being strategically more familiar with the terrain than your enemy or having the "home" advantage for reinforcements (though those definitely help too)—it was having a respect for the land and natural space that surrounds you and seeing it all as a participatory ally in the good fight.

There is a sacredness to everything in the world, and all terrains (natural and urban) carry with them an energetic resonance. If you have ever felt just an indescribable surge of energy or weight of history from walking into a specific physical space, you have come into contact with the sacredness of that space. Such sacredness can be imbued into a physical space by any number of things: it having been the site of a traumatic or historical

204 "Three-Quarters of Australians Biased Against Indigenous Australians, Study Finds," *The Guardian*, June 8, 2020, https://www.theguardian.com/australia-news/2020/jun/09/three-quarters-of-australians-biased-against-indigenous-australians-study-finds.

event, a confluence of ley lines, even manually made so by an intentional blessing by a person with faith or magical knowhow.

So, for your takeaway challenge here, attempt to get in contact and ally with the sacredness of a space in which you or a community will engage in activism. If you have not done so in the past, it may be easier to begin by learning to see the sacredness of all spaces in which you exist throughout your day. No matter where you are, no matter how openly rural or over-run with urban steel and concrete your daily space may be, it possesses a sacredness for those who know how to tune themselves to its frequency. As you become more adept and become acquainted with familiar places, reach out to less familiar ones and grow your network of unseen allies.

By mastering this challenge, you will be able to help protect and aug-ment the energy of any activist movement that takes place in these spaces. Should you want to defend protestors from the zealous brutality of law enforcement, you can bless the space to be protective toward such activists of the good fight. You can also lend your magical and spiritual energy to help boost, amplify, and influence a site's already-inherent energy wherein an important speech will be made or important decisions are currently being made. Remember, you have more allies than just people and spirits—the very spaces of the land can be your allies, too, if you learn how to listen and familiarize yourself with them and their spiritual power.

Deities & Legends

JANDAMARRA

Jandamarra (known as "Pigeon" by the British colonists of the times) was a late-nineteenth-century Aboriginal Australian social and guerrilla leader of the Bunuba people in the Kimberly region of what is now Western Australia. He attained legendary folk hero status in Australia from his suc-cessful, three-year-long armed resistance leadership against colonial abuses toward native peoples, and, thanks to best-selling nonfiction books based on his own people's surviving oral history of him, much of his authentic legend has been preserved.

His story is an interesting one because, originally, he was a tracker for the British colonies' police forces, a position wherein he'd help colonial law enforcement find food and water out in the bush while also forcibly kidnapping and getting rid of "undesirable" Aboriginals who didn't submit to British territorial expansion. However, during one assignment to subdue resistance fighters from his own native Bunuba tribe who were causing hit-and-run economic damage to British cattle ranches, his tribespeople convinced him that the real bad guys were the British colonizers and that he would be forgiven for his crimes against his own people if he switched sides and fought against the British. So, Jandamarra defected from the colonial police force, killed his boss (the regional constable), and used his intimate understanding of British colonial society and police tactics to help the native peoples become more effective guerrilla fighters.[205]

Now as an outlaw who had sided with the Bunuba resistance, he helped ramp up their guerrilla activities. Hatred of him by colonial society became so intense that police forces began indiscriminately killing Aboriginal peoples regardless of whether or not they knew of or were associated with Jandamarra. For three years, his guerrilla raids continued, leading to rumors that Jandamarra had mystical powers and that no white man could ever defeat him because of this magic he possessed.

These rumors of being preternaturally protected were shared and believed by the white colonists themselves, and because of this they hired another Aboriginal tracker named Minko Mick (known to the British colonists as "Micki") to do what they believed no white man could do. Despite also being a native Aboriginal himself, Minko Mick was not ethnically Bunuba, and so he had no qualms with getting paid to help white law enforcement

205 Howard Pedersen, "Jandamarra (1870–1897)," *Australian Dictionary of Biography*, vol. 12, 1990, National Centre of Biography, Australian National University, accessed July 6, 2021, http://adb.anu.edu.au/biography /jandamarra-8822.

track down and put an end to the Bunuba hero Jandamarra. On April 1, 1897, Minko Mick found and shot Jandamarra dead. Still, Jandamarra's legacy lives on and is celebrated in films, novels, stage productions, and other media as a heroic folk figure of Aboriginal resistance in Australia.[206]

THE RAINBOW SERPENT

The Rainbow Serpent is a totemic deity found in the legends of numerous Aboriginal cultures throughout the Australian continent, and although the exact legends and details differ depending on which oral history is being told, this multicolored giant snake is *usually* associated with creation, destruction, water, and fertility. In modern times, the Rainbow Serpent has become a symbol of Aboriginal social movements for equality and environmentalism. Sometimes male, sometimes female, sometimes both, sometimes neither, and sometimes beyond humans' conception of physical gender, the Rainbow Serpent shaped the earth by carving rivers and mountains into the land, and surviving lore tells us that this deity can still be seen by humans in the form of a rainbow in the sky.

They control the life and death of the human race by controlling the rains, through which they bless the people with water when appeased and withhold it to create extensive droughts when displeased (also sometimes delivering excessive rains when angered via floods and cyclones). Because Australia is mostly arid, the importance of the Rainbow Serpent and their life-sustaining rains has made them a prominent part in legends and artwork for millennia.

Nowadays, in addition to these ancient legends, the Rainbow Serpent has been incorporated into new legends befitting the Aboriginal experience in modern Australia. These new legends revolve around issues of social justice and environmentalism such as associating the Rainbow Serpent's nonbinary gender and iconic multicolored appearance with the

206 Courtenay Rule, "On This Day in History: The Death of an Aboriginal Resistance Fighter," *Australian Geographic*, November 7, 2013, https://www .australiangeographic.com.au/blogs/on-this-day/2013/11/on-this-day-in -history-the-death-of-an-aboriginal-resistance-fighter/.

LGBTQ+ Pride flag in support of the Aboriginal queer struggle as well as the Rainbow Serpent lending themselves to the native peoples of Australia to be their symbol of anti-uranium mining, an industry whose extraction processes and products have led to large-scale human death and environmental degradation.[207]

VINCENT LINGIARI

An Aboriginal rights activist of the Gurindji people and former unpaid forced laborer in Australia's Northern Territory (aka: "slave," even though that wasn't the official word used by the Australian government at the time), Vincent Lingiari played a major part in leading one of the most culturally defining and legendary nationwide protests of First Nations Aboriginal peoples of Australia in their fight for sovereign control over the lands that were stolen from them.

His activism began in force in 1966 upon his organization and leadership of a massive labor strike of Aboriginal workers at a large, multinationally owned cattle station in the Northern Territory to protest the unequal pay and working conditions Aboriginal "employees" suffered in comparison to non-Aboriginal employees. The strike lasted nine *years*, and as it prolonged, it gathered popular attention. With increasing eyes, ears, and sympathy of the general public and various other non-Gurindji Aboriginals on this seemingly endless strike for equality, Lingiari knew that popular support and public pressure was on his side, prompting him to leverage this support and pressure by expanding the scope of his strike to include that the Gurindji peoples be given ownership of the land on

---

207 Tom Smith, "Rainbow Serpent: The Story of Indigenous Australia's God of Weather," Culture Trip, March 14, 2018, https://theculturetrip.com/pacific /australia/articles/rainbow-serpent-story-indigenous-australias-god-weather/; Georges Petitjean, "'Casting Ahead Serpent-fashion,' The Rainbow Serpent in Australia," in *Dangerous and Divine: The Secret of the Serpent*, ed. Wouter Welling (Amsterdam: Koninklijk Instituut voor de Tropen, 2012).

which the cattle ranch in question stood since it was originally their land anyway before it was stolen from them.[208]

The conservative-majority Australian government of the time, however, refused Lingiari's demands, and so in the upcoming 1972 national elections, the left-wing Labor Party (having been the minority party for the past twenty-three years) used the ongoing Aboriginal strike as a main election platform, saying that the Aboriginal people were justified in their anger and, if elected into the majority, the Labor Party would do what the conservatives hadn't and make things right with Aboriginals as well as enact a whole host of other progressive reforms for social justice. With an overwhelming majority of Australians at that point in favor of granting Aboriginal Australians their overdue rights, the Labor Party resonated with the people and was elected as the majority in parliament.

After three long years of the newly in charge Labor Party laying the groundwork, victory finally came to the strikers in 1975 when then-Prime Minister Gough Whitlam (who would later that same year be the first and only Australian Prime Minister to be fired from office by the Governor-General—the Queen's representative in Australia—due to a conservative political coup d'état in response to his progressive reforms) granted the Aboriginal Gurindji people ownership of the land on which the contested cattle station was built, and though this was a small concession compared to *all* Aboriginal peoples being given land reparations, it was a victory for Lingiari and established a precedent.[209]

Nevertheless, because Lingiari's strike had become such a cultural phenomenon and had drawn so much popular support for Aboriginal land reparations, the self-reinstalled-via-coup conservative-majority government bowed down under massive public pressure and passed the Aboriginal

208 Ted Egan, "Lingiari, Vincent (1919–1988)," *Australian Dictionary of Biography*, vol. 18, 2012, National Centre of Biography, Australian National University, accessed July 6, 2021, http://adb.anu.edu.au/biography/lingiari-vincent -14178.

209 "Vincent Lingiari the leader," Australian Broadcasting Corporation, accessed June 19, 2020, https://education.abc.net.au/home#!/digibook/618856 /vincent-lingiari-the-leader.

Land Rights Act of 1976, which gave the Aboriginal peoples of Australia's Northern Territory (no other states or territories, just those with sovereign claims in the Northern Territory) ownership over much of their ancestral lands and the right to negotiate or deny business ventures on said land.

Unfortunately, though, in 2005, the Australian government took a hatchet to the landmark Aboriginal Land Rights Act. Specifically, they removed certain protected land from Aboriginal ownership and gave private businesses more power and sway over Aboriginal councils in land-use negotiations... basically overturning and reversing much of the progress made since Lingiari's legendary strike.[210]

210 Michael Dodson and Diana McCarthy, "Communal Land and the Amendments to the Aboriginal Land Rights Act (NT)," Australian Institute of Aboriginal and Torres Strait Islander Studies, 2006, n.p., https://aiatsis.gov.au /sites/default/files/research_pub/dodsonm-mccarthyd-dp19-communal-land -amendments-aboriginal-land-rights-act_0_1.pdf.

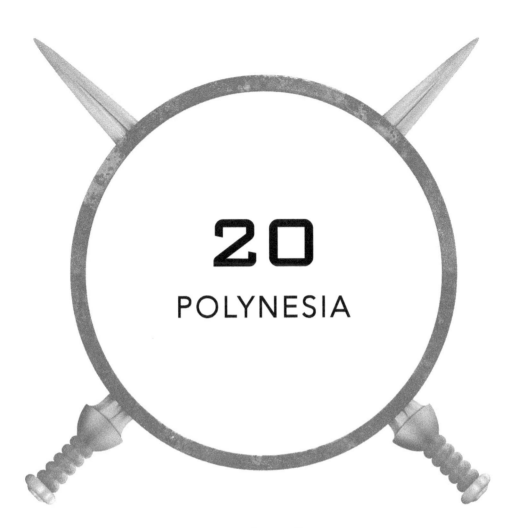

20

POLYNESIA

Cultural

The Magic of Mana

Of all the Polynesian peoples of all the islands in the Pacific, the Māori are, perhaps, the most well-known for their warrior culture (as often demonstrated by their national rugby team's performance of the intensely martial traditional *haka* dance before each match). In fact, long before the British arrived to colonize their homeland of *Aotearoa* (now known as New Zealand), the Māori had centuries of martial experience from inter-tribal wars due to a mix of overpopulation pressures on limited food resources and the desire to increase one's *mana*, one's spiritual life-force energy.

Mana, however, is not exclusive to the Māori. Across many Polynesian cultures, this concept of "mana" played a big part in war and resistance efforts because (in overgeneralized terms) the more mana a person possessed, the more spiritual potency and influence they had (somewhat akin to "clout" and "prestige" mixed with "vitality" and "strength" but with deeply religious undertones).

So, if a warrior was, let's say, injured or took part in a losing conflict, then they'd lose face, lose prestige, lose mana (and by extension, lose mana for their entire tribe). Thus, in order to reclaim their warrior and tribal mana, they'd have to redeem themselves by taking back the mana lost (usually via armed conflict or physical force). This led to endless cycles of martial revenge, though it's important to note that the Māori didn't regard all this inter-fighting as "war"; rather, it was seen as a necessary cosmic balancing act: mana was taken from me, and to balance out my mana deficit, I must take it back from someone else…ad nauseam.[211]

Women of Peace

And while the men usually made war, it was often the women who made the peace. The Māori belief was that men were too aggressive, too shortsighted to create armistice terms that would lead to lasting peace. However, if women were in charge of the peace negotiations, they'd think of the greater good and work things out so that the brokered peace would be long lasting.

These Māori ideals of peace as paramount and battle as only justified to reclaim spiritual mana proved to be advantageous to the British once they came to the islands in force. You see, initially, the Māori welcomed these foreigners because they traded powerful weapons to them (muskets) and taught them new agricultural techniques for higher production yields.

---

211 "Maori Warfare," Te Ruapekapeka, June 20, 2012, https://www.ruapekapeka
.co.nz/read/traditional-maori-warfare; Basil Keane, "Story: Riri—Traditional
Māori Warfare," *Te Ara—The Encyclopedia of New Zealand*, June 20, 2012,
https://teara.govt.nz/en/riri-traditional-maori-warfare.

Thus, since there was initially no affront to their mana, there was no reason to really attack or fully repulse these newcomers.

Meanwhile, the damage was already done. In addition to the devastation brought by disease, the introduction of guns into all the ongoing inter-tribal fighting ramped up the death tolls because the Māori were now able to more efficiently and effectively kill each other on a larger scale than ever before in their age-old attempts to balance their mana. Moreover, the new agricultural methods introduced to the islands destabilized traditional society, only to be made even worse by the newly introduced practice of land privatization. Of course, during all this, missionaries were also dividing the native peoples amongst each other ideologically and spiritually. So, when the British decided to fully commit to colonizing New Zealand in earnest, the fierce and highly trained Māori warriors were already greatly weakened from the inside out.[212]

Mercenary Marketplace

Many leagues north from New Zealand are the islands of Fiji and Tonga, both of which possessed a warrior class as a main pillar of their pre-colonial social structures. Although somewhat close to each other distance-wise (compared to the vast distances of endless ocean between other cultures of the Pacific), Fiji is technically a part of a distinct culture group within Oceania called "Melanesia" (named so by Europeans due to the native peoples having darker skin color, and thus more "melanin," compared to other Pacific Islanders) while Tonga is a part of Polynesia proper. This cultural difference made each an "exotic" to the other and a sought-after trade partner, especially in buying royal soldiers of fortune.

Both Fiji and Tonga were closely linked through commercial trade, so much so that the daughters of Tongan kings were reserved in marriage for the sons of Fijian kings, and these intercultural royal weddings developed

212   David Green, "New Zealand's 19th-Century Wars," New Zealand History, Ministry for Culture and Heritage, updated September 30, 2020, https://nzhistory.govt.nz/war/new-zealands-19th-century-wars/introduction; "Maori," Encyclopedia Britannica, updated November 9, 2020, https://www.britannica.com/topic/Maori.

a unique spiritual union ritual that combined both Fijian and Tongan religious and cultural beliefs. These marriages kept the two cultures spiritually linked to one another and were intended to ward off war between them.

In regard to their economic ties, in lieu of draining their treasuries to economically repay their debts to one another, Tongan and Fijian chieftains sold their elite warriors off as hired mercenaries to one another. This exchange of loaned-out soldiers became the preferred way to repay debts. Such a unique economic system of warrior lending also had the added benefit of preventing internal uprisings that could disrupt economic trade with one another. Thus, by helping each other militarily, they essentially helped themselves economically.[213]

Sacred Limitations

Warfare, as destructively horrid as it has always been, often held the opportunity for people in societies around the world to gain honor and prestige and climb the social ladder, and Polynesia was no exception. Still, battles in the South Pacific were often sacred affairs, and thus no matter how badly a warrior wanted to attain glory, honor, and mana through military service, very strict rules of engagement had to be followed. Any warrior who transgressed these sacred rules would not only *not* receive the honors and mana after which they were lusting, but they would *lose* whatever honor and mana they already had because of their disrespect for the rules.

The micro-islands of Tuvalu had many such sacred limitations on war. Aside from not killing women and children, a warrior could only engage in combat with another warrior of equal strength. Concealing weapons was also not allowed; if your opponent did not visually see you bring a weapon into battle, you couldn't use it. Furthermore, in terms of large-scale armies, a battle could only take place if each side was evenly matched

---

213   "Pre-History," Tropical Fiji, South Pacific Holidays, accessed July 7, 2020, http://www.tropicalfiji.com/about_fiji/culture/prehistory/; John Spurway, *Ma'afu, Prince of Tonga, Chief of Fiji: The Life and Times of Fiji's First Tui Lau* (Canberra: Australian National University Press, 2015), 81, 395.

in the quantity of warriors they had. An overwhelming force might easily win, but there'd be no perceived sense of "spiritual victory" in such a win and thus no mana gained from it. Disregard for the sacred limitations on war would only disgrace and spiritually damage the family line of all those who took part in the transgression.[214]

Tattoo Rebellions

With war being such a high-risk, high-reward endeavor, warriors wanted the most protection they could get, and here in Polynesia, one essential form of divine protection in war was tattoos. Now, tattooing was done for all sorts of sociopolitical and religious reasons such as status and kinship signifiers, commemoration for individual achievements, spiritual wards, and more, but amongst the Tahitian people of the Society Islands in what is now French Polynesia (or more accurately, the Mā'ohi people, as they refer to themselves), tattoos were extremely valued for their magical powers in war.

Mythically, tattoos were seen as a gift to humans from the gods, and so, traditionally, to get a tattoo for frivolous or capricious reasons or just for art's sake was not done. Every image of ink under your skin was a link to the Divine, and in a culture without writing, it was a sacred way to carry ancestral lineage and stories into the living present. In terms of war, tattoos relayed to others one's accomplishments and triumphs in the line of duty (somewhat akin to modern military badges and medals adhered over the breast of an officer's formal uniform).

These tattoos and the spiritual powers of prowess and protection they gave to Mā'ohi warriors did not go unnoticed by French colonists (even though they regarded the tattoos' effects as psychosomatic, these effects were, nevertheless, a potent phenomenon they recognized). So, to hit the Mā'ohi right in the psyche, French missionaries successfully lobbied

---

214   International Committee of the Red Cross, *Under the Protection of the Palm: Wars of Dignity in the Pacific* (Suva, Fiji: ICRC Regional Delegation in the Pacific, 2009), https://www.icrc.org/en/doc/assets/files/other/wars-of-dignity-pacific -2009.pdf.

Pōmare II (the then-King of the Mā'ohi who had recently converted to Catholicism) to outlaw all tattooing.

This made tattoos the defining symbol of native resistance, and though illegal, getting new tattoos became code for being part of the underground resistance. As French power grew in the Society Islands (aided by this native, now-Catholic absolute monarch), much of the sacred associations of tattoos became lost to time. It wouldn't be until the 1980s that tattooing as a sacred art would see a revival among the Mā'ohi.[215]

Holistic Warriors

At the northernmost point of Polynesia are the Hawaiian Islands. Now a peaceful archipelago that bills itself as a paradise-on-earth tourist destination, the early history of Hawai'i was filled with intense inter-tribal and inter-island wars. Despite all the conflict, though, Hawaiian warriors were far from overaggressive brutes (as warriors around the world tend to be stereotyped). No, Hawaiian warriors were well-trained to be a complete human being—in touch with both their masculine and feminine sides in equal measure as well as skilled in wisdom and the arts just as much as physical strength and martial discipline. In many ways, to be a warrior in Hawai'i was to be the modern equivalent of a Renaissance man.

For all Hawaiian warriors, it was important to be proficient in the *Kapu Ku'ialua* (or *lua*, as it was often shortened), a traditional martial arts style native to Hawai'i. Those most proficient in the lua were also the most proficient in killing. Through a series of calculated strikes to specific nerve centers, their opponent would become paralyzed, allowing the warrior time to quickly dislocate various joints in the body, break major bones, and then finish them off with a snapping of the spinal column. Conversely, those same warriors had to know how to heal and repair bodies just as efficiently as they could damage them. Thus, massage, herbal medicine,

215 "Tahiti and French Polynesian Culture," The Islands of Tahiti: Tahiti Tourisme, accessed June 26, 2020, https://tahititourisme.com/en-us/tahiti-culture/; Lars Krutak, "Embodied Symbols of the South Seas: Tattoo in Polynesia," Lars Krutak: Tattoo Anthropologist, June 3, 2013, https://www.larskrutak.com /embodied-symbols-of-the-south-seas-tattoo-in-polynesia/.

the mending of bones, and chiropractic techniques had to be in your wheelhouse if you wanted to be recognized as a great warrior in Hawai'i.

However, the best warriors were also seen as those who, in addition to martial prowess, could compose the most beautiful poetry, dance the most elegantly, and surf the highest waves. Any man can kill, but not every man can excel in all aspects of human life. To be a person with such holistic excellence signified you had great spiritual mana within you, and those with the most spiritual mana were often recruited to be the elite warriors for Hawaiian chieftains.[216]

Polynesian Takeaway:
THE WELL-ROUNDED WARRIOR

Woe to the warrior whose life is nothing but war. That is no way to live, and despite any romanticizing of the way of the warrior or the glorification of "the cause," those whose entire life is nothing but fighting, struggling, and facing the horrors of battle will wear out quickly and suffer the psychological consequences of sustained presence amidst the mêlée. Like any person, a warrior needs outlets, they need hobbies, they need escapes, some sort of cathartic way to not have their entire being and personality be intertwined with the rough miseries of warfare.

To the native Hawaiians, their warrior history emphasized the value of a holistic, well-rounded life. A complete warrior to them (and the most honored, revered, and praised ones) was one who was adept in healing just as much as killing, the mind just as much as the body, artistic creation just as much as violent destruction.

This idealization of the ultimate warrior as a well-rounded human is often lost to many in the West who believe that being a soldier and "warrior-ing" substitutes for a personality. Those who only think about weapons, war, brutality, and their constant "self-image" as a tough warrior are not "true" warriors. Similarly, those who *only* engage in war-themed entertainment in

---

216 Naomi Sodeta, "Hawaii: Way of the Warrior," *Hana Hou! Magazine*, April/May 2003, https://warriorpublications.wordpress.com/2013/02/02/hawaii-way-of -the-warrior/.

video games, movies, books, and conversation in their free time are not very well-rounded in their psyche. All this is not healthy and, as the warriors of Hawai'i understood, makes for ineffective and low-tier individuals. The best, truest warriors are those who enjoy and know how to disengage from all things associated with war and violence when there is no need for it. After all, it comes as little surprise to notice that those who most fervently glorify warfare are rarely those who actually fight in it.

So, for your takeaway challenge here, find outlets for personal development and self-betterment that are not all linked to the same thing. You may be passionate about the social justice movement you're organizing or participating in, but you cannot let that cause become your whole life and occupy every waking moment in your mind. It will grind you down and wear you too thin for effective action.

Likewise, the same can be true for your magical and spiritual practices. Having your life, all of your hobbies, and your entire personality be your "tradition" or your "faith" is not a well-rounded individual. It's okay to love and be frequently involved in your spiritual practice or your faith community, but, again, those "traditions" and "faiths" are not personalities and only a small aspect of the totality of you. They are a *part* of your life, not your *entire* life. The wise among us know that by having many outside interests, those interests ultimately serve to enhance our main passions. After all, the warrior who can only do warrior-related things is forever inferior to the warrior who can do warrior-related things *and* incorporate the varied talents of their other interests into their warrior arsenal. Remember, you are a *warrior*, not the *war*.

Deities & Legends

KING KAMEHAMEHA I

In all of Hawaiian history, arguably no other chief has been as singularly influential as King Kamehameha I (also known as "Kamehameha the Great"). Originally the chieftain of just the Big Island of Hawai'i, King Kamehameha I, through his military expertise and charisma, was able to unify all the Hawaiian Islands under his singular rule, move the political capital to Honolulu, and keep his kingdom united during an era of tremendous cultural changes.

Born in the early to mid 1700s, his birth was seen as mystically auspicious because it coincided with the passing of Halley's Comet over Hawai'i (something that only happens every seventy-five years or so). From a young age, Kamehameha I (whose name means "Lonely One" due to his growing up in exile to escape the then-king's politically motivated blood hunt for him) was militarily ambitious, and when he grew into adulthood, fortune would give him a powerful advantage over his rivals: European aid. Assistance that would later come back to bite the West in the butt.[217]

When Kamehameha I became ruler of the Big Island, he incorporated British guns into his army and also allowed the British to assist him with advisors, firearm provisions, and shipwrights who helped him build an armada of cannon-equipped ships. Through this essential help, the British had unknowingly played right into Kamehameha I's plans.

You see, once the islands were united under Kamehameha I, Britain and the rest of Europe could no longer play all the squabbling Hawaiian chieftains off one another. Hawai'i was now a united front under a powerful central government and had an army equipped with and trained in European weaponry and military tactics. With this power, Kamehameha I maintained Hawaiian independence as a neutral buffer kingdom that would be unwise for any European power to invade, since that would risk igniting a war with a fellow European superpower.[218]

As a king to his people, he was both very severe and very progressive. An autocratic ruler who demanded complete obedience from his subjects, he, nevertheless, created a code of laws (known as the "Law of the Splintered Paddle") that was based on prohibiting excessive punishments and

217 "Kamehameha I: King of Hawaii," Encylopædia Britannica, updated May 4, 2020, https://www.britannica.com/biography/Kamehameha-I.

218 "Kamehameha the Great," National Park Service, updated February 28, 2015, https://www.nps.gov/puhe/learn/historyculture/kamehameha.htm; "The Story of King Kamehameha I," Hawaii Tourism Authority, accessed June 27, 2020, https://www.gohawaii.com/culture/history/king-kamehameha.

protecting the most vulnerable in society. In practice, this meant his various governors of each island could not dispense punishment without just cause, and even then, they could only give sentences that befit the crime and not in excess of it. Moreover, all citizens had the natural right to feel safe everywhere in and out of their homes within the kingdom, and thus it was the responsibility of his governors to make that so by keeping their territories in a state of perpetual peace.[219]

ʻORO

Among the peoples of the Society Islands, ʻOro was the god of war and peace. To the Māʻohi on the island of Tahiti, however, ʻOro was also worshipped as the main supreme deity. Accompanied by his three daughters into battle, ʻOro was greatly feared and respected as the most powerful god in the pantheon and the one who could aid in aggression as well as bestow protection from harm, but when there was no war to be had, he was celebrated as divine patron of the fine arts.[220]

ʻOro was also regarded as the chief patron and legendary founder of a secret religious society of traveling bards and players among the Māʻohi called the Areoi (sometimes spelled "Arioi"). In many ways, though, the Areoi weren't really so much of a "secret" society as they were a closed fraternal order (although they did allow women to be members).

The perception of "secrecy" that surrounded the Areoi came about mostly because a lot of their rituals and traditions were kept secret from the public at large and *especially* from the Europeans who came to their islands. However, it would be this ability to keep a secret under the personal protection of ʻOro

---

219 Hawaiʻi Legal Auxiliary, "The Law of the Splintered Paddle: Kānāwai Māmalahoe," University of Hawaiʻi, accessed June 27, 2020, https://www .hawaii.edu/uhelp/files/LawOfTheSplinteredPaddle.pdf; "Kamehameha I: King of Hawaii," Encylopædia Britannica.

220 Te Rangi Hīroa [Peter Henry Buck], *Anthropology and Religion* (New Haven, CT: Yale University Press, 1939), n.p.; Robert D. Craig, *Dictionary of Polynesian Mythology* (Westport, CT: Greenwood Publishing Group, 1989), 193–194.

that would be what kept Mā'ohi traditions (such as sacred tattooing) alive during the times of heavy colonialism and French Catholic evangelism.[221]

TŪMATAUENGA

In Māori society, Tūmatauenga (sometimes just called "Tū") is the chief deity of war and of food procurement and preparation (such as agriculture, hunting, fishing, and cooking). He also played a big part in the Māori creation myth wherein he took an oppositional stance against his divine siblings on how to deal with their parents (who were the earth and sky gods locked in an eternal embrace that essentially crushed everyone and everything between them, including their children).

According to legends, Tūmatauenga was a bit extreme in that he wanted to solve this problem by killing their parents despite his siblings just wanting to forcefully separate them. The other siblings won out, but one brother (Tāwhirimatea, god of tempests) objected to the forced separation of their parents and started attacking his siblings. Among them, only Tūmatauenga was strong enough to beat him to a standstill.[222]

After this, Tūmatauenga became upset at his siblings for not agreeing to his initial plan of killing their parents and for being too weak to help him battle against Tāwhirimatea, and so now *he* began savagely taking his revenge on his siblings and everything over which they held divine patronage. All the divine siblings and their descendants easily succumbed to Tūmatauenga, and so, as the last one standing, his descendants were the ones left to populate the earth (we humans). He went on to teach us how to hunt animals and grow crops so that we (his children) could be

---

221 Hutton Webster, *Primitive Secret Societies: A Study in Early Politics and Religion* (New York: Macmillan Company, 1908), 164–171; Te Rangi Hīroa [Peter H. Buck], *Arts and Crafts of the Cook Islands* (New York: Kraus Reprint Co., 1971), n.p., http://nzetc.victoria.ac.nz/tm/scholarly/tei-BucArts.html.

222 Edward Tregear, "Tu," *The Maori-Polynesian Comparative Dictionary* (Wellington, NZ: Lyon and Blair, 1891), 540.

independent and not reliant upon the divine help of his despised siblings or any other weak god for these life-sustaining skills.[223]

In modern times, respect for Tūmatauenga is still greatly upheld in New Zealand military culture. In fact, the official Māori name for the New Zealand Army is *Ngāti Tūmatauenga* ("Tribe of Tūmatauenga"). The army also has its own official, national *marae* (a sacred holy clearing protected by Tūmatauenga) wherein traditional Māori ceremonies are performed. Additionally, the New Zealand Defense Force has its own Māori cultural advisor to help the New Zealand military grow spiritually in respect to and in honor of Tūmatauenga.[224]

223 George Grey, "Children of Heaven and Earth," in *Polynesian Mythology & Ancient Traditional History of the New Zealanders: As Furnished by Their Priests and Chiefs,* Sacred Texts, 1854, https://www.sacred-texts.com/pac/grey/grey03.htm.
224 "Ngāti Tūmatauenga," NZ Army, New Zealand Defense Force, accessed March 20, 2020, http://www.army.mil.nz/culture-and-history/ngati-tumatauenga.htm.

21

OCEANIC MAGICAL COMMUNITY

WILD WITCHERY

Making our way to the Australian capital of Canberra, it's here we meet our next guest warrior, Jarrah, an Aussie explorer of magic and all things spiritual who has a particular affinity toward the element of earth and the teachings of the natural world. He has been invited here to come and talk to us about the significance of one social justice endeavor we have not yet discussed, one that is very near and dear to the peoples of Australia: wildlife activism.

Yes, we humans may be masters of the Earth, but we inhabit this planet with countless other living beings besides ourselves. As we expand farther and farther into the fewer and fewer remaining "wild" places of the globe and turn them into parking lots, pastures, and other profit-producing tracts of logged and leveled land, where are the animals to go? Australia, in particular, has been on the leading edge of environmental activism for quite some time now, and with a native array of some of the most rare and unique animals found nowhere else, the protection of animal rights and the natural ecosystems they inhabit are much more important and urgent.

So, to give us the current status on animal and eco-activism going on down here in Australia, I'm going to step aside and let Jarrah provide not only the authentic Australian perspective and his own magical endeavors toward wildlife conservation, but also all the earth magic goings-on of Aussie Neopagans and spellworkers who have had to adapt their magic to a land wherein the rules (as taught by Northern Hemisphere traditions of magic) often don't apply. Of course, though, should you be interested in learning more, feel free to follow Jarrah's Australian adventures on Instagram via @jarrahwell as well as his earth-focused woodcrafting via @danewoodburning.

Many people became aware of the plight of wildlife in Australia during the bushfires of 2019–2020, especially of the koalas who were particularly impacted. But Australia has a long history of environmental activism, especially since the protests against the Franklin Dam project in Tasmania in the 1970s, which led to the creation of the world's first green political party.

Another issue for many Aussies, and for those that travel here, is our very strict quarantine laws for imported animals as well as for animal and plant products, as we have seen the devastation caused by the introduction of foreign animals to our ecosystems. You'll find Aussies agree with these laws here, as there is a common awareness of the uniqueness and vulnerability of our flora and fauna. Feral rabbits are rampant throughout the country, as are foxes, feral camels roam our arid regions, and carp are responsible for the decline of native freshwater fish in our waterways.

There is also a general awareness here of the inextricable connection between the land, animals, and the spirit world through the beliefs of the indigenous peoples of Australia and "The Dreaming." While I am not indigenous myself and do not claim any right to this ancient knowledge, it does further inspire me to seek out the spiritual side of our native Austra-

lian nature and wildlife. I am fascinated with so many Australian animals, among my favourites are dugongs, numbats, wombats, rock wallabies, and gang-gang cockatoos, but on a spiritual level I feel particularly connected to the echidna and try to connect with its spirit.

For those in spiritual, neo-pagan, and witchcraft circles in Australia, we are aware that much of the magickal teachings and literature available to us is based on the nature and seasons of the northern hemisphere. This can make it harder to connect at times when, for example, our Wheel of the Year has Samhain in April and the spirits that inhabit this land, apart from the introduced species, are also very different from what most people encounter. To help adapt our magick to the land, some of us connect the cardinal directions with different elements to those in the northern half of the world. I feel that this increases the need for us to be even more connected and understanding of the environment that we are in since a lot of what is taught by northern hemisphere writers and practitioners is not really applicable here.

I try to use my magick practice in order to help the conservation of our native wildlife. As a practical measure, I firstly donate money where I can, to organisations who are established in working in this area. Spiritually, I spend time in the bush, listening, looking, feeling, and smelling everything I can and being open and receptive to whatever things I may learn along the way. I also have pictures of certain native animals framed at home to use as a focus for meditation and to serve as a constant reminder that we are not separate from our environment but a part of it, along with every other living creature, plant, and mineral on this land that we live on. Even something as simple as giving thanks to the land and acknowledging and supporting the indigenous, traditional owners of this land and their insep-arable connection to it can go a long way.

—*Jarrah*

A CRY FOR SOVEREIGNTY

The struggle for Native independence and national self-sovereignty is not an endeavor that was suddenly achieved during the twentieth century when much of the Western nations gave up their colonial territories (most of them, at least). Native peoples and separatist movements whose home-lands have become incorporated into modern countries (through force or dubious political maneuvering) are still fighting hard to reclaim what was stolen from them. One such homeland in which such a cry for sovereignty is gaining momentum is here in Hawai'i.

To give some background, up until the summer of 1959, Hawai'i was an occupied territory of the U.S. because of its strategic military and com-mercial position in the Pacific Ocean (and it only became a territory in the first place by way of the U.S. Marines and agricultural corporations forcing the indigenous Queen Lili'uokalani to abdicate her throne and dissolve the sovereign Kingdom of Hawai'i). Many Native Hawaiians still regard modern statehood as a continuation of this occupation, and they are still awaiting their due justice.

One such Native Hawaiian is the warrior I've arranged for us to meet here today. His name is Pua Ishibashi, and he is a husband, father, and co-founder of the Aloha 'Āina Party that was established in 2020. As the Chairperson of this new political party, Pua is on the front lines of this native sovereignty movement for Hawai'i because, in addition to plat-forms such as environmentalism, freedom of worship, acceptance of all people regardless of one's demographics, and transparency in government, the Aloha 'Āina Party is deeply committed to Ho'oponopono ("make right what is wrong"). In particular, they advocate for the sovereignty of Native Hawaiians and Hawaiian nationals.

Like everything in politics, research the party on your own. Choose whether or not you personally support the Aloha 'Āina Party in regard to their various platforms and keep them accountable for the pledges and promises they make on the campaign trail. I'm not saying that I am vouch-ing for or even in agreement with *everything* about this nascent political party (but then again, who 100 percent agrees with everything about *any* political party?) nor am I personally endorsing them; however, politics has always been one of the most important theatres of war, and with enough votes and "good" people in political office, warfare can be prevented, wrongs can be righted, and the need for activism becomes lessened since those in power have the welfare of the people at heart.

The reason Pua Ishibashi is here today is not to give us a lecture on politics or pander for your votes and sympathy. No, I've asked him here to recount, from a Native Hawaiian perspective, what it's like living in an occupied territory that was once his people's homeland and to tell of his people's ongoing pursuit of the sovereignty that was stolen from them by the point of a U.S.-Marine-issued rifle. This is an account of the times from a Native Hawaiian perspective and from someone who is doing something to create his desired change in the world by organizing and fighting for his cause in the realm of politics. Ultimately, *you* influence politics with your vote, but only the voter who listens to the cries of the oppressed can truly know toward what ends their votes are going.

I was born in the Territory of Hawaii in 1957. My mother Mona, was also born in the Territory in 1937, as was her mother Emma in 1910. My great grandmother Mary, was born in the Kingdom of Hawaii in 1884, under the rule of King Kalākaua. She witnessed firsthand the Overthrow of Queen Liliuokalani in 1893 (age 9), establishment of the Republic of Hawaii in 1894 (age ten), Annexation in 1898 (age 14), and Hawaii becoming a Territory in 1900 (age 16). My great-grandmother Mary passed in 1954 at the age of 70, waiting for justice. Hawaii became the 50th State in 1959.

I feel sad and often cry when I think of the Overthrow of the Kingdom of Hawaii. I feel pain and betrayal, knowing what America did to my people, land, and country. Stealing our country and national identity, disenfranchising us from our land, language, dance, resources, and culture. And marginalizing my people economically, politically, socially, and spiritually. Yes, the Overthrow causes me great pain and even anger. But, fortunately for me, I have been able to process this and move from anger and depression to "What can I do to help my people move forward?" However, for many Native Hawaiians, addressing the Overthrow continues to be a struggle.

What happened to our kupuna (elders) and keiki (children) during and subsequent to the Overthrow was akin to being kidnapped, assaulted/

raped, and left for dead. Compounding the act was the fact that it was perpetuated by an America that was previously respected and trusted, a Nation believed to be a friend. The Overthrow resulted in mass feelings of depression, being overwhelmed, hopelessness, despair, inadequacy, and inferiority. In addition, feelings of mistrust for the government, political system, educational system, and even religious institutions. Feelings that continue to be held by many Native Hawaiians today.

Psychologists call this "Historical Trauma." As defined by the U.S. Department of Health & Human Services, "Historical trauma is multigenerational trauma experienced by a specific cultural, racial or ethnic group."[225] It is common knowledge that Native Hawaiians have the worst statistics among all ethnic groups in Hawaii. This includes, but is not limited to: low income, poverty, homelessness, poor education, substance abuse, physical and sexual abuse, teen pregnancy, mental health issues, poor education, poor health, disproportionate incarceration, infant deaths, and suicide.[226]

Why are Native Hawaiians at the top of everything bad and at the bottom of everything good? Why does the Native Hawaiian community continue to struggle for over one-and-a-quarter century after the Overthrow? I believe the Overthrow is the root cause for the symptoms we suffer from today. That we, as a people, continue to suffer from Historical Trauma, a trauma so deep and lasting that it continues to impact Native Hawaiians today.

So what can be done? How can we fix the current Hawaiian condition and reverse devolving trends? The answer is simple and straightforward. I believe our ability to heal and move forward as a people and nation will be in direct proportion to making things pono *(correct and balanced) once again. We must* ho'oponopono *(make right what is wrong) and have restitution (restore what was lost/taken). Only this will satisfy justice and the desires*

---

225 "Trauma," U.S. Department of Health & Human Services, accessed September 7, 2021, https://www.acf.hhs.gov/trauma-toolkit/trauma-concept.

226 "Be Aware: Suicide Epidemic Native American Youth," I Love Ancestry, accessed July 8, 2021, https://iloveancestry.com/topics/activism/invisible -truth/native-american-indian-suicide-epidemic/.

of our kupuna *(ancestors). The restoration of a sovereign and independent Nation of Hawaii. Only this will mend the broken hearts and spirits of our people. Only this will heal us from the inside out.*

Sovereignty must be our quest, from the mountain to the sea, from the classroom to the courtroom, from the voting ballot to peaceful civil disobedience, we must press forward the fight and never give up!

—Pua Ishibashi

PART 7

THE AMERICAS

*If there is no justice for the people, let
there be no peace for the government.*
EMILIANO ZAPATA

22
LATIN AMERICA

Cultural

SOUTH AMERICA

South America, from its tropical north all the way down to its Patagonian south, is a massive landmass. Unfortunately, though, this region of the world all too often gets glossed over whenever it appears in history books. The arrival of the Spanish around the middle of the second millennium CE is when many people think that the history of this continent officially began, as if everything that came before was either irrelevant or just a prelude to colonization. In reality, pre-colonial South America was inhabited by many diverse peoples who were at each other's throats for imperial power and for the defense of their homelands before Europe ever knew this place existed. And just like anywhere else, magic and spirituality played a big part in how these peoples went to war with and resisted one another.

The Mighty Mapuche

It's fitting that we start our trek through Latin America at the Southern Cone of South America because down here is where we'll find some of the *fiercest* resistance fighters on the continent: the Mapuche. Native to central and southern Chile as well as parts of southwestern Argentina, the Mapuche were originally composed of various small agricultural villages all sharing a similar culture, but whenever outsiders arrived in an attempt to be their new overlords, the Mapuche united and achieved seemingly impossible victories.

The first invaders were the Inca who had a massive, well-trained army. The Mapuche knew that, as rural farmers, they needed to adapt to survive against such an imperialistic juggernaut, and so they put inter-tribal squabbles with their neighbors aside to come together against this common enemy. Each separated village joined in an alliance to provide a united resistance, they trained themselves in guerrilla tactics, and they absolutely never stopped being an expensive pain in the wallet to the Inca. Yes, the Inca were stronger, but because the Mapuche never backed down and kept up armed resistance (however small-scale they could), the Inca war effort proved more costly than it was worth, resulting in the abandonment of the campaign and never conquering the Mapuche or their lands.[227]

One major contributing factor to the resilience of the Mapuche amid such unfavorable odds was their high spiritual reverence for herbal medicines and the shamans who concocted them. These religious leaders were called *machi*, and they specialized in healing magic, mediumship, and tribal advisory on matters of war and peace. Though mostly female, male machi

---

227   Inca Garcilaso de la Vega, *Comentarios reales: Segunda parte* (San Francisco: Wikimedia Foundation, 1616), https://es.wikisource.org/wiki/Comentarios _reales_-_Segunda_parte; Osvaldo Silva Galdames, "¿Detuvo la Batalla del Maule la Expansión Inca Hacia el Sur de Chile?" *Cuadernos de Historia* 3 (July 1983): 7–25.

were often genderqueer due to the need to transcend beyond the binary of male/female when performing rituals. So, when in the midst of a resistance movement, the Mapuche heavily relied on the machi and their *extensive* training in the spiritual science of medicine to heal the wounded and get them into fighting shape again given how outnumbered the Mapuche often were.[228]

Naturally, when the Spanish arrived next, the Mapuche were well prepared and knew how to dig their heels into the soil for a long resistance. Yet, they also adapted to their new European foes, learning how to ride horses and using them in war. Because of their resilience, ability to adapt to changing times, and their dedication (for centuries) to, once again, never giving up armed resistance, the Spanish (like the Inca before them) found the conquest of Southern Chile too costly to be worth it, and the Mapuche were never conquered by the Spanish Empire.[229]

It wasn't until Chile declared its independence from Spain in 1818 that the Mapuche would ultimately lose the good fight. Originally given sovereignty over their own protected lands within the borders of newly established Chile in the early 1800s, by the late-1800s the Chilean government wanted that land back for economic exploitation, and they used a loophole in the constitution to do so.

This loophole (which was finally closed in the early 1970s under the socialist presidency of Salvador Allende, but was then reopened after a military coup d'état led to Allende's suicide and presidential usurpation by the U.S.-backed conservative military dictatorship of Pinochet) centered around the fact that the Mapuche are not recognized in the constitution at all. Since they are not recognized by the constitution, they technically "don't exist" according to the government and right-wing interpretations

228 Maria Costanza Torri, PhD., "Medicinal Plants Used in Mapuche Traditional Medicine in Araucanía, Chile: Linking Sociocultural and Religious Values with Local Heath Practices," *Complementary Health Practice Review* 15, no. 3 (2010): 132–148, https://journals.sagepub.com/doi/pdf/10.1177/1533210110391077; G. G. Bolich, *Conversing on Gender* (Raleigh: Psyche's Press, 2007), 248–249.
229 "Mapuche," Encyclopedia Britannica, updated January 14, 2020, https://www .britannica.com/topic/Mapuche.

of the Chilean legal system. This means they, as a people, technically have no legal rights to land, property, or protection. Unable to stand up to the industrialized army of Chile with its modern weapons, the Mapuche were summarily rounded into reservations and, to this day, continue to be oppressed and economically indebted to multinational creditors for even the basic necessities of life.[230]

Ruthless River

Up in the large (yet vanishing) rainforest apothecary of the world lies the basin of the Amazon River, which snakes through this jungle land and touches countless native peoples, all of whom call this humid hot spot of biodiversity home. And while Brazil (as well as modern corporations and capital venture stockholders) has had firm geopolitical control over a majority of the Amazon rainforest for the past centuries, many of its native peoples still remain uncontacted by and unknown to the modern world. Unlike the Mapuche, though, this was not because of some strong resistance efforts, but rather by the grace of how impenetrable the Amazon jungle is.

Nevertheless, that does not mean there has existed a utopian Shangri-La here beneath the rainforest canopy—quite the opposite. Modern anthropology is finding evidence that, prior to any European arrival, an estimated one-third of all deaths here were caused by violent conflicts. The reasons, unsurprisingly, are due to the same reasons we've been killing each other everywhere else since prehistory: jealousy, conflicting religious beliefs, accusations of witchcraft, attempts to get ahead in society, resource accumulation, and fear of those who are different. In fact, inter-tribal violence here in the Amazon was found to be decisively *more* fatal when the conflict was between two peoples of different cultures or spiritual beliefs.[231]

---

230 Jane Chambers, "Chile's Mapuche Indigenous Group Fights for Rights," BBC, November 26, 2020, https://www.bbc.com/news/world-latin-america -55042838.

231 University of Missouri-Columbia, "Amazonian Tribal Warfare Sheds Light on Modern Violence, Says Anthropologist," ScienceDaily, 2012, https://www .sciencedaily.com/releases/2012/10/121002145448.htm.

What makes all this extra fascinating (albeit depressingly so) is that many of the current uncontacted Amazonian tribes whom we know about have ways of life similar (though not exactly the same since *all* peoples evolve and adapt through time) to their ancestors who arrived here around 10,000 years ago. One could argue that perhaps *that* is us at our most elemental core if you strip back all the complications and societal expectations of modern life. It's very telling that despite the relative "simplicity" of life back in 8000 BCE, uncomplicated by computers, cars, urbanization, and organized religion, there was *still* so much prejudicial violence toward "differentness."

Nevertheless, despite history and anthropology showing an ingrained, global human tendency of inherent wariness toward those who are different (since rolling up into the territory of a different tribe in times past was a good way to get yourself killed), that same wariness that might have kept us alive in more violent, less interconnected times doesn't really have a place in modern times. A globally interconnected world is very different from a world of isolated tribal villages. So, keeping a psycho-behavioral relic from 10,000 years ago such as fear of "differentness" just doesn't make sense anymore, even if it made survival sense in times long past.

Children of the Sun

No examination of resistance, war, or martial magic in South America is complete without talking about the Inca. Before we get into it, though, it's important to wrap your head around just how uniquely impressive the Inca Empire was in comparison to many other empires around the globe. Their empire (which they referred to as "Tawantinsuyu," which roughly translates to "The Four United Regions," while "Inca" is really just the Quechua word for "king," which the Spanish used to refer to everything about the empire) was extraordinarily built across extremely inhospitable regions of the continent without major rivers or arable land. What's even more amazing, though, is that they built their highly populated, multicultural empire without the invention of writing, the use of iron tools, the creation of the wheel, or even the luxury of beasts of burden to aid in manual labor. They also had no concept of money, but more on that a bit later.[232]

How on earth did they manage to become such a powerhouse and maintain imperial control over their conquered subjects, you ask? Well, it was all thanks to the magic of divine right and big government. This is because, in Inca religious cosmology, the sun was not only the supreme deity in the pantheon but also the ancestral progenitor from whom the Inca people literally descended. First amongst these children of the sun, of course, was the emperor, the perceived most-direct descendent of the sun. Being the most holy person in existence, the emperor held absolute rule, and so an ultra-strong, heavily centralized government was utilized to facilitate his divine commands.[233]

No Money, No Problems

Still, how did the Inca stay in power and squash all rebellions that popped up against their imperial rule? Ironically, through a lack of money. You see, the Inca (though *vastly* wealthy by our standards of gold and resources) had no currency of any form, yet they still had a tax system. Instead of money, every person in the empire had to pay their taxes either in foodstuffs or in the form of human labor in public projects for a portion of the year.

This human labor option of tax payment allowed the emperor to relocate individuals to various parts of his culturally diverse empire to perform their tax service. Because peoples of different cultures and religious beliefs were less likely to put aside personal prejudices and unite together in rebellion, this forced dilution of cultures, and antagonistic mixing of peoples throughout the empire effectively diminished the number of populous uprisings against the Inca government.

---

232 "Inca (n.)," Online Etymology Dictionary, accessed June 30, 2020, https://www.etymonline.com/word/inca.

233 "Religion in the Inca Empire," Boundless World History, Lumen Learning, accessed June 30, 2020, https://courses.lumenlearning.com/suny-hccc-worldcivilization/chapter/religion-in-the-inca-empire/.

Simply put, the conquered fought against each other for Inca scraps rather than target their unified rage toward the Inca who were seated at the banquet table. No matter how much a conquered people hated their Inca overlords, they were just too suspicious of other cultures and prejudiced toward other conquered peoples to be able to work together in united revolt (a powerful tactic still well in use by the powers that be to get minority groups and others they oppress to fight amongst themselves instead of uniting against the real enemy).[234]

State Property

The military power of having no currency system goes further than that, though. The lack of money made the empire, in many ways, the oft-romanticized state property communist ideal that nations in the twentieth century seemed to profess to be (yet never really lived up to). Uniquely, there were no marketplaces in the Inca Empire wherein people could exchange goods or services, and no money, established currency, or barterable private property with which to do it even if there were. Every single thing in the empire, instead, was owned by the divine emperor and provided to his people by the central government based on need.

Each town center had its own state-owned warehouse of sorts wherein the locals would deposit surplus food, tools, and clothing (and all the things one would sell at a marketplace once one's own needs were met), and then if anyone needed anything they couldn't produce themselves, they could simply go to this warehouse to receive the item for free. Money didn't exist in the empire simply because there was not a need for it. And this leads to the warrior might of the money-less Inca: ease of military logistics and not having to finance a standing army.

Because the Inca Empire was so state-centralized and so geographically far-flung, the farther a revolt was from the capital, the more difficult it would've been to put down. That's where these state-owned warehouses

<hr>

234 "Inca Empire Overview," Khan Academy, May 10, 2017, https://www .khanacademy.org/humanities/world-history/medieval-times/maya-aztec -and-inca/v/inca-empire-overview.

came into play. The emperor's troops didn't have to worry about being weighed down by and carrying lots of supplies over vast distances everywhere. Instead, the royal army could quickly move throughout the empire unburdened, hopping from town center to town center along the way, and get their supplies as needed from each warehouse. The divine rulers and royal government never had to worry about how to finance, equip, or feed their troops at any time anywhere throughout their empire—complicated logistics and expenditures that slow down any army and have broken the backs of many an empire the world over.[235]

Dead Men Don't Share

As amazing as the Inca Empire was, one of the *most* amazing things is that it only existed for a little over one hundred years (the empire, mind you, not the culture, which pre- and post-dates the actual empire). Yes, all the massive imperialistic expansionism, revolutionary economic practices, grand construction projects that have become wonders of the world, and all the rest were done within the entire span of only three or so generations. As we know, the arrival of the Spanish with their guns, germs, and steel put a sudden end to everything, but the Inca's own afterlife beliefs worked against them and held part of the blame for their downfall, even perhaps (because historians love to theorize alternate timelines) sowed the seeds of their own impending doom had the Spanish never arrived at all.

I go into much more details about Inca mysticism on death and the afterlife in my book *Morbid Magic: Death Spirituality and Culture from Around the World*, but for our warrior focus here, the main problematic factor was state ownership of everything by the ruling emperor. Yes, that same state property concept that helped build and maintain the Inca Empire also had an extreme caveat in the religious fine print. You see, in Inca spiritual belief, ownership of something continued on after death, and because all

235 Cogito, "Peak of the Incan Empire," Kings and Generals, May 24, 2018, YouTube, 11:56, https://www.youtube.com/watch?v=3aYeUOVgbck; Terence N. D'Altroy, *The Incas* (Malden, MA: Blackwell Publishing, 2003), n.p.

state property was owned by the emperor (all the resources, land, and goods acquired under his rule), he continued to own them in the afterlife.

This meant that the next emperor could not have access to the previous emperor's wealth and supplies and thus had to start all over again to accumulate power. Because of this, the empire had to *constantly* expand every time there was a new ruler. Each monarch needed to conquer more land, more resources, and more people beyond what his ancestors had already conquered.

This is why the Inca Empire spread so quickly by any historical standards, yet constant expansion left little time to consolidate rule. Each emperor was too preoccupied with getting *new* land that their dead predecessors didn't already own from beyond the grave, and so no national unity was established that would pacify the conquered peoples into having a sense of shared identity. Thus, with always needing to instigate constant, expansionist wars farther and farther away, the military might of Inca rulers was already stretched dangerously thin by the time the Spanish came along. And, assuming Europe never came to the Americas, at what point would the empire not have been able to militarily expand anymore, thus destroying itself from the impossibility of unlimited growth?[236]

MESOAMERICA

Though empires and imperialism over native peoples by native peoples is nothing new in the pre-colonial Americas, the relatively small region of Mesoamerica is unique for having had such a concentration of them. Two of the biggest ones have names that are still recognized the world over: "Aztec" and "Maya." These empires have become infamous for the ways in which their spiritual cosmology incentivized them toward battle and conquest, and so powerful were these spiritual outlooks that even the Spanish Empire could not fully douse the flames of their resistance. Instead, Europe had to compromise and acquiesce as a syncretic faith emerged, one that allowed the polytheistic magic of these bellicose empires to survive under the outward guise of Catholicism.

236 Cogito, "Peak of the Incan Empire."

Blood Born

Journeying up into the central region of Mexico, we find the lasting legacy of the Aztec Empire ("Aztec" being a modern name given to the empire of the ruling indigenous people of the area who called themselves the "Mexica" [pronounced meh-SHEE-kah], from whom the modern nation of "Mexico" gets its name). Alongside the Norse Vikings and medieval Mongols, the Mexica were some of the most battle-glorifying, hawkish, and bellicose people in the history books. Their bloody infamy, however, was not completely undeserved. In fact, their imperialistic expansionism at the point of an obsidian-studded club would be what brought them to glory just as much as what, ironically, brought them down.

The shedding of blood, particularly in the form of human sacrifice, was absolutely essential for the Aztec world to function. You see, in Mexica mythos, humans owed their entire existence on this earth to the mythological act of the gods sacrificing themselves so that humans could live, and because of this, humans were forever indebted to the gods on a primal, blood level.

Furthermore, blood sacrifices were essential to keep the sun rising every day. This was because their chief deity, Huitzilopochtli (god of, among other things, the sun and war), was in a constant battle with darkness (literally and figuratively). Without regular sacrificial blood offerings from us humans to help him rise in his fight every day, the darkness would win and eternal night would consume the land. Thus, to ensure the sun would rise every day and ensure the continuation of the universe as they knew it, the Aztec Empire made continual offerings of human blood through rituals of human sacrifice.[237]

Flower Wars

So what do all these human sacrifices and blood debts to the gods have to do with the Aztec war machine? Everything. Undoubtedly, the Mexica

---

[237] Dave Roos, "Human Sacrifice: Why the Aztecs Practiced This Gory Ritual," History, October 11, 2018, https://www.history.com/news/aztec-human -sacrifice-religion.

were supremely effective at conquering their neighbors and establishing an iron-fisted empire stretching across central and southern Mexico, but the problem was that there were always too few captured prisoners of war whom they could offer as sacrifices (warriors being the *most honorable* sacrificial offering). Wars of conquest tended to favor killing over capturing, and since the elaborate intricacies of Aztec human sacrifice rituals required a *live* offering, total war was just too unconducive for a steady supply of captured warrior blood.

Enter the flower wars. These wars were self-contained "friendly" faux-wars that were created for the purpose of obtaining live prisoners of war and fought between different regiments within the Aztec military (and also against armies of select neighbors whom they purposely never conquered so as to essentially "farm" prisoners of war from them). Sort of similar to modern "war games," the point was not to destroy, but rather simply to beat and capture your opponent in a realistic, war-like controlled scenario without actually killing them.

By being able to stage these flower wars whenever necessary, the Mexica were able to always obtain a safe supply of sacrificial warrior blood to keep the universe going. Naturally, it was not ideal to diminish their own troop numbers through sacrifices, but when there were no enemy warriors to be captured, these flower wars allowed the empire to always have coveted warrior blood on hand for sacrifice. They also provided crucial, real-world, regular training for the Aztec military, which kept them constantly in top form as well as allowed individual soldiers to earn warrior prestige and honors when there was no war of conquest to be had. In fact, the primary way in which to gain rank in the Aztec military was to capture opponents because anyone can kill, but only the skilled can capture.[238]

---

238 "The Aztec Empire: Society, Politics, Religion, and Agriculture," History on the Net, accessed July 3, 2020, https://www.historyonthenet.com/aztec-empire -society-politics-religion-agriculture; Chris Muscato, "What Is an Aztec Flower War?" Study.com, August 8, 2017, https://study.com/academy/lesson/what-is -an-aztec-flower-war.html.

Honor could also be obtained by being on the losing side of an expansionist or flower war. To the warrior-worshipping Mexica, death on the battlefield or death from being sacrificed as a captured prisoner of a flower war was *the* ultimate honor, and it ensured access into the best afterlife destination. Similar to the Norse Vikings, the Mexica believed that only such a war-related death could grant a soul access to eternal paradise. With disease and accidental death from daily life always a possibility, these flower wars offered soldiers more opportunities of being killed in action or captured as a sacrifice to the gods, thus allowing them avenues into paradise during times of peace.[239]

Simply the Best

Couldn't the Mexica have just selected some (un)lucky person at random from their vast Aztec Empire or used their many slaves to maintain a safe sacrificial blood supply, you may be wondering? Why did they have to stage these elaborate faux-wars to capture their own warriors when enemy warriors were not available? The answer…only the best would do when making a sacrifice for the supreme sun god. Contrary to popular belief, the Mexica were not indiscriminate in ritualistically sacrificing people. The offering had to be *worthy* enough for the honor. To offer the blood of the lower classes or some commoner nobody to fuel Huitzilopochtli's celestial war efforts in holding back infinite night was seen as supremely disrespectful.

Though there is evidence of occasional sacrifices from all social strata and ages, the "best" of society was always preferred. Simply being among the aristocracy was one way to be seen as part of the Mexica cream of the crop, though there were others, such as being extremely beautiful. The Mexica being a war-worshipping people, however, they considered warriors to be the "best" and most honored people in society and considered

239 Luz Espinosa, "Mictlán: el lugar de los muertos," Cultura Colectiva, September 23, 2014, https://culturacolectiva.com/letras/mictlan-el-lugar-de-los-muertos/; Diego Durán, *Historia de las Indias de Nueva-España y islas de Tierra Firme* (London: Forgotten Books, 2018), n.p.; Fray Diego de Landa, *Relación de las cosas de Yucatán* (Mexico City: Miguel Ángel Porrúa, 1982), n.p.

the battlefield as the "best" place to display one's talents. Thus, the sacrificial blood of a warrior who was captured on a battlefield was one of the greatest offerings they could make to a god of war (their chief god) and why these flower wars were so important in times of peace.[240]

The Quality of Mercy

Undeniably, the Aztec Empire was a super-effective, imperialistic war machine, but conquering and ruling are two quite different things. As rulers, the Mexica were tremendously cruel, demanding, and unmerciful. They held supreme dominion over their neighbors by forcefully conquering them and then taxing them heavily (on their food supplies as well as a blood tax on their best individuals for sacrifices). Like any conquered peoples living under the economic and political boot of a punishing foreign power, the native non-Mexica peoples of central and southern Mexico wanted their oppressors gone.

By the time Hernán Cortés arrived, hatred for the Mexica was at an all-time high, and so because of this, many of the conquered peoples within the Aztec Empire gladly helped these strange foreigners whose goal was the same as theirs: bring down the regional hegemon of the Mexica. Thus the Mexica's iron-fisted, merciless rule via extreme oppression ultimately served to make their conquered subjects willing allies to Spain, providing invaluable military personnel, intelligence, and logistical aid to the small band of Spanish conquistadors far beyond what these outnumbered men could have done on their own as strangers in a strange land.

Had the Mexica not been so cruel and, instead, were more merciful in their rule over their subjects, perhaps Hernán Cortés's men would not have had the invaluable support and local aid they desperately needed

---

240 "The Aztec Empire: Society, Politics, Religion, and Agriculture."; David L. Carrasco, "Human Sacrifice in Aztec Culture," Serious Science, October 13, 2016, http://serious-science.org/human-sacrifice-in-aztec-culture-6995.

to overthrow the Aztec Empire, and though it's all speculation, it's not improbable.[241]

City Pride

Unlike that of the Inca and Mexica, the Maya Empire had already risen and fallen long before the Spanish ever arrived in the Americas (around half a millennium before). They also lasted longer too. While the Inca and Mexica had their empires last in prominence for only about one hundred years each, the Maya Empire was in power for about six hundred years (around 300–900 CE). Most amazingly, they managed to endure for such a long time amid seemingly incessant internal conflicts and warfare.

The thing to keep in mind about the Maya (especially in how they differ from the Inca or Mexica) is that they were never a united empire with a central government. Rather, they more resembled the city-states of Mesopotamia or ancient Greece wherein a single city acted autonomously as a sovereign state that just so happened to have similar linguistic, orthographic, cultural, and spiritual beliefs with other cities in the same geographic region. This held many advantages on helping them endure for so long, most especially since there was no central city or king that their enemies (or themselves) could conquer that would bring the whole thing down. However, the lack of a strong central government and lack of unity among the various cities also meant more frequent and violent in-fighting amongst each other.[242]

Mesoamerican Star Wars

Of all the Maya conflicts, the star wars are, perhaps, the best examples of how spirituality, practicality, and imperialism all meshed together. The

---

241   Christopher Minster, "Hernan Cortes and His Tlaxcalan Allies," ThoughtCo., October 1, 2019, https://www.thoughtco.com/hernan-cortes-and-his -tlaxcalan-allies-2136523; "This Day in History: Aztec Capital Falls to Cortés," History, updated August 11, 2020, https://www.history.com/this -day-in-history/aztec-capital-falls-to-cortes.

242   Cogito, "Rise of the Maya," Kings and Generals, July 12, 2018, YouTube, 15:23, https://www.youtube.com/watch?v=sK9yv5wAoY0.

name of these wars comes from the glyph used in the Maya writing system to describe them (which showed a distinctive planetary star in it), and because the Maya *had* a writing system (the only native peoples in the Americas currently known to have had a fully developed writing system prior to European arrival), their inter-fighting and spiritual history comes to us from their own hand, unadulterated by Spanish monks, soldiers, or settlers.

These star wars were periodic military campaigns that coincided with the astronomical movements of the planet Venus. You see, to the Maya, Venus was the celestial body associated with war (so much so that when the glyph for "Venus" was written in battle records, it was Maya shorthand for "total destruction"), and so military conquests were scheduled around the transit of Venus to better be in sacred alignment with the war planet's military influence. For example, when Venus was in its "evening phase" (visible in the early evening twilight), this was seen as an auspicious omen for a military victory, and thus many of the major Maya star wars coincided with when Venus was in its "evening phase."[243]

Regardless of religious Venusian blessings, the reasons the Maya went on military campaigns were always practical. Unlike the Inca and Mexica, religious or spiritual motives didn't really factor into being justifiable reasons for conquest. Nevertheless, because Maya military campaigns were heavily coordinated around the spiritual transit of celestial bodies, religious priest-astronomers were usually in charge of making all the plans for the entire campaign, right town to battle strategy. So, in a way, even if spirituality wasn't a *reason* for war, it pretty much dictated everything else about it.[244]

---

243 Erik Vance, "Have We Been Misreading a Crucial Maya Codex for Centuries?" *National Geographic*, August 23, 2016, https://www.nationalgeographic.com /news/2016/08/maya-calendar-dresden-codex-venus-tables-archaeology -science/; Simon Martin and Nikolai Grube, *Chronicle of the Maya Kings and Queens: Deciphering the Dynasties of the Ancient Maya* (London: Thames & Hudson, 2000), n.p.

244 Maria C. Gomez, "Maya Religion," World History Encyclopedia, July 29, 2015, https://www.worldhistory.org/Maya_Religion/.

Leagues of Their Own

When it came to the actual fighting, Maya warriors often formed leagues composed of many city-states working together in a temporary alliance of self-protection. This helped to prevent wars because even if Venus was right in that sweet spot in the sky, rarely was your army going to have only one enemy on which to focus; you had to take into account all the other city-states that were members of whatever united league your enemy was in at the time. Humans being humans, though, war still happened, but even if the biggest, baddest leagues in all Maya culture declared war on one another, the duration of the campaigns were often very short affairs.

They were short for practical reasons more so than spiritual ones because the environment just didn't allow for extensive campaigning. The Maya lived in thick, swampy jungle that was hard to traverse, and with the lack of pack animals (like horses) and lack of rotary transportation equipment (like carts), all supplies for the entire campaign had to be manually carried by the warriors themselves (porters were often also used, but even then, it would get to a point where you'd have to bring along more porters just to carry enough supplies for the original porters, and so on). A war campaign beyond two weeks' marching distance from one's city-state was just not feasible or worth it. Thus, Maya warfare was a short, nearby, secular affair, albeit always strategized by the religious elite.[245]

Latin American Takeaway:
REVERSAL OF FORTUNE

The wheel of fortune is always turning, and whether you're standing triumphantly upon its uppermost arc or being painfully crushed beneath its lowermost curve, it won't last. This is a bitter lesson people often forget, generation after generation. Our human tendency to observe what is around us and assume "This is how it'll always be" tends to skew our vision into the future. It's an oppressively disempowering thing to believe

---

245 Cogito, "Maya Star War: Tikal—Calakmul War," Kings and Generals, July 26, 2018, YouTube, 16:08, https://www.youtube.com/watch?v=heeOSwoBOjk.

when we're going through a time of severe troubles, and it's a dangerously optimistic thing to believe when we're in a time of peace and power.

For the Mexica, their culture lived through a complete rotation of the wheel of fortune. Starting off as a wandering band of persecuted refugees from northern Mexico, they settled a new homeland and, through severe violence and merciless brutality, became the most powerful empire in the region. They were on top of the world, their rule was universal law, and no one came close to threatening them thanks to the overbearing power of their military.

Thinking they were untouchable and that these days of glory would last into forever, they saw no need to show kindness or mercy toward anyone. However, when the unexpected happened (a small band of Spanish warriors arriving), their conquered and oppressed subjects joined forces with these unforeseen strangers to successfully accomplish the unthinkable: the fall of the Aztec Empire. With that, the Mexica once again found themselves back at the bottom, crushed under the same wheel of fortune upon which they had previously stood as kings.

But what if the Mexica had not assumed that their absolute rule was going to last forever? What if the Mexica understood that a reversal of fortune is a real possibility for every person, empire, and culture? Would they have been more merciful in their rule?

After all, the various people we manipulate, betray, mistreat, and step on to climb the ladder of success and victory are the same people we will see again on our inevitable descent downward. If they wanted to, they have the ability to catch us or at least soften our impact upon the hard ground...but have we given them any reason to do so during our ascent to and time at the top?

So, for your takeaway challenge here, train yourself to become aware that no victory or defeat lasts forever, and a reversal of fortune awaits commoner, emperor, and warrior alike. Also be sure to be kind on your ascent upward and during your time at the top. You may be the biggest, baddest, most influential activist, social media influencer, or magical practitioner around, but if you rose to that position through the stepping on of others or use your apex clout to dismiss, harm, or invalidate those beneath you, then beware. Although they might not have the power to bring you down right now, they certainly won't be there to help you keep your balance or defend you on your descent as the wheel of fortune continues to roll forward.

Deities & Legends

BULUC CHABTAN

Buluc Chabtan (historically known as "God F" due to the Maya writing system not having been deciphered when archaeologists were needing to categorize their finds, and so the gods were just given a distinctive letter by which to differentiate them) is the intense Maya deity of war, violence, and sudden or unexpected death. Despite not being an admired or favorite deity of the Maya, he was nonetheless frequently worshipped out of fear as a tactic to curry favor and endear themselves to his good side. Warriors prayed to him for success in battle, but everyone also prayed to him so as to not unexpectedly drop dead, suffer from violence, or become an unlucky fatality of war.

He was often accompanied by a Maya death deity, *Ah Puch*, and so wherever "war" went, "death" often followed. Meanwhile, in nonmilitary affairs, Buluc Chabtan's sacred day was the seventh day of each month, and on that day a stag or a human would be sacrificed to him (especially an enemy prisoner of war if one was available). Though unlike the honor it was to be a sacrifice to the other gods, his sadism and brutality made being sacrificed to him unwanted and greatly feared.[246]

HUITZILOPOCHTLI

Although many gods in the Mexica pantheon had warrior and battle aspects to them, as befitting a culture that glorified militarism, it was

---

246 Daniel Collazos, "Buluc Chabtan," Mitos, Leyendas Y Símbolos, July 23, 2019, https://mitoyleyenda.com/mitologia/maya/buluc-chabtan/; Austin Cline, "Buluc Chabtan: Mayan God of War," Learn Religions, July 22, 2017, https://www.learnreligions.com/buluc-chabtan-buluc-chabtan-god-of-war-250382.

Huitzilopochtli who was the official god of war (as well as the sun, the Aztec capital city of Tenochtitlan, hummingbirds, and more). Due to his immense popularity, he takes part in many myths, but one of the most famous was in the founding myth of the Aztec Empire itself. According to legends, it was believed that he guided the refugee Mexica people on where to found the capital city of their future empire by telling them (in dreams) that the location would be where an eagle could be seen eating a snake from atop a cactus that had grown out of a rock (both the foundation myth of Mexico City and the origins of the central emblem on the modern Mexican flag).[247]

Originally, Huitzilopochtli was a minor hunting deity back when the Mexica were a band of nomadic refugees from the north, but once they settled down and started an empire based on military conquest, he gained more martial aspects and more popularity to the point where he was promoted as chief deity. In fact, the plumage with which he was often depicted (due to his patronage of hummingbirds) became a symbol of nobility and status in the Aztec empire as the upper classes began wearing ornate feathers on their person and clothing so as to look more like him, or at least in the style of him.[248]

The month sacred to Huitzilopochtli closely coincided with our modern month of December, during which the people celebrated his most important festivals and celebrations. In today's Catholic Mexico, December is synonymous with Jesus Christ's birthday month and a days-long celebration called *Las Posadas* (literally "the inns," a nine-day festival wherein each night local children reenact the Gospel story of the wanderings of Joseph and the heavily pregnant Virgin Mary for a place to stay the night and of their eventual lodging in a barn wherein Jesus was born).

247 Wu Mingren, "Huitzilopochtli: The Hummingbird War God at the Forefront of the Aztec Pantheon," Ancient Origins, updated July 25, 2018, https://www .ancient-origins.net/myths-legends-americas/huitzilopochtli-0010426#main -content.

248 Nicoletta Maestri and K. Kris Hirst, "Huitzilopochtli," ThoughtCo., updated October 18, 2019, https://www.thoughtco.com/huitzilopochtli-aztec-god-of -the-sun-171229.

The reason why this ritualized, inn-seeking story of *Las Posadas* is so heavily emphasized in Mexican culture (in comparison to the rest of the Catholic world that venerates the same Gospels), is due to it being a replacement ritual for the days-long Mexica celebration in honor of Huitzilopochtli's winter solstice birthday. Yes, much like Our Lady of Guadalupe being a Catholic appropriation of the Mexica "Mother Earth" goddess *Tonantzin*, so, too, is *Las Posadas* a Catholic appropriation of a birthday party ritual in honor of the Mexica war god, Huitzilopochtli.[249]

VICHAMA

To the Inca, Vichama (alternately called "Atipa") was the god of war and vengeance who created the sexes and the patriarchal, oligarchic class stratification of humankind. All of these associations come from the epic tale of his birth, and though there are many versions of this legend (all of which vary in regard to important plot points), a basic retelling goes something like this:

After having created the first man and woman on earth, Pachakamaq (the primal deity who created all of existence, alternatively known from other legends as Viracocha) soon became disinterested with these first humans and set about creating and paying more attention to new ones. The first man eventually died, and the first woman, in her grief and in knowing Pachakamaq no longer cared about her, asked the sun to do something to ease her loneliness. So, the sun impregnated her with his rays, but this enraged Pachakamaq (because the sun was stepping into *his* dominion of creation). Summarily, Pachakamaq killed the baby once it was born, but the sun later created a new baby to give to the mother fashioned from the umbilical cord of the murdered baby. This *second* baby was Vichama.

As Vichama grew older, he left his mother to start his own life as an adult. With him away, Pachakamaq saw his opportunity to take revenge on Vichama's mother for having deliberately gotten pregnant again against his wishes all those years ago, and so he murdered her. Upon hearing of this, Vichama swore revenge, which he eventually enacted through the killing of all the other humans Pachakamaq had made by turning them into stone. This first-of-its-kind mass genocide retribution led to him being given the divine dominion over war and vengeance.

Now with no humans left in the world, Vichama asked his father (the sun) to recreate a new humanity not fashioned by Pachakamaq's malice. The sun obliged and laid a golden egg, a silver egg, and a bronze egg all from which the modern human race emerged. Out of the golden egg came the male nobles. Out of the silver egg came the wives of the nobles. And out of the bronze egg came everyone else. Thus, the Inca understood themselves to be the stratified children of the sun, justified men's superiority over women, and regarded unequal disparity between the aristocracy and the plebian masses as sacred, all thanks to the vengeance of the god of war.[250]

250 "Pachakamaq y Vichama, una historia de venganza," *Un rincón en la historia,* March 27, 2018, https://unrinconenlahistoria.wordpress.com/2018/03/27 /pachakamaq-y-vichama-una-historia-de-venganza/; "El Mito de Vichama," *Inti Land Tours,* accessed July 5, 2020, https://unrinconenlahistoria.wordpress.com/.

23

NATIVE NORTH AMERICA

Cultural

CENTRAL PLAINS & WESTERN DESERTS

A region of the world made internationally famous through the western-genre films of directors like John Ford and Sam Peckinpah, the tallgrass prairies and sagebrush-carpeted mountains of the Central Plains and American West have imbued a sense of magic and wonder toward these places in modern imagination. However, the unfortunately maligned depictions of the native peoples of these regions and their violent clashes with the U.S. cavalry in these same films have also influenced modern imagination. Though these clashes were, indeed, violent, they were resistance efforts to defend ancient homelands from merciless invaders, and like the resistance movements in South America, the ones here were also aided by ancestral spirituality and ritual.

Many Happy Returns

Trekking up from Latin America into the expansive plains of Texas, Oklahoma, and bits of Kansas, Colorado, and New Mexico, we find ourselves in Comanche territory. The Comanche peoples are not a single organized tribe, but rather a generalized grouping of many tribes who all share similar (though not the exact same) culture, language, and spiritual beliefs. One such common belief was in the accumulation of *puha* ("medicine power"). This power is similar to the Polynesian concept of "mana" we explored earlier in the sense that the more spiritual puha one had, the more potence one possessed in clout, prestige, physical power, and spiritual command. Puha was present in all things, but two specific plants were regarded as having intrinsically high levels of puha: peyote and cedar.

Cedar, in particular, was the favored medicine during times of war and used to bestow power and spiritual blessings to Comanche warriors returning home from war (in traditional ceremonies that still continue to the present day for modern Comanche military vets). In these Cedar Ceremonies, a feather is used to waft cedar smoke onto the returning warriors so as to spiritually counteract the horrific memories of things they had seen and bore witness to in battle. Its medicine focuses on mitigating the effects of what we would now call post-traumatic stress disorder (PTSD), and it did so by specifically targeting any negative thoughts or nightmares the returning warrior might have lingering in their psyche after coming home.[251]

Aside from the Cedar Ceremony, the enactment of other welcome-home war rituals depended upon the success of the returning Comanche warriors. If the warriors were successful in their military endeavor, a special victory ceremony would be held, most notably the "Shakedown Dance" wherein women of the tribe danced in praise of the returned warriors and,

---

251 "Comanche Tribal Members Perform Ceremony for Troops," ABC 7 News: KSWO, Gray Media Group, updated May 24, 2010, https://www.kswo.com /story/12478667/comanche-tribal-members-perform-ceremony-for-troops/.

in return, the warriors would gift these women who were performing the sacred dance with gifts from their spoils of war. If, however, the returning warriors had been unsuccessful or lost a man in battle, there would be no celebratory ceremonies or rituals, and the warriors would quietly return to civilian life without much pomp or acknowledgment of their failure.[252]

Ghost Dance I: The Desert Genesis

Moving up into the high desert of Nevada's Great Basin, we find the origins of the mystical Ghost Dance that reignited a revolution against U.S. imperialism over native peoples. Originally, the Ghost Dance was a late-1860s Northern Paiute ceremonial ritual developed by a respected seer named Wodziwob who claimed that if his people would perform a specifically choreographed dance as taught to him from his visionary journeys in the spirit realm, then this kinetic ritual would raise their ancestral dead (a particularly timely message since an epidemic had just recently killed a significant swath of their population).

This original Ghost Dance movement eventually died out, but it was revived twenty years later in the late-1880s when a messianic Paiute "prophet" named Wovoka (who incorporated Protestant and Mormon beliefs into his mystical world view) claimed that if his people would perform a version of the Ghost Dance specifically choreographed exactly how God (yes, the Christian God) had revealed it to him, it would not only resurrect their dead ancestors, but it would also supernaturally force all the white invaders in western Nevada to leave, thus creating a new golden age of Paiute self-sovereignty. (Mind you, this is the same prophet who believed himself to literally be the second coming of Jesus Christ and even had self-inflicted stigmata.)[253]

252 Gregory R. Campbell, "Chapter 7: Comanche Historical Ethnography and Ethnohistory," National Park Service Ethnobotany Report, University of Montana Department of Anthropology, 2004, http://files.cfc.umt.edu/cesu /NPS/UMT/2004/Campbell_Etnobotony%20Report/chapterseven.pdf.

253 "Ghost Dance," Encyclopedia Britannica, updated March 2, 2021, https:// www.britannica.com/topic/Ghost-Dance.

Ghost Dance II: The Prairie Apocalypse

Despite its very aggressive and sensationalist message of how this magical ritual would force a mass exodus of white settlers from the region, Wovoka insisted that this be a peaceful movement (or, rather, Wovoka insisted that *God* insisted on pacifism). The magic would do all the work, while anyone who acted violently toward whites would risk compromising the magic. However, word of this Paiute Ghost Dance spiritual resistance movement spread to other First Nations peoples across North America who were in the midst of active, violent oppression by a post-Civil War U.S. government, and like a game of "Telephone," the original message of peace and pacifism became lost along the way the further it was passed along.

Most notably, the Sioux and the Lakota of the Northern Great Plains became renewed with resistance vigor upon hearing of this Ghost Dance that the Paiute out in Nevada were doing to kick out their white oppressors. The Sioux understanding of this ceremonial ritual (or at least the understanding that became most popular) was that, if correctly performed, it would bring about an apocalyptic annihilation of all white people (not just kick them out but eradicate them completely). Once word of this Sioux version of the Ghost Dance reached white settlers, they became frightened as all hell, and this fear of the Sioux Ghost Dance had a ripple impact in instigating the massacre of the Lakota at Wounded Knee.

After this defining slaughter at Wounded Knee, the Ghost Dance movement lost momentum. The people felt betrayed by Wovoka due to the Ghost Dance ultimately not resulting in native self-sovereignty and due to the notorious ineffectiveness of the protective "Ghost Shirts" that he promised, if worn, would make the wearer impenetrable to bullets. Furthermore, as an unfortunate side effect of the Christian overtones and evangelistic delivery of Wovoka's Ghost Dance to these various tribes, it subsequently assisted in helping to convert the native people who believed most fervently in it to Christianity and to assimilate into white culture after the fact.[254]

EAST COAST & ARCTIC NORTH

Unlike the invaders from across the ocean, the native peoples of the American East Coast and Canadian Arctic often held strict codes of honor when it came to war and self-defense. Battles had to be fought on the spiritual plane just as much as the physical one, and the things one did to win a war often had ripple effects into the spiritual world. But despite having these extra complications to consider that European colonists often did not have to concern themselves with, it also allowed the native peoples of these regions additional avenues of attack via the spiritual world that would take their monotheistic enemies by surprise.

Spiritual Bloodstains

Among many of the First Nations Native American tribes of the U.S. Southeast, fighting and warfare were not regarded as all-out, anything-goes, the-ends-justify-the-means affairs. Playing a big part in why peoples of this region were extremely conscious toward reining in the cruelest and most brutal aspects of war was their spirituality. Details, of course, vary from tribe to tribe, but in general, the soldiers of these tribes of the Southeastern woodlands needed to remain spiritually clean throughout the conflict lest they allow their souls to become impure and tainted by crossing the line on what was spiritually taboo in war.

Before any military campaign, it was important that a warrior be as spiritually pure and clean possible. So, for the native peoples living in what is now generally defined as the Southeastern United States, it was common for many tribes to hold days-long departure ceremonies wherein the warriors isolated themselves from society in their chief's home, fasting and drinking

---

254 Catherine S. Fowler and Don D. Fowler, "Great Basin Indian: Religion and Ritual," Encylopædia Britannica, updated November 16, 2020, https://www .britannica.com/topic/Great-Basin-Indian/Religion-and-ritual; James Mooney, *The Ghost-Dance Religion and Wounded Knee* (New York: Dover Publications, 1973), n.p.; "Ghost Dance," Encylopædia Britannica.

herbal potions to spiritually cleanse themselves for the battles ahead. The more spiritually "pure" one was, the more preternaturally protected and physically potent they were believed to be in battle.

Within war itself, two taboos in particular were the most egregious and damning toward one's spiritual purity: having sex and killing another human. The sexual abstinence was, arguably, the easier of the two to avoid, and its adherence led to significantly lower incidents of enemy women being raped by the Southeastern Native Americans in comparison to the European and American settlers in the region. The killing part proved more difficult since, undeniably, killing is a major component to war. Taking a human life, even if justified in the context of self-defense and resisting oppression, stains the killer's spirit. Thus the purifying departure ritual helped to mitigate the severity of spiritual staining by giving each warrior a pure slate on which to start the campaign.

Because of the inevitable killing that comes part and parcel with engaging in war, many tribes of the Southeastern woodlands also conducted purifying rituals upon their warriors' return to help undo, as much as possible, the spiritual staining they received. These rituals mirrored the purifying departure rituals except women of the tribe were encouraged to help motivate the returning warriors who were quarantined in the chief's home by singing songs to them from outside. Still, because of the arduous austerity involved in the pre- and post-rituals of purification from battle and the inevitable stains on one's spiritual soul, war itself was never an ideal option among Southeastern tribes nor an endeavor set about capriciously.[255]

Matrilineal Mourning Wars Revisited

From the perspective of matrilineal tribes further up in the Northeastern U.S., the concept of war was not always one of conquest and self-defense but also one of filling a spiritual void in the tribe left by the untimely death

---

255 Wayne E. Lee, "Peace Chiefs and Blood Revenge: Patterns of Restraint in Native American Warfare, 1500–1800," *The Journal of Military History* 71, no. 3 (July 2007): 701–741, https://www.sjsu.edu/people/ruma.chopra/courses /H173_MW_S12/s2/Lee_Patterns_warfare_Indians.pdf.

of someone. These are often post-historically given the name "mourning wars" and were most famously waged among the Iroquois whose confederacy of Mohawk, Oneida, Onondaga, Seneca, Cayuga, and Tuscarora tribes lived on the vast swath of land in what is now considered Upstate New York and had a sphere of influence stretching from Illinois and Kentucky to Ontario and Québec. And while we've explored these spiritual mourning wars in my previous book *Morbid Magic* from their mourning perspective, we're going to revisit them again here from a war perspective.

It is believed that when an Iroquois tribesperson is murdered, a certain spiritual imbalance is left in the wake of this death, and it is up to the ruling matriarch to return balance to her tribe. If the killer is a fellow tribesperson, then financial reparations have to be made to energetically counterbalance the loss, but if the killer is not from the same tribe, then there is no way to internally balance out the wrong that has been done. This is when a mourning war is declared, and its intention is to refill the spiritual and demographic void left by the murder through taking a hostage from the offending tribe and assimilating them into the victim's family.

Although called a "war," this was really just a one-off kidnapping mission. The tribe's warriors would seek to kidnap a member of the killer's family and bring them back to the matriarch of the victim's family. What next awaited the kidnapped person was entirely dependent upon the grief of this matriarch.

If the matriarch (after talking with the hostage) was still too engulfed in her grief and sorrow or committed to vengeance, the hostage would be tortured before being forcibly adopted into the matriarch's family (effectively replacing the deceased victim in reparation and restoring energetic balance to the tribe). If, however, the matriarch was able enough to feel sympathy for this kidnapped person (who was often personally innocent, their only crime being a relative of the actual murderer), they would be spared the torture and lovingly welcomed as a new adopted member of the matriarch's family. Regardless of whether the matriarch chose vengeance or mercy, the kidnapped would never be allowed to return home since their forced adoption was the only thing that could return energetic balance back to the tribe.[256]

Arctic Astral Attacks

Warfare, oppression, and humans hating other humans whom they deem "different" from themselves are never isolated occurrences, and when such evil happens anywhere, it affects everyone everywhere as its injuries ripple out all over the globe. For the Inuit peoples of North America whose homelands stretch from western Alaska to eastern Greenland, the icy cold remoteness of their expansive tundra and boreal forests does not protect them from or make them immune to the militaristic depravity of humanity that occurs elsewhere on earth. However, just because oppression and invasions are happening in lands far away from them doesn't mean they can't be allies in the war effort against such evil, and, in fact, Inuit shamans have actively helped peoples' resistance efforts throughout the world thanks to their command over the magic of astral projection.

To the various Inuit tribes here along the Arctic Circle, having purposeful and controlled out-of-body experiences that allow one's soul to travel anywhere in the universe (including spirit realms) is not unusual. Most commonly, this astral projection is done to seek out valuable information not available in their immediate community (such as how to heal a sick person whose ailment has no known cures, how to end a string of bad luck in hunting, etc.), and it is intended for the greater good of the tribe, not so much for personal benefit. However, in terms of human conflict, if news of peoples being oppressed outside the community reached the ears of tribal

---

256 Michele Meleen, "Native American Death Rituals," Love To Know, accessed July 10, 2020, https://dying.lovetoknow.com/native-american-death-rituals; Margaret Haig Roosevelt Sewall Ball, "Grim Commerce: Scalps, Bounties, and the Transformation of Trophy-Taking in the Early American Northeast, 1450–1770," University of Colorado Department of History, 2013, https://scholar.colorado.edu/concern/graduate_thesis_or_dissertations/c821gj859.

leaders, they could deploy warriors to the front lines (and behind enemy lines) through this same power.[257]

One of the most notable recorded instances of this was during WWII. Hearing of the ongoing fascist atrocities of the Nazis in Europe pained the Inuit community living on the tiny island of Igloolik in the Canadian arctic, and in early 1945, they grew frustrated with how the anti-fascist Allies had still not yet put an end to the Nazi leader. So, the more emboldened members of the community decided that if they could astrally project their spirits into Nazi headquarters, they could act as stealth assassins for the Allies and put an end to Hitler and his evil regime. The effects and details of this astral assassination mission are not fully known, including whether or not the tribespeople on Igloolik went through with this mission; *however*, coincidentally in spring of that same year, Hitler was, indeed, dead, killed by his own hand. Did these anti-fascist Inuit allies help bring this about through their influence in the astral realm? Anything's possible...[258]

Native North American Takeaway:
DEHUMANIZER

One of the most important lessons a warrior must learn (lest it destroy our humanity and doom to failure the cause for which we took up the mantle of warrior in the first place) is the ability to recognize the hatred within ourselves and root it out before it *becomes* us. Many "negative" emotions are all right to have because they motivate us as warriors: anger inspires the desire for change, vengeance inspires action, even rage has its place to give that extra "oomph" into specific endeavors...but hate...hate is only a corrosive, dehumanizing vitriol that consumes and eats away at whoever possesses it, even if it is justified hate.

---

257 Daniel Merkur, *Becoming Half Hidden: Shamanism and Initiation Among the Inuit* (New York: Routledge, 2013), n.p.

258 Zacharias Kunuk, Norman Cohn, and Pauloosie Qulitalik, "Nunavut (Our Land) Episode 4: Tugaliaq (Ice Blocks)," Igloolik Isuma Productions, 1995, 28:55, http://www.isuma.tv/isuma-productions/tugaliaq-ice-blocks.

Many Native American tribes are in this precarious position of being fully justified in so-called "negative" emotions for all the centuries of continued injustice from which they and their people still suffer. They are, indeed, rightly justified in any feelings of hate they have toward past and present systemic oppression, but that is the one emotion that always leads to self-ruin, little gain, and a loss of humanity. If left unchecked and allowed to fester within our psyche, regardless of culture, it becomes an unspoken legacy of hatred passed down from generation to generation wherein children learn to develop and accept that uncomfortable bitter feeling in their gut for "others" as a natural, normal, and acceptable part of life. (One First Nations example is the still ongoing Cree vs. Inuit feud of distrust and derision toward one another due to cultural misunderstandings that happened centuries ago.)[259]

A battle, protest, ritual, or any other social justice endeavor enacted out of a sense of righting wrongs, establishing equality, or lifting up the oppressed is a *very* different beast than those same endeavors being enacted out of a sense of hatred. A fight *for* something is inspiring and magical, but a fight *against* something is embittering and never-ending (just as being "pro-peace" and "anti-war" are completely different mindsets).

When you take action based on that feeling of hate, you think you are in control and using it as a tool, but you aren't. Hate has become you, and it rules you. You may believe you're using your hatred as fuel for your crusade, but when hate for your enemy is all you talk about, speak about, dream about, and dedicate all your human energy toward, hate is who's *really* in control … you are no longer human, merely a body being wielded by hate.

Because you are not in control, you cannot make good decisions on the battlefield, in online discussions, at protest marches, or even in spellwork. And when your enemy points to you, singling you out (and thereby the cause you stand for) as hateful and primarily motivated out of a desire for

259 Zacharias Kunuk and Neil Diamond, *Inuit Cree Reconciliation*, Kingulliit Productions, 2013, 46:34, http://www.isuma.tv/en/InuitCreeReconciliation /movie.

destruction more so than creation, they'll be right, and you'll lose allies and popular support, even if your feelings are fully justified.

So, for your final takeaway challenge here, search deep in your soul for hatred and remove it at all costs. Rarely are we transparently honest with ourselves and can admit that we have feelings of "hate" toward anyone. Although we might harbor hatred within us, we've learned to convince ourselves that the emotion isn't really hatred or that, at the very least, it's justified. "That's just how those people are." "It's always been like this." "Everyone I know agrees with me." "This is what I was taught and how I was raised." These are all latent forms of learned hatred, and hate by any other name still smells as foul and rotten.

"Negative" emotions can be good, but never hate. If you are joining a movement or beginning a ritual out of hatred or being "against" or "anti" something (as opposed to "pro" whatever its positive opposite is), whether you realize it now or not, you've fertilized the seeds of your own undoing. So, examine your motivations for all the things you do. You may, indeed, be fully justified, but if hate for the enemy is what's motivating you more than the manifestation of a better world for the oppressed, then God bless the cause for which you fight because you may just be what unintentionally brings it down…if you live long enough to see the consequences of your actions, that is.

Deities & Legends

TOYPURINA

Toypurina was the medicine woman of the Tongva tribe who became a revolutionary icon when, in 1785, she led her people in armed resistance against the Spanish Franciscan missionaries and their infamous string of missions along the California coast stretching from San Diego to Sonoma. Specifically, her revolt was targeted at Mission San Gabriel, which was erected on stolen Tongva land in Southern California as a religious way-point for the newly founded city of Los Angeles.

Daughter of the tribe's chief, Toypurina held great political power throughout what is now the Los Angeles Basin, but her role as medicine woman for the tribe granted her even more influence and clout since she also held spiritual sway within the region as well. Extremely intelligent, she saw the Franciscan priests and monks arriving in her territory for what they were: Spain's spiritual shock-troop army sent ahead of colonists to subdue the local populations. Often more so than in other Spanish religious settlements, those in California (led by the fanatically zealous, and now, as of 2015, canonized Catholic "saint" Junípero Serra) were particularly brutal since Serra was of the opinion that only the natives' souls mattered, not their bodies. Thus, his missionaries could be as sadistic as they liked toward the native peoples, and if a native person died an early death, all the better because it meant their soul arrived in heaven that much sooner.[260]

In addition to brutal physical treatment and exploitive slave labor, the missionaries controlled the lives of the Tongva people through coercive baptisms and land privatization that left the non-baptized Tongva unable to feed themselves. It all came to a head, however, when the missionaries officially prohibited all Tongva from performing ritual ceremonial dances. Having stepped into dictating the traditions her people's spiritual life on top of their physical one was the last straw, and the twenty-five-year-old Toypurina rallied a massive armed rebellion against the missionaries to tear down Mission San Gabriel.

The strategy was that Toypurina would utilize her divine influence in the spirit realm to magically immobilize the missionaries while her soldiers went in and did the physical damage. However, the assault on Mission San Gabriel was put down just as quickly as it started thanks to the betrayal by the converted Tongva people who endeared themselves to the enemy and told the Spanish of Toypurina's plot. She and her soldiers were arrested, and an inquest ensued wherein she was, again, betrayed by her

260 Caitlin Harrington, "The Lesser-Told Story of the California Missions," Hoodline, March 20, 2016, https://hoodline.com/2016/03/the-lesser-told-story-of-the-california-missions/.

people and outed as the rebellion's leader (the leader being the one person the missionaries could legally execute). Toypurina courageously refused to deny her role as leader of the rebellion and expressed no guilt, shame, or repentance for any of it.

Still, Toypurina was clever, and she managed to avoid execution, first by requesting that she be baptized so as to be able to enter heaven (a bureaucratic process in the Catholic faith, which took some time) and then by marrying a landed Spaniard who ensured her protection. Eventually, she moved to Northern California with her husband and lived a full life. Nowadays, Toypurina is immortalized in street art and murals throughout Los Angeles, especially by the Chicanx and Latinx communities of the city who empathize with her heroic action and rebellion against oppression.[261]

TWIN WAR GODS OF
THE PUEBLO PEOPLES

In the deserts of the Southwest, the preeminent war gods of the Pueblo peoples were often a pair of twin boys. For context, it's important to understand that the "Pueblo" peoples is not a single tribe in and of itself, but rather, it's a generalized term to describe various tribes in the U.S. Southwest who all share a similar culture, mythos, and agricultural practices, though each tribe has its own very different language and important nuances in their culture, spirituality, and diet (similar to how the descriptor "Celts" is used to label a vast array of different-yet-similar peoples throughout Europe).

In what is now known as Arizona, one of the Pueblo tribes who worship the twin war gods is the Hopi. To the Hopi, the twins' names are Pö-ökang-hoya and Palö-ngao-hoya, and they are the grandchildren of Spider Woman (an "earth goddess" archetypal deity, sometimes called Spider

---

261 Maria John, "Toypurina: A Legend Etched in the Landscape of Los Angeles," PBS: KCET, May 15, 2014, https://www.kcet.org/history-society/toypurina-a -legend-etched-in-the-landscape-of-los-angeles; Cecilia Rasmussen, "Shaman and Freedom-Fighter Led Indians' Mission Revolt," Los Angeles Times, June 10, 2001, https://www.latimes.com/archives/la-xpm-2001-jun-10-me-8853-story .html.

Grandmother). Being young boys, they have a reputation for being a bit mischievous, but they are, nonetheless, supremely skilled warriors. It's believed that in threatening times, the twins will become more serious and, under the guidance of their grandmother (who keeps them in line), will help protect the Hopi people.[262]

Another well-known Pueblo tribe to have these twin boys as their deities of war are the Zuni of what is now known as New Mexico. Unlike their Hopi counterparts, these Zuni twins were much more severe in nature, being created by Sun Father to specifically protect the Zuni from all that intend to do them harm. Armed with lightning and celebrated during the winter solstice, these twins are highly revered, so much so that it is considered offensive to ever dress as them or imitate them in any way, even out of intended respect in a sacred ceremony.[263]

WHITE BUFFALO CALF WOMAN

White Buffalo Calf Woman is a deity of protection and peace who exists in the mythos of a number of Native American tribes of the Great Plains, though she is arguably best known to outsiders through the lore of the Lakota. She plays a major role in many Lakota myths and even continues to be an important figure, albeit she's now heavily syncretized with Christian aspects from centuries of evangelism and religious conversion.

To the Lakota, buffalo (or, more accurately, "bison" since buffalo are only native to Africa and Asia) were supremely important because they provided many of the essentials necessary for human survival on the plains (food, clothing, shelter, tools, etc.). But it was White Buffalo Calf Woman who taught them that not just the buffalo but all of nature was sacred and

262 H. R. Voth, *The Traditions of the Hopi* (Chicago, Field Columbian Museum, 1905), https://www.sacred-texts.com/nam/hopi/toth/index.htm; Don Talayesva, "The Giant and the Twin War Gods," *The Unwritten Literature of the Hopi*, ed. Hattie Greene Lockett (Tucson: University of Arizona Press, 1933), https://www.gutenberg.org/files/15888/15888-h/15888-h.htm#The_Giant.

263 "One of the Twin Gods of War [Ahayuta]," The Archive for Research in Archetypal Symbolism, accessed July 26, 2020, https://aras.org/one-twin -gods-war-ahayuta.

that even the animals, plants, and the earth should be treated with dignity and respect on par with humans.[264]

To help maintain dignity for all life, she endowed the Lakota with the sacred peace pipe as a divine tool with which to end wars by ceremonially officializing peace treaties. According to legend, she taught the Lakota many rituals and prayers to help maintain peace, but before she left back into the spiritual realm in the form of a white buffalo calf, she promised to return to the Lakota some day and bring with her peace on earth (a storyline co-opted by Christian missionaries to liken her to a Christlike prophet whose anticipated Second Coming conveniently fell in line with Christian teachings of Christ's return on Judgment Day).[265]

264 Mindy Weisberger, "Bison vs. Buffalo: What's the Difference?" Live Science, December 23, 2017, https://www.livescience.com/32115-bison-vs-buffalo -whats-the-difference.html; "White Buffalo Calf Woman," Encyclopedia.com, August 7, 2020, https://www.encyclopedia.com/environment/encyclopedias -almanacs-transcripts-and-maps/white-buffalo-calf-woman.

265 "Legend of the White Buffalo," Aktá Lakota Museum & Cultural Center, accessed July 26, 2020, http://aktalakota.stjo.org/site/News2?page =NewsArticle&id=8862; Natalia Klimczak, "White Buffalo Calf Woman— Healer, Teacher, and Inspirational Spirit for the Lakota People," Ancient Origins, November 13, 2016, https://www.ancient-origins.net/history-ancient -traditions/white-buffalo-calf-woman-healer-teacher-and-inspirational-spirit -lakota-021067; Shannon Smith, "White Buffalo Calf Woman: The Sacred Lakota Figure Has Evolved Over Time, But She Hasn't Gone Away," Native Daughters, February 2010, https://shannonmariesmith.files.wordpress.com /2010/02/native-daughters-shannon-design.pdf.

24

LATINX & NORTH AMERICAN MAGICAL COMMUNITY

THE STEREOTYPICAL WARRIOR

So far, many of the contemporary warriors we've met throughout our journey have shared with us their advice on how to become and be seen as a more effective warrior, and while that is the very thing most of us are wanting to learn, some of us need help with the exact opposite: how to handle life when all the world seems unable to see the kindness and peacefulness inside you, instead having stereotyped you as an over-aggressive, brutish warrior.

For this unique lesson, I've brought along my friend Luis Carazo, a Colombian-born American SAG-AFTRA actor who has often been typecast as the "tough Latino bad guy" because of his ethnicity and physical appearance. It's quite possible you've already seen him in films and TV since he's been on everything from *Casa de mi Padre* with Will Ferrell, *S.W.A.T.,* *NCIS: Los Angeles, Criminal Minds,* and numerous tabletop RPG streaming shows, most notably as stoic Latino badass "Nines Rodriguez" in the hit series *Vampire: The Masquerade: L.A. By Night.* Hell, he was even the macho "man's man" guy in a number of commercials for the Lowe's hardware franchise … a *very* stereotypical "hypermasculinity" role, which just further emphasizes his typecasting. Take a look at his IMDb page and you'll see what I mean.[266]

Now, I've known Luis personally for a while, and I can tell you that, despite what his typecast filmography may present him as, he's actually a very fun-loving, compassionate optimist with a Paladin spirit who loves befriending elves and dragons, and you can even see this for yourself if you search his name on Twitter or Instagram. So listen well as he gives you some first-person advice on what it's like when life has stereotyped you as an aggressive, "ethnic" brute even though your greatest strength is not in your biceps but in your heart.

> *Dark, swarthy, passionate, fiery. These are some of the ideas or impressions people put on me upon first contact. I admit, there are worse things than having people assume you are fiery and passionate. Some of it is due to ste- reotyping. I am, after all, a Latino male in the U.S., and there is certainly a handful of stereotypical assumptions thrown my way here and there.*
>
> *The biggest negative one is that people often assume that I am not smart. They are surprised to learn that I know things about art, or obscure film and music. I am often told that I am well-spoken as though it was an unexpected surprise. Sometimes people ask me where my accent went. I have had folks try to point out tiny moments in my speech where they think an accent comes out. And I also know that on first impression people think I am quite brooding and stand-offish.*
>
> *All that can certainly be due to some kind of "foreignness" about my appearance that people are perceiving and responding to. It's the kind of nagging thing they can't quite put their finger on about me, like a math*

266 "Luis Carazo," IMDB, www.imdb.me/luiscarazo.

problem they can't quite solve standing in the flesh right before them. And it is the thing that always precedes the inevitable "So, where are you REALLY from?" question.

But maybe some of people's preconceptions of me can be due to other aspects of my appearance (my build, my beard ... haha, you might be surprised about the assumptions people might make about you based on the length and bushiness of your beard. Bushy beard = MAN). So, I guess people sometimes assume I am a not very smart, standoffish meathead that has something foreign about him. Which I find hilarious.

In casting I do sometimes get somewhat pigeonholed as a gangster or drug cartel baddie, but the second I put on a flannel shirt, BOOM I am now stereotyped as a lumberjack cowboy thing. Or as in L.A. By Night, this version of idealized badassery that my character Nines Rodriguez embodies. It's odd how it warps what someone else sees in me. I mean, I have actually had people think I am much taller than I actually am and that my voice is deeper than it actually is. People have assumed I served in the military, assumed I had tattoos.

In real life I am a complete softy, but I have been in fights. I have jumped out of my car to get in a dude's face when I thought they were out of line, I have head-butted somebody at a bar and broken his nose (he had it coming, the bartender even gave me a nod afterward). But I can count those moments on one hand, the moments where I have backed off, backed down, or chickened out will outnumber those. By a lot.

But what I've also done is diffuse tension with compassion. Imagine some dude puffing his chest in a moment of needing to prove himself, but instead of being met back with some "tough guy" attitude, he is met with a calm that isn't threatening or challenging or condescending. I have talked tempers out of people. That is definitely something people don't expect from me, at least people who do not know me well.

I think people are often surprised by my vulnerable and sensitive side. But I think they are even more surprised by my complete ownership of it. I have had people, especially men, say to me that they felt threatened by my willingness to be vulnerable. They usually become reactive towards me because of it, and eventually it melts away as I gain their trust or build a kind of rapport with them. Some of my strongest male friendships in one way, shape, or form had to jump this hurdle in our relationship at one point.

And this aspect also shows up in casting. On occasion, I get to explore a role that appears strong, but in intimate moments gets to show weakness, which of course requires a different kind of strength. Those are some of my favorite, because they feel more human. I guess that feeds into a sort of running theme in my life, people think I am tougher than I actually am, but that idea of toughness gives me an "in" of some sort and the unexpected left hook I throw them is actually from the heart and not at all an actual fist. And the true toughness came to me the day I owned it and stopped apologizing for it. I can't think of anything more personally warrior-esque than that.

—Luis Carazo

BALANCING THE SCALES
THROUGH BRUJERÍA

I know what you're thinking: "This book needs more special guest warriors who are unabashedly all for enacting personal retribution against those who have wronged us," right? Don't worry; I hear you, and that's exactly why I've invited our next warrior here. Not only are you about to get an unapologetic crash course on how Brujería balances out the scales of just comeuppances, but you're also about to be schooled by a Bruja on how Brujería regards the pacifist "harm none" credo of more Wiccan magical traditions.

This Bruja, Katrina Rasbold, is someone I've known for years now, and she has a number of books if you're wanting to learn more spellwork involving such magical retribution. But in addition to being an author, she's also a known public speaker, shop owner, and professional Bruja and healer. And believe me, she definitely knows how to get something done the way it needs to get done in regard to magical manifestations. After all, your enemies and the world's oppressors aren't going to self-handicap themselves by taking the moral high road, and so if you don't want to be at a disadvantage and prefer victory over so-called "honorable" defeat, pay close attention.

In Brujeria, our clients come to us under the cloak of secrecy to solve their problems and tell their children to be good or the Brujas will get them. And guess what? We might. You never know which of the stories are real and which ones are empty threats. We won't get you as children, though. We will wait until you're grown up enough to make mistakes that cause someone to want you out of their life.

My Wiccan friends wince when they visit and see the kinds of spell work I have cooking on the altar for other people. What they don't get is that an attitude of "harm none" comes from a place of tremendous privilege. The intent is admirable, but when it comes to practical application, sometimes you burn down the house and salt the earth to build something better. "Harming none" presumes that you are comfortable taking a repeated beat down and doing nothing about it. Most people are not that Christ-like and that is when they come to me.

My practice is a blend of faith and science. I have faith that God, The Universe, and all that is Divine can use me as a vessel to create change in the life of a person who seeks out my services. Whether I choose to or not depends on how they present their case. The science part is Newton's Third Law of Motion: "For every action, there is an equal and opposite reaction." Actions have consequences.

If you screw over your business partner, leave your long-suffering first wife for the trophy bride of your mid-life crisis dreams, or sleep with your best friend's husband, then I just might be that equal and opposite reaction. Nothing says people cannot be agents of karma, and if I get tapped by the person you harmed to balance the scales on their behalf, then yeah, the Brujas are coming for you ... or at least this one is.

I have no problem holding people accountable for their actions and will gladly stand in front of the right client and go to battle on their behalf. I think back to grade school when the older brothers and sisters would wade in on behalf of the younger ones who could not defend themselves. If I can do that for someone, why would I not? If I walked in on a person harming my kids, my spouse, or one of my friends and I had a weapon available to stop it and chose not to, am I really going to have some kind of moral and ethical crisis over it? No, I am going to act.

There is a reason why we have "DUME" (Death Unto My Enemies) candles, "Destroy Everything" candles, and "Bitch Be Gone" candles. There is a reason why people revere divine figures such as Marta Dominadora (Martha the Dominator), Kali Ma, and Santa Muerte. They are powerful forces in the world that refuse to be oppressed or painted as victims.

Warrior magic is not about drawing in love, light, prosperity, and safety. In a world where people are able and willing to further their own causes by disadvantaging others, we need a counterbalance and that does not always fit into a socially accepted box of defensive magic. Warrior magic shows that sometimes, the best defense is a great offensive, and if I have to be offensive to take care of the people who trust me to take up the battle for them, so be it. I am in it to win it.

—Katrina Rasbold

SPIRITUAL HOUSECLEANING

In war and conflict, oftentimes we humans believe that if attacked, the only way to overcome the attacker is to attack back with more force, and though this is definitely one way to win, it's not the only way. In fact, when faced against a more powerful attacker, it's just not going to be possible for the "weaker" defender to overpower them through direct confrontation. Alternate routes to victory are the only routes to victory in such a case.

This is also true when talking about attacks from spiritual forces and spectral entities. How do you combat against a harmful being from beyond the grave when they have supernatural powers? Well, to help answer this question, I've asked my Navajo friend Brian Simpson to come and give us an example from one of his more memorable encounters in the spirit realm when he banished a ghost who was haunting a mother and her children inside their home. He did this not through direct magical force, but rather, by enlisting the aid of his spirit guides to help provide him with an alternate path to victory.

For those of you not familiar with Brian, he is a Native American from Northern Arizona who practices different forms of spirituality and is trained in different spiritual traditions as well as in his Tribe's ancestral spiritual traditions. If you *are* familiar with him, it's mostly likely through his cult hit YouTube series "Toad and Broom" wherein he's one half of the magical duo sharing advice, tutorials, and stories on how to improve your spellwork and become more effective in your magical endeavors.

In regard to his own magical endeavor of cleansing that haunted house through indirect, albeit very effective, means, well…I'll let him tell you all the details about it himself.

I looked back at my body that was still beating the drum I use for ceremonies; it was a bit unnerving at first when I heard the voice of the disgruntled spirit I had been called to help with. A male spirit approached me, aggressively demanding to know who I was when suddenly one of my guides stood between us to keep the spirit back.

A week prior to this, I had gotten a call asking for my spiritual help. A homeowner had a possible ghost in her house that was scaring her children to the point where the children refused to be inside by themselves because of it. Having accepted, I was now looking at this ghost and asked it, "Who are you?" The male spirit looked at me confused for a second and aggressively responded that he lived there and that this was his house. I asked him what he remembered last, and he told me that a friend came over and they were shooting up together and then he woke up here after he had fallen asleep.

I stood there in the spirit world looking directly at this spirit and trying to quickly think of a solution when I glanced over at my guide and asked it to get someone to help him cross over. My guide left, the spirit and I spoke, and he told me how he was mad because everyone in the house was ignoring him. That's when, suddenly, he noticed a door that was not there before.

We heard a knock from the door, and he asked me what it was. I told him to answer it because it might be for him. As he opened the door, bright light came through; there in the doorframe was a silhouette of a short woman, stocky and wearing a dress. Her hair was tied up in a bun, she wore glasses on her round face. I asked the male spirit who the woman was, and he said that she was his aunt who had passed away when he was a teenager and that he used to run away from home to her house when he was a kid. When she died, he felt alone and started doing drugs.

She extended her hand to him and said it was time for him to come with her, and as she reached out, other silhouettes started to come forward from off in the distance. He walked closer and took her hand. Where there were feelings of anger and hostility there was now peace, love, and reunion. As he walked through the door, it closed and faded away leaving a blank astral wall where the door had suddenly appeared. I stood there with my guide looking at the wall and my guide let me know my work was done, so I went back into my body.

I could feel myself sitting on the floor of the living room of the woman's house as I slowly opened my eyes, fighting off the disoriented and dizzy feeling I get when I return. As I gathered my bearings, I saw her kids staring at me with confused looks on their faces through the thin clouds of sage and cedar smoke I had used to cleanse the space.

—*Brian Simpson*

TAKIN' IT TO THE STREETS

Sometimes modern times do require modern solutions, and though the wisdom of the ancients and spellwork from extinct civilizations can still be helpful, if we cannot adapt them to the current issues facing us in this day and age, then they won't be as much help as they could be. That's why I've invited an "insider" friend of mine who is very involved in modern resistance movements through his extensive street activism.

His name is David Salisbury, and he's a queer activist and Feri initiate who works at a U.S. nonprofit for civil rights in Washington, D.C., though you might already know him from his book *Witchcraft Activism* (among several others) or from all the events he has done around the country teaching about the intersection of advocacy and magic. Right now, he's here to not just tell us what it's like being an activist witch on the front lines of protests and marches, but also to teach us how to bless and protect spaces where activism for justice is about to go down.

I've been doing street activism (marches, protests, dramatic demonstrations) for most of my life. My first action was a union workers' rally my father took me to when I was just 11. I was in awe of the whole spectacle; chanting, songs, colorful signs, and the amount of people all gathered in one place for one purpose: to create change.

Although I'm now engaged in a variety of advocacy tactics, event advocacy or "street activism" is my favorite. In many ways it's a form of performance art where the creativity of the people is channeled into a powerful tool to get a message heard. With the amount of news and messaging bombarding us all every day, protesting and marching are some of the few tools at our disposal to help us rise above the noise.

As a witch and magic worker, I also consider these actions to be a form of community ritual. As with any magical working, these actions can be powerful while also holding a degree of risk. Over the years I've been in many situations around unlawful arrests of activists, chaotic crowd conditions, and even weather hazards like heat exhaustion. At a recent Black Trans Lives Matter *march, several of us fainted while marching in 100 degree weather for many miles on end. The warrior spirit of the activist, for better or worse, often provides us with the courage we need to continually show up and press on.*

No matter how crushing the world can seem, the bravery of the people I see in the streets fighting back will forever inspire my mission and my magic. Out of that inspiration I've developed many charms, blessings, and prayers over the years designed to bless such actions and to protect the people performing them. This is one of my go-to favorites.

To Bless and Protect an Advocate's Space Before an Action:

Stand at the general center of the space that you wish to have protected. Allow your breathing to slow and let your personal attention turn to the natural land around you. Take in any observations as you merge your full attention to the land. When you feel truly connected to the site, speak the invocation:

Spirits of space; the east, south, north, and center
Of flora, fauna, faerie, and stone
I call your favorable attention unto me
A steward of the land cries out to you
Awaken for the defense of this your domain
And the people within.
Hail to your holy names!

Move to the far north of the space and walk clockwise, tearing off pieces of bread and placing them discreetly as you walk. In place of bread I might also pour out spring water, particularly over stones and at the roots of any nearby trees. Walk slowly and solemnly, feeling the impact of your gifts.

When you return again to the north, focus deeply on the land and any buildings on it. When you feel satisfied, you may resume normal awareness and prepare to participate in the action.

If the spirits of the land were satisfied with your call and gifts, they should set to work with their own way of defending the space against chaos, attack, and harmful influence.

—David Salisbury

COMING TO AMERICA

To close out this book, I thought the best story to share would be one of hope and optimism. The tale of the American Dream realized, an immigrant's journey, determination, and warrior-like spirit persevering against the odds in a strange new land called the United States. This is the story of my friend from Russia, Yuri Sire.

Orphaned in St. Petersburg amid the tumultuous times of the fall of the Soviet Union and the chaotic re-building of a new nation from its totalitarian ruins, Yuri is someone who was given a new opportunity by being adopted into a home across the world in Southern California. Not only did he have to grow up and face the difficulties of school, prejudice, and teenage drama that all American kids face, but he had to do it all while learning a new language, adapting to an unfamiliar culture, overcoming the stigma of "differentness," and surviving the trauma of having escaped a bad situation in another country to strive for the very things most of us take for granted here … trauma to which most of his classmates, coworkers, and many of us could never relate.

Yuri's story, though shining with the warrior spirit, is not a unique one. People from all over the world are still escaping hardships and coming to the U.S. and elsewhere to find refuge. They have to work twice as hard to achieve half as much as those of us who won the uterine lottery by simply being born here, however imperfect "here" is. This is the story of many immigrants who have come to the U.S. as told through the example of one who did not let the events of his past embitter him, but rather propel him … one whom I have the honor to know personally and call my friend.

At the age of 14, I made America my new home. I had to learn English very fast having had only a basic foundation of it back in Russia. Nevertheless, when I was 18, in my English class, my teacher somehow magically chose my writing works as the #1 example that she printed out to hand out to all my classmates to teach them English. My family and I were very proud of such an achievement as it symbolized the overcoming of the language barrier by mastering the new language beyond expectations and better than the native speakers. Ultimately, I was already trying to create a better life for myself and my family.

What no one knew was that this was a way for me to start a completely new life in a different country with a different family so as to build something more meaningful, thus surpassing triumphantly my biological parents who utterly trashed their lives with bad habits like smoking, alcohol, drugs, lousy diet, poor sanitary conditions, and the list goes on … Sadly, they died at a young age due to extremely unhealthy lifestyles of self-abuse and neglect, leaving my younger brother and me orphaned in St. Petersburg, Russia … By the time I was 14, there was no biological family member left in my family except for my brother. They all passed away …

My noble goal was to NEVER become like my oblivious, reckless parents! In all honesty, they had always been awful role models for me—so much so, that I had to REINVENT a complete new version of myself and had to scrutinize to become the best version of myself—the process of which started when I was as young as 13. It is the true story of how and why I became adopted by an American who became my new father and gave me and my brother a new life here in the United States. He taught me so many things and gave me a fair chance with so many opportunities I never had in Russia and all with so much care, support, and respect, that I will never forget his legacy.

Being an adopted immigrant in America, inevitably, had to be propelled with a more extraordinary spirit like that of a tenacious World War Russian soldier who never gave up defending the honor, the dignity, and freedoms of the fellow people. Same way, I never gave up on myself and my new family dignity by trying to become the best version of myself defying the daunting odds of my heavy past while at the same time trying to invent new business ventures that would hopefully one day help "save the world" to make it a better place for all.

In a way, my extreme past events and my sad childhood family tragedies had severely impacted my view on life—to such an extent that somehow it created the spirit of a warrior who would have a persistent, benevolent drive to keep innovating new ways to succeed with a desire to help the world in a significant way … pay it forward for my father, the American man who helped me from half-way around the world when I needed it most.

—Yuri Sire

POST-MISSION
DEBRIEFING

*Hope has two beautiful daughters; their
names are Anger and Courage. Anger at
the way things are, and Courage to see
that they do not remain as they are.*
ST. AUGUSTINE OF HIPPO

Now that our global reconnaissance trek throughout history and the world has been accomplished, you are officially drilled, trained, and armed with the knowledge on how to be the best warrior you can be in making this world and the world for generations to come a better place. Knowing, however, is only half the battle. A warrior who fights the good fight without this knowledge is doomed to fail, but a warrior who fights with *only* this knowledge will never achieve victory. Always remember that action is the key ingredient to all magic and movements, for even if someone has all the knowledge in the world but does not actively apply that knowledge, what good does having such knowledge actually do for anyone?

Who am I to tell you all this, though, right? Well, I guess since we traveled so far together, I should probably tell you a little bit about me, your guide throughout this extensive mission we've undertaken. Perhaps you've heard about me as the writer and author of LGBTQ+ multicultural history or the licensed mortuary professional who explores the morbid and macabre, and while those are both true, I have also long been a warrior for social justice on the international stage. You see, before becoming an author, I had lived and worked in the cities, jungles, and pampas of South America, in countries which, not very long ago, were all under *severe* military dictatorships wherein people just "disappeared" on the regular. And while it would be unwise for me to get too much into it (and for you to know too much about it), it's probably safest to just say that during my time there, I had been involved in a number of guerrilla activist groups for the progressive ideals of women's bodily sovereignty, queer equality, indigenous rights, ecological habitat preservation, and economic retribution.

I have to say, though, while in the thick of it all on the ground level or organizing peoples into a united force, the most frustrating obstacles to victory that we kept on encountering were people who possessed the drive, passion, ability, and knowhow to be some of the greatest, most influential warriors for justice, yet were too timid or selfish to utilize those skills for the greater good. And you know why? They feared that they'd no longer look like a knight in shining armor if they got their hands dirty with actual, effective activism.

But you know what? A knight in shining armor is just a warrior who has never had their metal or their mettle tested. *Real* warriors and *real* change only come from those whose armor is dirtied with mud, dented with arrows, and nicked everywhere from blows they have suffered while in the fray of the good fight.

For this, I point back to the quote that opened this final debriefing. Those words are just as true now as they always have been. Hope, though essential to the human spirit, gets nothing done on its own. It is invaluable in keeping the human spirit uplifted and counteracting the devastating paralysis of depression, but it doesn't actually *do* anything that effects change. People hope for things all the time. The sick hope to get well. The poor hope to rise out of poverty. The persecuted hope for a day when they can live in peace. But hope alone never achieves anything.

Looking back into the societal justice movements throughout the world that have had the most impactful, long-lasting gains, it's quick to see that anger has been the most effective motivating force for positive change. Anger over despotism led to global revolutions for representative governments. Anger over enslaving other human beings led to the abolitionist movements and a long-overdue amending of the U.S. Constitution. Anger over being treated as second-class citizens led to the civil rights and women's liberation movements of the '60s and '70s. Anger over unjust laws and police prejudice led to the Stonewall riots, the queer rights movement, and recently the Black Lives Matter movement. Sure, hope gave them inspiration, but their anger and other "unpopular" emotions are what motivated them to do something about it and achieve progress.

The funny thing about humanity, though, is that we don't ever take meaningful action until we hit rock bottom. We try to soothe our anger and convince ourselves that things aren't that bad, that they'll just get better on their own, and that there's no need to ever be angry since anger solves nothing. On an individual level this may be true at times, but on a global, societal level, the unbearable just gets more unbearable without action. We're all too comfortable to watch the world burn from the contented safety of our television sets and computer screens so long as we have our coffeemakers, video games, smartphones, and other modern luxury items to distract us and make us think *those people's* problems will never affect *us*. For some reason, we just never truly believe we're in hot water until it's already boiling... at least so long as the warm water leading to the boil is comfortable.

Trying to keep our aggressive warrior emotions in check, we hope that our lives and the world at large will just become a better place on its own, but if all (or at least a majority) of the people who want to and can make a better, more inclusive future temper their frustrations and sit on the sidelines in the hope that things will magically change on their own (having deluded themselves into thinking that the timeline of the universe is cosmically pre-destined to march forward only toward equality and justice)... then nothing changes.

The oppressors of the world preach high-road pacifism as the only means to combat them because they know it doesn't lead to lasting change, only to minor, temporary gains that shut us back up for a bit longer. All the while, the hopeful, positive people of the world with action-less good intentions sit and wonder why things seem to be getting progressively worse. Taking anger-fueled action guided by hope, that's what gets results, and *that's* why the powers that be want to shame us into thinking it's "bad."

To give a bit more spiritual insight into where I'm coming from, for most of my educational life, I attended private Catholic school in which "Religion Class" was mandatory every year from kindergarten to twelfth grade. Throughout these years, one lesson always surprised me because of how iconoclastic it seemed; it was the lesson on anger as a virtue. Specifically, that famous Gospel passage wherein Jesus told people that they needed to "turn the other cheek" most exemplified this virtuous anger.

In popular consciousness, "turning the other cheek" has come to erroneously mean passively taking other people's abuse via taking the high road of "forgiveness" and not outwardly confronting people and shutting them down. What I unanimously learned from the various nuns, monks, and priests who were my religion teachers for thirteen years was that the *true* meaning of the "turn the other cheek" story was that of defiance. You weren't supposed to turn your cheek as an offering for your abuser to strike you again knowing there'd be no retaliation. You were supposed to turn your check as an assertive act of insubordination, daring the abuser to try that again and see what the consequences will be for them now that they've been warned.

Regardless of what you think of Catholicism or how humans have "interpreted" Jesus's words and actions, Jesus was undeniably an action-oriented rebel. He defied the status quo, spoke out openly against injustice, publicly stood up for the poor and maligned, and even unleashed his anger in the form of physical violence in the Temple by overthrowing tables and grabbing a makeshift whip to literally "lash" out at those who angered him. And never once did he apologize or tell his followers that he shouldn't have done that and regretted it. He used his anger over the way things were to motivate himself to action. Yes, he prayed and had "magical" powers, but he also organized, publicly stood up to oppressors, and followed up his prayers with physical action.

As magical workers, we have a greater burden of responsibility toward the greater good than the general populace. With magic, there really is not much that we cannot achieve in this world, and with such power, we are obligated to stand up for the powerless and make the world a better place for all. It's a fight for survival—maybe not for you personally, but for many people all around you.

The fact that oppressors are allowed to stay in power until the next "election cycle" or any set amount of time dictated by the powers that be is essentially a death sentence to society's most vulnerable. Break out the hexes and the justified "harmful" magic—whatever gets results and permanently removes bigotry and injustice from positions of power as soon as possible. There are good people going through hell and dying because you are strolling along on the high road, wanting to keep your armor shiny and clean.

After all, what good is taking the high road if it means the oppressor wins? Tell me, which better serves the greater good: getting a moral victory by not allowing anger to get to you thereby allowing the oppressor to continue harming countless others, many of whom may be too weak to withstand such brutality… or getting down and dirty in your anger resulting in morally ambiguous tactics that remove an abusive oppressor from power and help lift their crushing boot off of the necks of those dying under the pressure? The high road is only available to those with *tremendous* privilege, those whose entire existence isn't on the line should they lose. It is a luxury that the vulnerable of society cannot afford.

And let me ask you this: you think abusive oppressors in positions of power will always play fair? Absolutely not. They will do whatever it takes to stay in power and continue their bigoted and harmful agendas. Those who are oppressed, by tying their own hands with always having to take the moral high road (as propagandized to them by the ruling elite), are constantly at a disadvantage. Once bigotry and injustice are removed from positions of power, only then can the high road be followed. Until then, we're in the fight for our lives. Losing means the death of inclusiveness and justice, and with all that on the line, we must do whatever it takes to achieve victory and right the wrongs of the ruling elite. A victory is still a victory no matter how it is achieved, and a loss is still a loss no matter the losing party's "intentions" or "morally superior" tactics.

All the positive thinking in the world and magical "good intentions" don't achieve as much as the smallest action. If that action is fueled by the emotions of justified anger toward intolerance, oppression, and bigotry, then that action, that spell becomes exponentially more powerful. Now, don't get me wrong. Positive thinking is powerful, too, but its power lies in energizing you to get up, take action, and believe that victory is attainable. Anger and courageous action, however, are what truly tip the scales toward victory.

Take a look around you at the world right now. It's full of positive-thinking people who play the part of Pollyanna and don rose-tinted glasses to view the world around them. Some do this out of self-preservation since the reality of the world is too overwhelmingly sad and painful to bear. Animals are going extinct, the environment is degrading, the gap between the rich and poor is widening, war is always happening somewhere, families are being displaced, and people are literally starving. Why are we passively allowing all this? How can our consciences be at ease for choosing the moral and magical high road if *this* is the result of that choice?

If you call yourself a worker of magic, a warrior, then own it. If you have the knowhow to help shape the universe and enlist the aid of the Divine to help alleviate human, animal, and ecological suffering, then why are you not doing so with your entire emotional arsenal? Why are you focusing on spells to quell your inner anger and uncomfortable emotions when you could be doing spells that *use* your anger and those emotions? Even after the spellwork is complete, why are you not out there on the streets in protest, bankrolling worthy causes, or helping organize the masses and following up your magic with concrete physical actions? If you meet the Universe halfway, results really do come more quickly.

Direct action gets satisfaction, and while it's true that a steady stream of soft droplets can erode a mighty boulder, we don't have that time. There are people suffering *now*! They cannot wait for the passive, non-direct tactics of the high road to eventually affect change sometime maybe in the future. If you are not on the end of your rope wherein desperate action is the only course of action, then you live a fortunate and sheltered life of supreme privilege compared to the majority of people on this earth.

You need to get angry. You need to embrace your inner warrior because there are people out there who need you to take action right now. Their misery and hardship are being prolonged because we're scared of speaking up and taking a stand, erroneously thinking any magic or activism that's not "white light happy" is somehow immoral or unjust. I'll tell you what's immoral and unjust: people being shot dead because of the color of their skin, people being denied equal rights because of whom they love, people being forced into medical jeopardy because they don't have sovereignty over their own bodies or the income to afford good health. *That* is immoral and unjust. Us sitting on the sidelines hoping these things will resolve themselves is immoral and unjust. Us ignoring that we have the power to fight back and expedite the alleviation of human suffering is immoral and unjust.

Again, a river of water can, over time, change an entire landscape dramatically, but a volcano's forceful eruption and river of hot, seething lava does it a hell of a lot faster. If you want to see change in your lifetime and help those who are suffering now, get angry and do something with that anger. Most of us are fighting for scraps because we're not angry enough to march up to the table and take the food we deserve as human beings. The oppressors will never give us enough scraps to become strong enough to sit at that table.

Imagine if we de-shamed the emotions that spark a warrior to fight in defense of what is good and right. Yes, these emotions feel uncomfortable, but that's because the discomfort is meant to get you to move. Peace and sympathy toward the enemy only enable the enemy. Remember, slavery only became abolished *after* a war. Queer rights were only granted *after* the queer community of color gave the government riots. Democracies in countries throughout the globe were established only *after* people took to the streets in revolution. The powers that be never give people what they deserve out of sheer kindness or because it's the "right thing to do." The people always must take it for themselves. Again, justice is not a fruit that suddenly falls from the tree once it is ripe; we have to make it fall and grab it ourselves before it withers on the branch.

Don't lose your temper, *use* your temper. It's up to you, to all of us. The Divine instilled us with anger and rageful warrior emotions just as much as "positive" emotions. I don't believe that was an accident, and I don't believe the Divine made a mistake in giving us the ability to feel those emotions or intended for us to forego their usefulness in creating change. So, the question ultimately is: what are *we* going to do about it? Temper them for a personal moral victory at the expense of the most downtrodden and vulnerable, or harness them into the fuel needed to overcome oppression and injustice? The choice is ours every single moment of every single day.

And I will say this before we part ways and the battle begins. This fight will be eternal. I say this not to be cynical but to motivate you. That utopia will never happen in our lifetimes or in the lifetimes of those generations to come. In fact, "utopia" is Greek for "no place" and was popularized by the Tudor-era theologian St. Thomas More in his satirical book of the same name as a sardonic nod to how a peaceful heaven on earth cannot exist anywhere humans exist.

Still, peace exists in this moment here and now because people like you and me are out here maintaining it. Anything, if left to its own devices or neglected, falls apart. Modern justice and all our modern equalities and rights are here because someone in the past was once angry at the lack of them and was willing to sully their armor in battle if it meant achieving something better for future generations to come. Your spirit, your wand, your hands, your wallet, your vote each and every day are what's keeping evil at bay.

There is no neutrality in the good fight. If you choose to do nothing in the hopes of waiting for the "perfect" candidate, the "safest" strategy, or some knight in shining armor to come save the day, you have still made a choice. You are that knight, that hero you've been waiting for—that the world has been waiting for! Now get out there, get angry, and make it happen. I'll see you on the battlefield!

BIBLIOGRAPHY

Abel, Ernest L. *Death Gods: An Encyclopedia of the Rulers, Evil Spirits, and Geographies of the Dead.* Westport, CT: Greenwood Press, 2009.

Addison, Charles G., Esq. *The History of the Knights Templars, the Temple Church, and the Temple.* London: Longman, Brown, Green, and Longmans, 1842. https://www.gutenberg.org/files/38593/38593-h/38593-h.htm.

al-Ṭabarī, Abū Jaʿfar Muḥammad ibn Jarīr. *The History of al-Tabari, vol. 9: The Last Years of the Prophet.* Translated by Ismail K. Poonwala. Albany: State University of New York Press, 1990.

Allam, Lorena, and Nick Evershed. "The Killing Times: The Massacres of Aboriginal People Australia Must Confront." *The Guardian.* March 3, 2019. https://www.theguardian.com/australia-news/2019/mar/04/the-killing-times-the-massacres-of-aboriginal-people-australia-must-confront.

Allen, Mark W., Robert Lawrence Bettinger, Brian F. Codding, Terry L. Jones, and Al W. Schwitalla. "Resource Scarcity Drives Lethal Aggression Among Prehistoric Hunter-Gatherers in Central California." *Proceedings of the National Academy of Sciences of the United States of America* 113, no. 43 (October 10, 2016): 12120–12125. https://www.pnas.org/content/113/43/12120.

Alvarado, Denise. *The Magic of Marie Laveau: Embracing the Spiritual Legacy of the Voodoo Queen of New Orleans.* Newburyport: Weiser Books, 2020.

Amin, Osama Shukir Muhammed. "Goddess Al-Lat and an Elderly
God from Hatra." World History Encyclopedia. June 4, 2019.
https://www.worldhistory.org/image/10861/goddess-al-lat-and-an
-elderly-god-from-hatra/.

Andrews, Evan. "8 Things You May Not Know About the Praetorian
Guard." History. August 29, 2018. https://www.history.com
/news/8-things-you-may-not-know-about-the-praetorian-guard.

Asprey, Robert Brown. "Guerrilla warfare." *Encyclopedia Britannica*.
Updated March 24, 2021. https://www.britannica.com/topic
/guerrilla-warfare/Strategy-and-tactics.

Assmann, Jan. *The Search for God in Ancient Egypt*. Translated by David
Lorton. Ithaca: Cornell University Press, 2001.

"The Aztec Empire: Society, Politics, Religion, and Agriculture."
History on the Net. Accessed July 3, 2020. https://www
.historyonthenet.com/aztec-empire-society-politics-religion
-agriculture.

Baker, Jordan. "The Beaver Wars and the Mourning Wars: A Tale Of
Two Wars." *East India Blogging Co.* (blog), July 11, 2019. https://
eastindiabloggingco.com/2019/07/11/beaver-wars-mourning
-wars/.

Ball, Margaret Haig Roosevelt Sewall. "Grim Commerce: Scalps,
Bounties, and the Transformation of Trophy-Taking in the Early
American Northeast, 1450–1770." University of Colorado
Department of History. 2013. https://scholar.colorado.edu
/concern/graduate_thesis_or_dissertations/c821gj859.

Beam, Christopher. "The Rise and Fall of Shaolin's CEO Monk."
Bloomberg Businessweek. December 28, 2015. https://www
.bloomberg.com/news/features/2015-12-28/the-rise-and-fall-of
-shaolin-s-ceo-monk.

Bekhrad, Joobin. "The Obscure Religion that Shaped the West." BBC.
April 6, 2017. http://www.bbc.com/culture/story/20170406
-this-obscure-religion-shaped-the-west.

Berndt, Ronald M., and Robert Tonkinson. "Australian Aboriginal Peoples." *Encyclopedia Britannica*. Updated April 19, 2018. https://www.britannica.com/topic/Australian-Aboriginal.

Beyer, Catherine. "Are Voodoo Dolls Real?" Learn Religions. January 25, 2019. https://www.learnreligions.com/are-voodoo-dolls-real-95807.

Bezertinov, Rafael. "Deities." In *Tengrianizm: Religion of Türks and Mongols*. Translated by Norm Kisamov. Lubbock: Texas Tech University Press, 2000, 71–95. http://www.hunmagyar.org/turan/tatar/turk.html.

Bishop, Kyle. "The Sub-Subaltern Monster: Imperialist Hegemony and the Cinematic Voodoo Zombie." *The Journal of American Culture* 31, no. 2 (June 2008): 141–152. https://onlinelibrary.wiley.com/doi/pdf/10.1111/j.1542-734X.2008.00668.x.

Blakemore, Erin. "What Was the Neolithic Revolution?" *National Geographic*. April 5, 2019. https://www.nationalgeographic.com/culture/topics/reference/neolithic-agricultural-revolution/.

Bolich, G. G. *Conversing on Gender*. Raleigh: Psyche's Press, 2007.

Bouglé, Célestin. *Essays on the Caste System*. Translated by D. F. Pocock. Cambridge: Cambridge University Press, 1971.

Braudy, Leo. *From Chivalry to Terrorism: War and the Changing Nature of Masculinity*. New York: Vintage, 2005.

Brix, Lise. "Why Danish Vikings Moved to England." ScienceNordic. February 23, 2017. https://sciencenordic.com/denmark-society—culture-videnskabdk/why-danish-vikings-moved-to-england/1442885.

Broadbridge, Anne F. "The Rise and Fall of the Mongol Empire." TED-Ed. August 29, 2019. YouTube, 5:00. https://www.youtube.com/watch?v=wUVvTqvjUaM.

Broadie, A., and J. Macdonald. "The Concept of Cosmic Order in Ancient Egypt in Dynastic and Roman Times." *L'Antiquité Classique* 47, no. 1 (1978): 106–128. https://www.persee.fr/doc/antiq _0770-2817_1978_num_47_1_1885.

Brooks, Robin, and Hyacinth Simpson. "Ogun: God of Iron." Ryerson University. 2012. https://www.ryerson.ca/olivesenior/poems/ogun .html.

Buchanan, Rebecca, ed. *Dauntless: A Devotional for Ares and Mars.* Bibliotheca Alexandrina, 2017.

Budnik, Ruslan. "Dahomey Amazons—The Only Elite All-Female Warrior Regiments." War History Online. October 10, 2018. https://www.warhistoryonline.com/instant-articles/dahomey -amazons.html.

Burgess, Ann Wolbert, Albert R. Roberts, and Cheryl Regehr. *Victimology: Theories and Applications.* Burlington: Jones & Bartlett Learning, 2009.

Cairns, Rebecca, and Jennifer Llewellyn. "CCP Social Reforms." Alpha History. September 23, 2019. https://alphahistory.com /chineserevolution/ccp-social-reforms/.

Campbell, Gregory R. "Chapter 7: Comanche Historical Ethnography and Ethnohistory." National Park Service Ethnobotany Report. University of Montana Department of Anthropology. 2004. http:// files.cfc.umt.edu/cesu/NPS/UMT/2004/Campbell_Etnobotony%20 Report/chapterseven.pdf.

Caprio, Betsy. *The Woman Sealed in the Tower: A Psychological Approach to Feminine Spirituality.* New York: Paulist Press, 1982.

Carelli, Francesco. "The Book of Death: Weighing Your Heart." *London Journal of Primary Care* 4, no. 1 (July 2011): 86–87. https://www .ncbi.nlm.nih.gov/pmc/articles/PMC3960665/.

Carrasco, David L. "Human Sacrifice in Aztec Culture." *Serious Science.* October 13, 2016. http://serious-science.org/human-sacrifice -in-aztec-culture-6995.

Carrasco Cara Chards, María Isabel. "The Ancient Aztec Celebration That Became A 9-Day Christmas Party." *Cultura Colectiva*. December 1, 2019. https://culturacolectiva.com/history/panquetzaliztli -aztec-origins-mexican-christmas-posadas.

Cartwright, Mark. "Mars." World History Encyclopedia. January 16, 2014. https://www.worldhistory.org/Mars/.

Cartwright, Mark. "Minerva." World History Encyclopedia. January 7, 2014. https://www.worldhistory.org/Minerva/.

Cartwright, Mark. "Mongol Warfare." World History Encyclopedia. October 10, 2019. https://www.worldhistory.org/Mongol_Warfare/.

Cartwright, Mark. "Sparta." World History Encyclopedia. May 28, 2013. https://www.worldhistory.org/sparta/.

Chambers, Jane. "Chile's Mapuche Indigenous Group Fights for Rights." BBC. November 26, 2020. https://www.bbc.com/news /world-latin-america-55042838.

Chan, Athena. "Why Guan Yu—Warrior God Known as Duke Guan— Is Worshipped in Hong Kong and Asia by Police, Gangsters…and Businessmen Alike." *South China Morning Post*. July 6, 2019. https:// www.scmp.com/news/hong-kong/society/article/3017346 /revered-police-gangsters-and-businessmen-warrior-deity-duke.

Chao-Fong, Léonie. "The Conquerors of Asia: Who Were the Mongols?" History Hit. January 15, 2020. https://www.historyhit .com/the-conquerors-of-asia-who-were-the-mongols/.

Chatland, Jan. "Descriptions of Various Loa of Voodoo." Webster University. Accessed August 8, 2021. http://faculty.webster.edu /corbetre/haiti/voodoo/biglist.htm.

Clark, Tim. "The Bushido Code: The Eight Virtues of the Samurai." Art of Manliness. Updated June 16, 2020. https://www .artofmanliness.com/articles/the-bushido-code-the-eight-virtues -of-the-samurai/.

Cline, Austin. "Buluc Chabtan: Mayan God of War." Learn Religions. July 22, 2017. https://www.learnreligions.com/buluc-chabtan -buluc-chabtan-god-of-war-250382.

Cogito. "Maya Star War: Tikal—Calakmul War." Kings and Generals. July 26, 2018. YouTube, 16:08. https://www.youtube.com/watch?v =heeOSwoBOjk.

Cogito. "Peak of the Incan Empire." Kings and Generals. May 24, 2018. YouTube, 11:56. https://www.youtube.com/watch?v =3aYeUOVgbck.

Cogito. "Rise of the Maya." Kings and Generals. July 12, 2018. YouTube, 15:23. https://www.youtube.com/watch?v =sK9yv5wAoY0.

Collazos, Daniel. "Buluc Chabtan." *Mitos, Leyendas Y Símbolos*. July 23, 2019. https://mitoyleyenda.com/mitologia/mexico/buluc-chabtan/.

Conner, Randy P., David Hatfield Sparks, and Mariya Sparks. *Cassell's Encyclopedia of Queer Myth, Symbol and Spirit*. London: Cassell & Co., 1997.

Cooper, Rabbi David. "2193 The Archangel Michael." Rabbi David Cooper. November 8, 2010. https://www.rabbidavidcooper.com /cooper-print-index/2010/11/8/2193-the-archangel-michael.html.

Craig, Robert D. *Dictionary of Polynesian Mythology*. Westport, CT: Greenwood Publishing Group, 1989.

Curry, Andrew. "The Rulers of Foreign Lands." *Archaeology*. Archaeological Institute of America (Sept–Oct. 2018). https://www .archaeology.org/issues/309-1809/features/6855-egypt-hyksos -foreign-dynasty.

Cutshaw, Jason. "Redstone Arsenal Celebrates St. Barbara Inductees." U.S. Army. February 11, 2020. https://www.army.mil/article /232637/redstone_arsenal_celebrates_st_barbara_inductees.

D'Altroy, Terence N. *The Incas*. Malden, MA: Blackwell Publishing, 2003.

Das, Subhamoy. "An Introduction to Lord Vishnu, Hinduism's Peace-Loving Deity." Learn Religions. Updated May 15, 2019. https://www.learnreligions.com/an-introduction-to-lord-vishnu-1770304.

Das, Subhamoy. "Lord Kartikeya." *Learn Religions*. May 7, 2019. https://www.learnreligions.com/lord-kartikya-1770301.

Dash, Mike. "Dahomey's Women Warriors." *Smithsonian Magazine*. September 23, 2011. https://www.smithsonianmag.com/history/dahomeys-women-warriors-88286072/.

De La Torre, Miguel A., and Albert Hernández. *The Quest for the Historical Satan*. Minneapolis: Fortress Press, 2011.

de Landa, Fray Diego. *Relación de las cosas de Yucatán*. Mexico City: Miguel Ángel Porrúa, 1982.

Department of Medieval Art and the Cloisters. "The Crusades (1095–1291)," New York Metropolitan Museum of Art. Updated February 2014. https://www.metmuseum.org/toah/hd/crus/hd_crus.htm.

Deshpande, Manali S. "History of the Indian Caste System and Its Impact on India Today." California Polytechnic State University Department of Social Sciences. 2010. https://digitalcommons.calpoly.edu/cgi/viewcontent.cgi?referer=https://www.google.co.in/&httpsredir=1&article=1043&context=socssp.

Desser, David, Joan Mellen, Stephen Prince, Tony Rayns, Donald Richie, and Tadao Sato. *Seven Samurai: Origins and Influences*. New York: Criterion Collection, 2006.

Diaz, Lizbeth. "Mexican Police Ask Spirits to Guard Them in Drug War." Reuters. Updated March 19, 2010. https://www.reuters.com/article/us-mexico-drugs/mexican-police-ask-spirits-to-guard-them-in-drug-war-idUSTRE62I3Z220100319.

Dodson, Michael, and Diana McCarthy. "Communal Land and the Amendments to the Aboriginal Land Rights Act (NT)." Australian Institute of Aboriginal and Torres Strait Islander Studies. 2006. https://aiatsis.gov.au/sites/default/files/research_pub /dodsonm-mccarthyd-dp19-communal-land-amendments -aboriginal-land-rights-act_0_1.pdf.

Duffy, Rich. "Bushido: Way of Total Bullshit." Tofugu. December 8, 2014. https://www.tofugu.com/japan/bushido/.

Duiker, William J. *Ho Chi Minh*. New York: Hyperion, 2000.

Duncan, Cynthia. "Resistance and Change in Cuban Santería." About Santería. Accessed May 7, 2020. http://www.aboutsanteria.com /resistance-and-change-in-santeriacutea.html.

Duncan, Cynthia. "Trance Possession." About Santería. Accessed May 7, 2020. http://www.aboutsanteria.com/trance-possession.html.

Durán, Diego. *Historia de las Indias de Nueva-España y islas de Tierra Firme*. London: Forgotten Books, 2018.

Duvalier, James. "The Importance of Dolls in Voodoo." James Duvalier. Accessed May 8, 2020. http://jamesduvalier.com/importance -dolls-in-voodoo/.

Eckley, Wilton. "Guerrilla Warfare." In *Magill's Guide to Military History*. Edited by John Powell. Pasadena, CA: Salem Press, 2001.

Egan, Ted. "Lingiari, Vincent (1919–1988)." *Australian Dictionary of Biography*, vol. 18. 2012. National Centre of Biography. Australian National University. Accessed July 6, 2021. http://adb.anu.edu.au /biography/lingiari-vincent-14178.

Elshaikh, Eman M. "The Rise of Islamic Empires and States." Kahn Academy. Accessed April 21, 2020. https://www.khanacademy.org /humanities/world-history/medieval-times/spread-of-islam/a/the -rise-of-islamic-empires-and-states.

Espinosa, Luz. "Mictlán: el lugar de los muertos." *Cultura Colectiva*. September 23, 2014. https://culturacolectiva.com/letras/mictlan-el -lugar-de-los-muertos/.

Fandrich, Ina Johanna. *The Mysterious Voodoo Queen, Marie Laveaux: A Study of Powerful Female Leadership in Nineteenth-Century New Orleans.* Lafayette, LA: University of Louisiana Lafayette Press, 2012.

Feinberg, Leslie. *Transgender Warriors: Making History from Joan of Arc to RuPaul.* Boston: Beacon Press, 1996.

Flaherty, Jordan. *Floodlines: Community and Resistance from Katrina to the Jena Six.* Chicago: Haymarket Books, 2010.

Flanagan, Damian. "Bushido: The Samurai Code Goes to War." *The Japan Times.* July 23, 2016. https://www.japantimes.co.jp/culture /2016/07/23/books/bushido-samurai-code-goes-war/# .Xtxl4KZ7mM8.

Fleener, Monica. "The Significance of the Coronation of Charlemagne." Thesis, Western Oregon University Department of History, 2005, 1–29. https://wou.edu/history/files/2015/08/Monica-Fleener.pdf.

Forell, George Wolfgang. *History of Christian Ethics, Vol. I: From the New Testament to Augustine.* Minneapolis: Augsburg Publishing House, 1979.

Fowler, Catherine S., Don D. Fowler. "Great Basin Indian: Religion and Ritual." *Encylopædia Britannica.* Updated November 16, 2020. https://www.britannica.com/topic/Great-Basin-Indian/Religion -and-ritual.

Frayer, Lauren. "Gandhi Is Deeply Revered, But His Attitudes On Race And Sex Are Under Scrutiny." NPR. October 2, 2019. https://www .npr.org/2019/10/02/766083651/gandhi-is-deeply-revered-but-his -attitudes-on-race-and-sex-are-under-scrutiny.

Gabriel, Richard A. *Muhammad: Islam's First Great General.* Norman, OK: University of Oklahoma Press, 2007.

Galton, David J. "Greek Theories on Eugenics," *Journal of Medical Ethics* 24, no. 4 (1998): 263–267. https://jme.bmj.com/content/medethics /24/4/263.full.pdf.

Garcilaso de la Vega, Inca. *Comentarios reales: Segunda parte*. San Francisco: Wikimedia Foundation, 1616. https://es.wikisource.org/wiki/Comentarios_reales_-_Segunda_parte_(Versi%C3%B3n_para_imprimir).

"The Garden of the Gods." Muangboran Museum. 2018. https://www.muangboranmuseum.com/en/landmark/the-garden-of-the-gods/.

Garlinghouse, Thomas. "Ancient Celts Decapitated Their Enemies and Saved Their Heads, Archaeologists Say." *Discover Magazine*. February 12, 2019. https://www.discovermagazine.com/planet-earth/ancient-celts-decapitated-their-enemies-and-saved-their-heads-archaeologists-say.

Gillan, Joanna. "Viking Berserkers—Fierce Warriors or Drug-Fuelled Madmen?" Ancient Origins. May 26, 2019. https://www.ancient-origins.net/myths-legends/viking-berserkers-fierce-warriors-or-drug-fuelled-madmen-001472.

Gnoli, G., and P. Jamzadeh. "BAHRĀM (Vərəθrayna)." *Encyclopedia Iranica*. Updated August 24, 2011. http://www.iranicaonline.org/articles/bahram-1.

Goldfarb, Lyn, and Margaret Koval. "The Roman Empire in the First Century." PBS. 2006. https://www.pbs.org/empires/romans/empire/soldiers.html.

Gomez, Maria C. "Maya Religion." World History Encyclopedia, July 29, 2015. https://www.worldhistory.org/Maya_Religion/.

González-Wippler, Migene. *Santeria, the Religion: Faith, Rites, Magic*. St. Paul, MN, Llewellyn Worldwide, 2002.

Green, David. "New Zealand's 19th-Century Wars." New Zealand History. Ministry for Culture and Heritage. Updated September 30, 2020. https://nzhistory.govt.nz/war/new-zealands-19th-century-wars/introduction.

Greenberg, David, Margaret MacMillan, Geoffrey Perret, Jean Edward Smith, and Jules Witcover. "Stretching Executive Power in Wartime." *The New York Times*. May 27, 2007. https://campaigningforhistory.blogs.nytimes.com/2007/05/27/stretching-executive-power-in-wartime/.

Geggus, David. "Sex Ratio, Age and Ethnicity in the Atlantic Slave Trade: Data from French Shipping and Plantation Records." *The Journal of African History* 30, no. 1 (March 1989): 23–44. https://www.researchgate.net/publication/231824532_Sex_Ratio_Age_and_Ethnicity_in_the_Atlantic_Slave_Trade_Data_from_French_Shipping_and_Plantation_Records.

Grey, George. "Children of Heaven and Earth." In *Polynesian Mythology & Ancient Traditional History of the New Zealanders: As Furnished by Their Priests and Chiefs*. Sacred Texts, 1854. https://www.sacred-texts.com/pac/grey/grey03.htm.

Groeneveld, Emma. "Odin." World History Encyclopedia. November 13, 2017. https://www.worldhistory.org/odin/.

Grout, James. "Sol Invictus and Christmas." Encyclopedia Romana. 2020. https://penelope.uchicago.edu/~grout/encyclopaedia_romana/calendar/invictus.html.

Handwerk, Brian. "What does 'Jihad' Really Mean to Muslims?" *National Geographic*. October 24, 2003. https://www.nationalgeographic.com/news/2003/10/what-does-jihad-really-mean-to-muslims/.

Hardy, Thomas A. "General's Legions: Marian Reforms and the Collapse of the Roman Republic." *Eastern Illinois University Department of History*. 2017. https://www.eiu.edu/historia/Hardy2017.pdf.

Harford, Tim. "The Warrior Monks Who Invented Banking." BBC. January 30, 2017. https://www.bbc.com/news/business-38499883.

Harrington, Caitlin. "The Lesser-Told Story of the California Missions." Hoodline. March 20, 2016. https://hoodline .com/2016/03/the-lesser-told-story-of-the-california-missions/.

Harrsch, Mary. "Eugenics in the Ancient World." Brewminate. February 17, 2017. https://brewminate.com/eugenics-in-the -ancient-world/.

Hass, Christopher. "Mountain Constantines: The Christianization of Aksum and Iberia." *Journal of Late Antiquity* 1, no. 1 (2008): 101– 126. http://users.clas.ufl.edu/sterk/junsem/haas.pdf.

Hastings, Christobel. "The Timeless Myth of Medusa, a Rape Victim Turned Into a Monster." *Vice.* April 19, 2018. https://www.vice .com/en_us/article/qvxwax/medusa-greek-myth-rape-victim-turned -into-a-monster.

Hataway, James Earl, Jr. "Zen and the Samurai: Rethinking Ties Between Zen and the Warrior." Master's thesis, University of Tennessee Knoxville, May 2006. https://trace.tennessee.edu/cgi /viewcontent.cgi?referer=https://www.google.com/&httpsredir =1&article=6006&context=utk_gradthes.

Hawai'i Legal Auxiliary. "The Law of the Splintered Paddle: Kānāwai Māmalahoem." University of Hawai'i. Accessed June 27, 2020. https://www.hawaii.edu/uhelp/files/LawOfTheSplinteredPaddle .pdf.

Hazra, Kanai Lal. *The Rise and Decline of Buddhism in India.* New Delhi: Munshiram Manoharlal Publishers Pvt. Ltd., 1995.

Hazzard-Donald, Katrina. *Mojo Workin': The Old African American Hoodoo System.* Champaign, IL: University of Illinois Press, 2012.

Heffron, Yağmur. "Inana/Ištar (goddess)." Ancient Mesopotamian Gods and Goddesses. Oracc and the UK Higher Education Academy, 2016. http://oracc.museum.upenn.edu/amgg/listofdeities /inanaitar/.

Heissig, Walther. *The Religions of Mongolia*. Translated by Geoffrey Samuel. Berkeley: University of California Press, 1970. https:// archive.org/details/bub_gb_OzDMbpw7EecC/page/n99/mode/2up.

Henley, Jon. "Why Genghis Khan Was Good for the Planet." *The Guardian*. January 26, 2011. https://www.theguardian.com /theguardian/2011/jan/26/genghis-khan-eco-warrior.

Herold, Andre Ferdinand. *The Life of Buddha*. Translated by Paul C. Blum. Sacred Texts, 1927. http://www.sacred-texts.com/bud/lob /index.htm.

Hickes, Martin. "Whatever Happened to the Knights Templar?" *The Guardian*. June 27, 2011. https://www.theguardian.com/uk/the -northerner/2011/jun/27/whatever-happened-to-the-knights -templar.

Hill, Jenny. "Montu." Ancient Egypt Online. 2015. https:// ancientegyptonline.co.uk/montu/.

Hoffman, Michael. "Understanding Heian Nobles' Snobbishness." *The Japan Times*. April 16, 2016. https://www.japantimes.co.jp/news /2016/04/16/national/history/understanding-heian-nobles -snobbishness/#.XtXBeTl7mM8.

Holland, Heidi. *African Magic: Traditional Ideas that Heal a Continent*. Johannesburg: Penguin Books, 2011.

Hollis, Matt. "Marian Reforms and Their Military Effects Documentary." Kings and Generals. December 13, 2018. YouTube, 14:19. https://www.youtube.com/watch?v=UIRS_PMeVVY.

Hollis, Matt. "Rise of Sumer: Cradle of Civilization DOCUMENTARY." Kings and Generals. March 14, 2019. YouTube, 13:45. https://www .youtube.com/watch?v=MHpmLrWBjnM&list=PLaBYW76inbX4 vEmC1vfsJDzQhs8M_ufQn&index=2&t=8s.

Hollis, Matt. "Watling Street 60 AD—Boudica's Revolt," Kings and Generals. June 6, 2019. YouTube, 17:01. https://www.youtube.com /watch?v=5xxUc3T1_As.

Hoyland, Robert G. *Arabia and the Arabs: From the Bronze Age to the Coming of Islam*. New York: Routledge, 2001.

Huda Dodge, Christine. "Angel Jibreel (Gabriel) in Islam." Learn Religions. February 5, 2018. https://www.learnreligions.com /angel-jibreel-gabriel-in-islam-2004031.

Hurley, Patrick. "Aurelian." World History Encyclopedia. March 20, 2011. https://www.worldhistory.org/Aurelian/.

Ignatow, Gabriel. *Transnational Identity Politics and the Environment*. Lanham: Lexington Books, 2007.

International Committee of the Red Cross. *Under the Protection of the Palm: Wars of Dignity in the Pacific*. Suva, Fiji: ICRC Regional Delegation in the Pacific, 2009. https://www.icrc.org/en/doc /assets/files/other/wars-of-dignity-pacific-2009.pdf.

Jacobs, Joseph, M. Seligsohn, and Mary W. Montgomery. "Michael." *Jewish Encyclopedia*. 1906. http://www.jewishencyclopedia.com /articles/10779-michael.

Jansen, Marius B., G. Cameron Hurst, Fred G. Notehelfer, Shigeki Hijino, Gil Latz, Yasuo Masai, Kitajima Masamoto, Taro Sakamoto, Takeshi Toyoda, Akira Watanabe. "Japan: The Heian period (794-1185)." *Encylopædia Britannica*. https://www.britannica.com/place /Japan/The-Heian-period-794-1185 (accessed Jun. 1, 2020).

Jarus, Owen. "Genghis Khan, Founder of the Mongol Empire: Facts & Biography." *Live Science*. February 10, 2014. https://www.livescience .com/43260-genghis-khan.html.

Jarus, Owen. "Guan Yu Biography: Revered Chinese Warrior." *Live Science*. February 25, 2014. https://www.livescience.com/43681 -guan-yu.html.

Jarus, Owen. "Spartacus: History of Gladiator Revolt Leader." *Live Science*. September 17, 2013. https://www.livescience.com/39730 -spartacus.html.

John, Maria. "Toypurina: A Legend Etched in the Landscape of Los Angeles." PBS: KCET. May 15, 2014. https://www.kcet.org/history -society/toypurina-a-legend-etched-in-the-landscape-of -los-angeles.

Johnson, Honor. "Morrigan." *The Order of Bards, Ovates and Druids*. Accessed May 2, 2020. https://druidry.org/morrigan.

Johnson, Todd. "Menelik II: Independence in the Age of Imperialism." NBC Learn. May 1, 2020. YouTube, 3:27. https://www.youtube.com /watch?v=wf2EYcKDEq8.

Kalensky, Patricia. "Stele representing the goddess Ishtar." *Louvre*. https://www.louvre.fr/en/oeuvre-notices/stele-representing -goddess-ishtar. (Site discontinued.)

Keane, Basil. "Story: Riri—Traditional Māori Warfare." *Te Ara—The Encyclopedia of New Zealand*. June 20, 2012. https://teara.govt.nz/en /riri-traditional-maori-warfare.

Kelly, Debra. "The Truth About the Legendary Shaolin Monk Warriors." Grunge. April 2, 2020. https://www.grunge .com/198843/the-truth-about-the-legendary-shaolin-monk -warriors/.

Kerkhove, Ray. "A Different Mode of War—Aboriginal 'Guerilla Tactics' in Defining the 'Black War' of South-Eastern Queensland 1843– 1845." Sovereign Union—First Nations Asserting Sovereignty, 2014. http://nationalunitygovernment.org/content/different-mode -war-aboriginal-guerilla-tactics-defining-black-war-south-eastern -queensland.

Kerkhove, Ray. "Tribal Alliances with Broader Agendas?: Aboriginal Resistance in Southern Queensland's 'Black War.'" *Cosmopolitan Civil Societies Journal* 6, no. 3, 2014. http://dx.doi.org/10.5130/ccs .v6i3.4218.

Kikoy, Herbert. "Sohei: The Warrior Monks of Medieval Japan." War History Online. July 28, 2018. https://www.warhistoryonline.com /instant-articles/sohei-the-warrior-monks.html.

King, Martin Luther, Jr. "A Study of Mithraism." *The Papers of Martin Luther King, Jr. Volume I: Called to Serve, January 1929–June 1951*. Berkeley, University of California Press, 1992, 211–225. https:// kinginstitute.stanford.edu/king-papers/documents/study -mithraism.

Kinnard, Jacob N. *The Emergence of Buddhism: Classical Traditions in Contemporary Perspective*. Minneapolis, MN: Augsburg Fortress, 2010.

Klimczak, Natalia. "White Buffalo Calf Woman—Healer, Teacher, and Inspirational Spirit for the Lakota People." *Ancient Origins*. November 13, 2016. https://www.ancient-origins.net/history -ancient-traditions/white-buffalo-calf-woman-healer-teacher-and -inspirational-spirit-lakota-021067.

Kloczowski, Jerzy. *A History of Polish Christianity*. Translated by Malgorzata Sady. Cambridge: University of Cambridge Press, 2000.

Knauft, Bruce M., Thomas S. Abler, Laura Betzig, Christopher Boehm, Robert Knox Dentan, Thomas M. Kiefer, Keith F. Otterbein, John Paddock, and Lars Rodseth. "Violence and Sociality in Human Evolution [and Comments and Replies]." *Current Anthropology* 32, no. 4 (Aug. –Oct. 1991): 391–428. https://www.jstor.org /stable/2743815?seq=1.

Koch, John C. *Celtic Culture: A Historical Encyclopedia*. Santa Barbara, CA: ABC-CLIO, 2006.

Kolo, Vincent. "China's Capitalist Counter-Revolution," Socialism Today, December 2007–January 2008. http://socialismtoday.org /archive/114/china.html.

Krutak, Lars. "Embodied Symbols of the South Seas: Tattoo in Polynesia." Lars Krutak: Tattoo Anthropologist. June 3, 2013. https://www.larskrutak.com/embodied-symbols-of-the-south-seas -tattoo-in-polynesia/.

Krygier, Rivon. "Did God Command the Extermination of the Canaanites? The Rabbis' Encounter with Genocide." Adath Shalom. Accessed April 19, 2020, 1–11. https://www.adathshalom.org/RK /about_the_extermination_of_the_Canaanites.pdf.

Kunuk, Zacharias, and Neil Diamond. *Inuit Cree Reconciliation*. Kingulliit Productions, 2013, 46:34. http://www.isuma.tv/en/InuitCree Reconciliation/movie.

Kunuk, Zacharias, Norman Cohn, and Pauloosie Qulitalik. "Nunavut (Our Land) Episode 4: Tugaliaq (Ice Blocks)." Igloolik Isuma Productions, 1995, 28:55. http://www.isuma.tv/isuma-productions /tugaliaq-ice-blocks.

Lallanilla, Marc. "How to Make a Zombie (Seriously)." *Live Science*. October 24, 2013. https://www.livescience.com/40690-zombie -haiti-are-zombies-real.html.

Lee, Wayne E. "Peace Chiefs and Blood Revenge: Patterns of Restraint in Native American Warfare, 1500–1800." *The Journal of Military History* 71, no. 3 (July 2007): 701–741. https://www.sjsu.edu /people/ruma.chopra/courses/H173_MW_S12/s2/Lee_Patterns _warfare_Indians.pdf.

Leiberman, Rabbi Shimon. "Kabbalah #11: Gevurah: The Strength of Judgment." Aish.com. Accessed April 20, 2020. https://www.aish .com/sp/k/Kabbala_11_Gevurah_The_Strength_of_Judgment.html.

Li, Yuhui. "Women's Movement and Change of Women's Status in China." *Journal of International Women's Studies* 1, no. 1, 3. January 2000. https://vc.bridgew.edu/cgi/viewcontent.cgi?article =1626&context=jiws.

Liebich, Don. "What Can the Islamic Golden Age Teach Us About Migration and Diversity?" Boise State University. Accessed April 22, 2020. https://www.boisestate.edu/sps-frankchurchinstitute /publications/essays/can-islamic-golden-age-teach-us-migration -diversity/.

Lile, Christopher. "Science Update: Chimps Start Wars for Power and Benefit from Play." Jane Goodall's Good News For All. July 11, 2018. https://news.janegoodall.org/2018/07/11/chimps-start -wars-power-show-disgust-feces-benefit-play/.

Lin, Derek, trans. *Tao Te Ching: Annotated & Explained*. By Laozi. Woodstock, VT: SkyLight Paths Publishing, 2006.

Locka, Christian. "Cameroon Has Been Using Witchcraft to Fight Boko Haram." The World. January 11, 2017. https://www.pri.org /stories/2017-01-11/cameroon-has-been-using-witchcraft-fight -boko-haram.

López-Muñoz, Francisco, Ronaldo Ucha-Udabe, and Cecilio Alamo. "The History of Barbiturates a Century after Their Clinical Introduction," *Neuropsychiatric Disease and Treatment* 1, no. 4 (Dec. 2005): 329–343. https://www.ncbi.nlm.nih.gov/pmc/articles /PMC2424120/#b74.

Louis, William Roger. *Imperialism at Bay: The United States and the Decolonization of the British Empire, 1941–1945*. Oxford: Oxford University Press, 1978.

Lynch, Patricia Ann. *African Mythology: A to Z*. Revised by Jeremy Roberts. Broomall: Chelsea House Publications, 2010.

Macdonald, Fleur. "The Legend of Benin's Fearless Female Warriors." BBC. August 27, 2018. http://www.bbc.com/travel/story/20180826 -the-legend-of-benins-fearless-female-warriors.

Maestri, Nicoletta, and K. Kris Hirst. "Huitzilopochtli." ThoughtCo. Updated October 18, 2019. https://www.thoughtco.com /huitzilopochtli-aztec-god-of-the-sun-171229.

Malandra, William M. "Zoroastrianism i. Historical Review up to the Arab Conquest." Encyclopedia Iranica. July 20, 2005. http://www .iranicaonline.org/articles/zoroastrianism-i-historical-review.

Mallowan, Max. "Cyrus the Great 558-529 B.C.)." In *The Cambridge History of Iran Vol.2: The Median and Archaemenian Periods*. Edited by I. Gershevitch, 329–419. Cambridge: Cambridge University Press, 1985.

Mandal, Dattatreya. "Ancient Celtic Warriors: 10 Things You Should Know." Realm of History. October 18, 2016. https://www .realmofhistory.com/2016/10/18/10-facts-ancient-celts-warriors/.

Mandal, Dattatreya. "The Ancient Egyptian Armies of the New Kingdom." *Realm of History*. June 16, 2017. https://www .realmofhistory.com/2017/06/16/10-facts-ancient-egyptian-armies -new-kingdom/.

Manzoor, Sarfraz. "Father to a Nation, Stranger to His Son." *The Guardian*. August 9, 2007. https://www.theguardian.com/film /2007/aug/10/india.

Mariani, Mike. "The Tragic, Forgotten History of Zombies." *The Atlantic*. October 28, 2015. https://www.theatlantic.com /entertainment/archive/2015/10/how-america-erased-the-tragic -history-of-the-zombie/412264/.

Mark, Emily. "Legalism." World History Encyclopedia. January 31, 2016. https://www.worldhistory.org/Legalism/.

Mark, Joshua J. "Mithra." World History Encyclopedia. February 11, 2020. https://www.worldhistory.org/Mithra/.

———. "New Kingdom of Egypt." World History Encyclopedia. October 7, 2016. https://www.worldhistory.org/New_Kingdom _of_Egypt/.

———. "Religion in the Ancient World." World History Encyclopedia. March 23, 2018. https://www.worldhistory.org/religion/.

Martin, Colin. "The Gods of the Imperial Roman Army." *History Today* 19, no. 4. April 1969. https://www.historytoday.com/archive /gods-imperial-roman-army.

Martin, Phillip. "Even with a Harvard Pedigree, Caste Follows 'Like a Shadow.'" *The World*. March 5, 2019. https://www.pri.org/stories /2019-03-05/even-harvard-pedigree-caste-follows-shadow.

Martin, Simon, and Nikolai Grube. *Chronicle of the Maya Kings and Queens: Deciphering the Dynasties of the Ancient Maya*. London: Thames & Hudson, 2000.

Mathew, Philip. "Marian Reforms." World History Encyclopedia. September 14, 2020. https://www.worldhistory.org/article/1598 /marian-reforms/.

McCoy, Daniel. "Valkyries." Norse Mythology for Smart People. Accessed May 2, 2020. https://norse-mythology.org/gods-and -creatures/valkyries/.

McCoy, Daniel. "Viking Raids and Warfare." Norse Mythology for Smart People. Accessed May 1, 2020. https://norse-mythology.org /viking-raids-warfare/.

McDermott, Alicia. "Sun Tzu: Famous Chinese Strategist and Philosopher." Ancient Origins. October 9, 2018. https://www .ancient-origins.net/history-famous-people/sun-tzu-0010817.

McDonald, Glenn. "The Rise and Fall of Islam's Golden Age." Seeker. September 4, 2016. https://www.seeker.com/the-rise-and-fall-of -islams-golden-age-1997288472.html.

Mdoda, Zama. "WHM: Dahomey Amazons Were Bad-Ass African Warriors." AfroPunk. March 8, 2019. https://afropunk.com/2019 /03/dahomey-amazons-african-warriors/.

Mehra, Bahrat, Paul A. Lemieux III, and Keri Stophel. "An Exploratory Journey of Cultural Visual Literacy of 'Non-Conforming' Gender Representations from Pre-Colonial Sub-Saharan Africa." *Open Information Science* 3, no. 1. January 15, 2019. https://doi.org /10.1515/opis-2019-0001.

Meleen, Michele. "Native American Death Rituals." Love To Know. Accessed July 10, 2020. https://dying.lovetoknow.com/native -american-death-rituals.

Merkur, Daniel. *Becoming Half Hidden: Shamanism and Initiation Among the Inuit*. New York: Routledge, 2013.

Mingren, Wu. "Huitzilopochtli: The Hummingbird War God at the Forefront of the Aztec Pantheon." Ancient Origins. Updated July 25, 2018. https://www.ancient-origins.net/myths-legends-americas /huitzilopochtli-0010426#main-content.

Minster, Christopher. "Hernan Cortes and His Tlaxcalan Allies." ThoughtCo. October 1, 2019. https://www.thoughtco.com/hernan -cortes-and-his-tlaxcalan-allies-2136523.

Mishra, Pankaj. "Ashoka the Great," *Boston Globe*. December 5, 2004. http://archive.boston.com/news/globe/ideas/articles/2004/12/05 /ashoka_the_great/.

"Mitra, Mithra, Mithras Mystery." The Iranian, in D. Jason Cooper, *Mithras: Mysteries and Initiation Rediscovered* (Newburyport: Red Wheel/Weiser, 1996), 1–8, September 11, 1997. https://iranian .com/1997/09/11/mithra/.

Mooney, James. *The Ghost-Dance Religion and Wounded Knee*. New York: Dover Publications, 1973.

Morris, Alan. "Path of the Soul #8: Strength of a Hero." Aish.com. https://www.aish.com/sp/pg/48909227.html.

Morris, Donald R. *The Washing of the Spears: The Rise and Fall of the Zulu Nation*. Cambridge: Da Capo Press, 1998.

Murasaki, Shikibu. *The Tale of Genji*. Translated by Edward G. Seidensticker. New York: Alfred A. Knopf, 2006.

Muscato, Chris. "What is an Aztec Flower War?" Study.com. August 8, 2017. https://study.com/academy/lesson/what-is-an-aztec-flower -war.html.

Muscato, Christopher. "The Roman Goddess Minerva: Importance & Mythology." Study.com. January 12, 2016. https://study .com/academy/lesson/the-roman-goddess-minerva-importance -mythology.html.

Muswellbrook Shire Council. "The Dreaming." Working With Indigenous Australians. Updated June 2020. http://www .workingwithindigenousaustralians.info/content/Culture_2_The _Dreaming.html.

Narayanan, Vasudha. "Freddie Mercury's Family Faith: The Ancient Religion of Zoroastrianism." The Conversation. November 3, 2018. https://theconversation.com/freddie-mercurys-family-faith-the -ancient-religion-of-zoroastrianism-105806.

Naumann, Sara. "A Brief History of the Shaolin Temple." *TripSavvy*. January 21, 2019. https://www.tripsavvy.com/brief-history -shaolin-temple-1495708.

Navarro, Vanessa M. "Aché, Music, and Spiritual Experience: The Concept of Aché and the Function of Music in Orisha Spirit Possession." Florida State University. April 11, 2013. 16–17. https://fsu.digital.flvc.org/islandora/object/fsu:183842/datastream /PDF/download/citation.pdf.

Newman, Chris. "African Spirituality's Influence on the Slave Experience in America." Thesis, Ohio State University, Dec. 2016, 1–28. https://kb.osu.edu/bitstream/handle/1811/78339 /AfricanSpiritualityInAmerica_ThesisPaper.pdf?sequence =1&isAllowed=y.

"Ngāti Tūmatauenga." NZ Army. New Zealand Defense Force. Accessed March 20, 2020. http://www.army.mil.nz/culture-and -history/ngati-tumatauenga.htm.

Nicholls, Christine Judith. "'Dreamtime' and 'The Dreaming'—An introduction." The Conversation. January 22, 2014. https:// theconversation.com/dreamtime-and-the-dreaming-an -introduction-20833.

O'Brien, Barbara. "Samurai Zen: The Role of Zen in Japan's Samurai Culture." Learn Religions. Updated January 13, 2018. https://www .learnreligions.com/role-of-zen-in-samurai-culture-449944.

O'Brien, Barbara. "Warrior Monks of Shaolin." Learn Religions. March 8, 2017. https://www.learnreligions.com/warrior-monks-of-shaolin -4123247.

O'Loughlin, Toni. "Recognition for Aboriginal Christians." *The Guardian*. July 28, 2009. https://www.theguardian.com /commentisfree/belief/2009/jul/28/uniting-church-aboriginal -australia.

Overton, Leonard C., and David P. Chandler. "Cambodia." Encyclopedia Britannica. Updated March 10, 2021. https://www .britannica.com/place/Cambodia/The-decline-of-Angkor.

Owunna, Mikael. "Drawing a Portrait of L.G.B.T.Q. Life." *The New York Times*. June 16, 2018. https://www.nytimes.com/2018/06/16/us /lgbtq-africans-share-their-stories.html.

Pedersen, Howard. "Jandamarra (1870–1897)." *Australian Dictionary of Biography*, vol. 12. 1990. National Centre of Biography, Australian National University. Accessed July 6, 2021. http://adb.anu.edu.au /biography/jandamarra-8822.

Penczak, Christopher. *Gay Witchcraft: Empowering the Tribe*. San Francisco: Red Wheel/Weiser, 2003.

Petitjean, Georges. "'Casting Ahead Serpent-fashion': The Rainbow Serpent in Australia." In *Dangerous and Divine: The Secret of the Serpent*. Edited by Wouter Welling. Amsterdam: Koninklijk Instituut voor de Tropen, 2012.

Petraeus, Gen. David. "'The Art of War': As Relevant Now as When It Was Written." *The Irish Times*. March 26, 2018. https://www .irishtimes.com/culture/books/the-art-of-war-as-relevant-now -as-when-it-was-written-1.3440724.

Poolos, Alexandra. "World: The True Meaning of the Islamic Term 'Jihad.'" Radio Free Europe/Radio Liberty. September 20, 2001. https://www.rferl.org/a/1097473.html.

"Pre-History." Tropical Fiji. South Pacific Holidays. Accessed July 7, 2020. http://www.tropicalfiji.com/about_fiji/culture/prehistory/.

Rangi Hīroa, Te [Peter Henry Buck]. *Anthropology and Religion*. New Haven, CT: Yale University Press, 1939.

Rangi Hīroa, Te [Peter Henry Buck]. *Arts and Crafts of the Cook Islands*. New York: Kraus Reprint Co., 1971. http://nzetc.victoria.ac.nz/tm/scholarly/tei-BucArts.html.

Rasmussen, Cecilia. "Shaman and Freedom-Fighter Led Indians' Mission Revolt." *Los Angeles Times*. June 10, 2001. https://www.latimes.com/archives/la-xpm-2001-jun-10-me-8853-story.html.

Rattini, Kristin Baird. "Who Was Ashoka?" *National Geographic*. April 1, 2019. https://www.nationalgeographic.com/culture/people/reference/ashoka/.

———. "Who Was Cyrus the Great?" *National Geographic*. May 6, 2019. https://www.nationalgeographic.com/culture/people/reference/cyrus-the-great/.

———. "Who Was Hammurabi?" *National Geographic*. April 22, 2019. https://www.nationalgeographic.com/culture/people/reference/hammurabi/.

Raupach, Kirsten. "'Black Magic' and Diasporic Imagination." *Current Objectives of Postgraduate American Studies* vol. 3, 2002. http://dx.doi.org/10.5283/copas.67.

Reese, Lyn. "The Trung Sisters." Women in World History. Accessed May 18, 2020. http://www.womeninworldhistory.com/heroine10.html.

Reese, M. R. "The Ancient Practice of Tengriism, Shamanism and Ancient Worship of the Sky Gods." Ancient Origins. December 2, 2014. https://www.ancient-origins.net/myths-legends-asia/ancient-practice-tengriism-shamanism-and-ancient-worship-sky-gods-002387.

Repp, Martin. "The Problem of 'Evil' in Pure Land Buddhism." In *Probing the Depths of Evil and Good: Multireligious Views and Case Studies*. Edited by Jerald D. Gort, Henry Jansen, and Hendrik M. Vroom. Amsterdam: Rodopi, 2007.

Ribeiro, Orquídea Moreira, Fernando Alberto Torres Moreira, and Susana Pimenta. "Nzinga Mbandi: From Story to Myth." *Journal of Science and Technology of the Arts* 11, no. 1 (September 10, 2019): 51–59. https://doi.org/10.7559/citarj.v11i1.594.

Rodgers, Greg. "Thaipusam Festival: Ritualistic Face and Body Piercing." Learn Religions. June, 19, 2020. https://www.learnreligions.com/what-is-thaipusam-1458358.

Roos, Dave. "Human Sacrifice: Why the Aztecs Practiced This Gory Ritual." History. October 11, 2018. https://www.history.com/news/aztec-human-sacrifice-religion.

Ross, Darius James. "Lithuania's Pagans Try to Turn Back the Clock." *The Baltic Times.* August 17, 2000. https://www.baltictimes.com/news/articles/1962/.

Rowell, S. C. *Lithuania Ascending: A Pagan Empire within East-Central Europe, 1295–1345.* Cambridge: Cambridge University Press, 2014.

Roy, Haimanti. "The Road to India's Partition." The Conversation. August 14, 2017. https://theconversation.com/the-road-to-indias-partition-82432.

Rule, Courtenay. "On This Day in History: The Death of an Aboriginal Resistance Fighter." *Australian Geographic.* November 7, 2013. https://www.australiangeographic.com.au/blogs/on-this-day/2013/11/on-this-day-in-history-the-death-of-an-aboriginal-resistance-fighter/.

Russell, Maj. Shawn. "Mao Zedong's 'On Guerrilla Warfare' and Joseph Kabila's Lost Opportunity." *Small Wars Journal.* July 10, 2012. https://smallwarsjournal.com/jrnl/art/mao-zedong%E2%80%99s-on-guerrilla-warfare-and-joseph-kabila%E2%80%99s-lost-opportunity.

Rzepa, Henry, Wyn Locke, Karl Harrison, and Paul May. "Barbiturates." Molecules in Motion: An Active Chemical Exploratorium. Accessed May 4, 2020. http://www.ch.ic.ac.uk/rzepa/mim/drugs/html/barbiturate_text.htm.

Sahner, Christian C. "How Did the Christian Middle East Become Predominantly Muslim?" University of Oxford. September 17, 2018. http://www.ox.ac.uk/news/arts-blog/how-did-christian -middle-east-become-predominantly-muslim.

Sanford, Whitney. "What Gandhi Can Teach Today's Protesters." The Conversation. October 1, 2017. https://theconversation.com /what-gandhi-can-teach-todays-protesters-83404.

Schroeder, Steven. "The Rise of Persia." Khan Academy. Accessed April 18, 2020. https://www.khanacademy.org/humanities/world-history /ancient-medieval/ancient-persia/a/the-rise-of-persia.

Shang, Yang. *The Book of Lord Shang: A Classic of the Chinese School of Law.* Translated by J. J. L. Duyvendak. Clark, NJ: The Lawbook Exchange, Ltd., 2003.

Shaw, Garry J. *War and Trade with the Pharaohs: An Archaeological Study of Ancient Egypt's Foreign Relations.* Barnsley: Pen & Sword Books, Ltd., 2017. https://www.academia.edu/37426621/War_and_Trade_With _the_Pharaohs?auto=download.

Shelton, Lillie. "The God of War." Johns Hopkins Archaeological Museum. Accessed April 14, 2020. http://archaeologicalmuseum .jhu.edu/the-collection/object-stories/egyptian-statuary-in-the -hopkins-archaeological-museum/the-god-of-war/.

Shirk, Adrian. "The Voodoo Priestess Whose Celebrity Foretold America's Future." *Zócalo Public Square.* November 28, 2018. https://www.zocalopublicsquare.org/2018/11/28/voodoo-priestess -whose-celebrity-foretold-americas-future/ideas/essay/.

Shōnagon, Sei. *The Pillow Book of Sei Shōnagon.* Translated and edited by Ivan Morris. New York: Columbia University Press, 1991.

Short, William R. "What Happened to the Vikings?" Hurstwic. Accessed May 1, 2020. http://www.hurstwic.org/history/articles /society/text/what_happened.htm.

Shrikumar, A. "Tracing the Roots of the Tamil God." *The Hindu*. Updated January 22, 2015. https://www.thehindu.com/features /metroplus/society/tracing-the-roots-of-the-tamil-god /article6808508.ece.

Silva Galdames, Osvaldo. "¿Detuvo la Batalla del Maule la Expansión Inca Hacia el Sur de Chile?" *Cuadernos de Historia* 3 (July 1983): 7–25.

Sinha, Ashish, Gayatri Kathayat, Harvey Weiss, Hanying Li, Hai Cheng, Justin Reuter, Adam W. Schneider, Max Berkelhammer, Selim F. Adali, Lowell D. Stott, and R. Lawrence Edwards. "Role of Climate in the Rise and Fall of the Neo-Assyrian Empire." *Science Advances* 5, no. 11. November 13, 2019. https://doi.org/10.1126 /sciadv.aax6656.

Smith, Shannon. "White Buffalo Calf Woman: The Sacred Lakota Figure Has Evolved Over Time, But She Hasn't Gone Away." Native Daughters. February 2010. https://shannonmariesmith.files .wordpress.com/2010/02/native-daughters-shannon-design.pdf.

Smith, Tom. "Rainbow Serpent: The Story of Indigenous Australia's God of Weather." Culture Trip. March 14, 2018. https:// theculturetrip.com/pacific/australia/articles/rainbow-serpent -story-indigenous-australias-god-weather/.

Snethen, Jessica. "Queen Nzinga (1583–1663)." BlackPast.org. June 16, 2009. https://www.blackpast.org/global-african-history/queen -nzinga-1583-1663/.

Sodeta, Naomi. "Hawaii: Way of the Warrior." *Hana Hou! Magazine*. April/May 2003. https://warriorpublications.wordpress.com/2013 /02/02/hawaii-way-of-the-warrior/.

Sotunde, Afolabi. "Ogun: Sacrifice to the Iron God." *Reuters*. September 23, 2015. https://widerimage.reuters.com/story/ogun -sacrifice-to-the-iron-god.

Spurway, John. *Ma'afu, Prince of Tonga, Chief of Fiji: The Life and Times of Fiji's First Tui Lau*. Canberra: Australian National University Press, 2015.

Steinsland, Gro, and Preben Meulengracht Sørensen. *Människor och makter i Vikingarnas värld*. Stockholm: Ordfront, 1998.

Stone, Leo. "Sohei: Buddhist Warrior Monks of Medieval Japan." Kings and Generals. October 15, 2020. YouTube, 21:15. https://www.youtube.com/watch?v=KHedbN-rL2Q.

Stratos, Anita. "Egypt: The Evolution of Warfare Part I." Tour Egypt. Accessed April 11, 2020. http://www.touregypt.net/featurestories/war.htm.

Strobridge, Truman R. "Shaka: Zulu Chieftain." History.net. October 2002. https://www.historynet.com/shaka-zulu-chieftain.htm.

Sturluson, Snorri. *The Poetic Edda*. Translated by Lee M. Hollander. Austin: University of Texas Press, 1986.

Sullivan, Richard E. "Charlemagne." *Encyclopedia Britannica*. Updated January 24, 2021. https://www.britannica.com/biography/Charlemagne/Religious-reform.

Sun, Chang. "The Changes of Mao Zedong Thoughts on Women's Liberation after the Founding of People's Republic of China." China University of Geosciences, Beijing. 2013.

Sun Tzu. *The Art of War*. Translated by Lionel Giles. Ballingslöv: Chiron Academic Press, 2015.

Sylvester, Phil. "12 Laws in Thailand: How to Stay Out of Jail." World Nomads. February 1, 2020. https://www.worldnomads.com/travel-safety/southeast-asia/thailand/a-travellers-guide-to-thailands-laws.

Szczepanski, Kallie. "What Was the Pax Mongolica?" ThoughtCo. April 2, 2019. https://www.thoughtco.com/what-was-the-pax-mongolica-195196.

Szostak, John D. "The Spread of Islam Along the Silk Route." University of Washington. July 29, 2002. https://depts.washington.edu/silkroad/exhibit/religion/islam/essay.html.

Tacitus. *The Annals*. Translated by Alfred John Church and William Jackson Brodribb. Internet Classics Archive. Accessed May 2, 2020. http://classics.mit.edu/Tacitus/annals.html.

"Tahiti and French Polynesian Culture." The Islands of Tahiti: Tahiti Tourisme. Accessed June 26, 2020. https://tahititourisme.com/en -us/tahiti-culture/.

Talayesva, Don. "The Giant and the Twin War Gods." *The Unwritten Literature of the Hopi*. Edited by Hattie Greene Lockett. Tucson: University of Arizona Press, 1933. https://www.gutenberg.org /files/15888/15888-h/15888-h.htm#The_Giant.

Talton, Benjamin. "African Resistance to Colonial Rule." African Age. 2011. http://exhibitions.nypl.org/africanaage/essay-resistance.html.

Templer, Robert. "Madame Nhu Obituary." *The Guardian*. April 26, 2011. https://www.theguardian.com/world/2011/apr/26/madame -nhu-obituary.

Tann, Mambo Chita. *Haitian Vodou: An Introduction to Haiti's Indigenous Spiritual Tradition*. Woodbury, MN: Llewellyn Publications, 2012.

't Hart, Marjolein. "Why Was Ethiopia not Colonized During the Late Nineteenth-Century 'Scramble for Africa'?" In *A History of the Global Economy: From 1500 to the Present*. Edited by Joerg Baten. Cambridge: Cambridge University Press, 2016.

Thomas, Kenneth R. "A Psychoanalytic Study of Alexander the Great." *Psychoanalytic Review* 82, no. 6 (December 1995): 859–901. https:// www.ncbi.nlm.nih.gov/pubmed/8657823.

Thompson, Ian. "The Black Spartacus." *The Guardian*. January 30, 2004. https://www.theguardian.com/books/2004/jan/31/featuresreviews .guardianreview35.

Thompson, James C. "Women in Sparta." Women in the Ancient World. Accessed April 28, 2020. http://www .womenintheancientworld.com/women%20in%20sparta.htm.

Torri, Maria Costanza, PhD. "Medicinal Plants Used in Mapuche Traditional Medicine in Araucanía, Chile: Linking Sociocultural and Religious Values with Local Heath Practices." *Complementary Health Practice Review* 15, no. 3 (2010): 132–148. https://journals.sagepub .com/doi/pdf/10.1177/1533210110391077.

"Trauma." U.S. Department of Health & Human Services. Accessed September 7, 2021. https://www.acf.hhs.gov/trauma-toolkit /trauma-concept.

Tregear, Edward. "Tu." *The Maori-Polynesian Comparative Dictionary*. Wellington, NZ: Lyon and Blair, 1891.

Tse-Tung, Mao. *On Guerrilla Warfare*. Translated by Samuel B. Griffith. New York: BN Publishing, 2007.

Tse-Tung, Mao. "Statement of the Problem." In On Protracted War. Yenan Association for the Study of the War of Resistance Against Japan. 1938. Accessed May 20, 2020. https://www.marxists.org /reference/archive/mao/selected-works/volume-2/mswv2_09.htm.

Tse-Tung, Mao. *Quotations from Chairman Mao Tse-Tung*. Translated by D. Weinberg. New York: BN Publishing, 2007.

Tsurugaoka Hachimangu. "Hachiman faith." *Tsurugaoka Hachimangu*. Accessed June 6, 2020. http://www.tsurugaoka-hachimangu.jp /hachiman_faith/ (site discontinued).

Tussing, Nigel. "African Resistance to European Colonial Aggression: An Assessment." *Africana Studies Student Research Conference*. February 12, 2017. https://scholarworks.bgsu.edu/cgi/viewcontent .cgi?article=1056&context=africana_studies_conf.

Tzabar, Rami. "Do Chimpanzee Wars Prove that Violence Is Innate?" BBC. August 11, 2015. http://www.bbc.com/earth/story/20150811 -do-animals-fight-wars.

University of Missouri-Columbia. "Amazonian Tribal Warfare Sheds Light on Modern Violence, Says Anthropologist." *ScienceDaily*. 2012. https://www.sciencedaily.com/releases/2012/10/121002145448.htm.

van Dijk, Jacobus. "The Amarna Period and the Later New Kingdom." In *The Oxford History of Ancient Egypt*. Edited by Ian Shaw, 311–312. Oxford: Oxford University Press, 2000.

Vance, Erik. "Have We Been Misreading a Crucial Maya Codex for Centuries?" *National Geographic*. August 23, 2016. https://www .nationalgeographic.com/news/2016/08/maya-calendar-dresden -codex-venus-tables-archaeology-science/.

Vandergriff, Tomi. "The Crucial Role Religion Played in the Conquests of Alexander the Great." *University of Wisconsin-Milwaukee Department of Religious Studies*. June 4, 2013. https://dc.uwm.edu/cgi /viewcontent.cgi?article=1001&context=rsso.

Veal, Clare. "The Feudal Photograph of a Democratic Dhammaraja: Secularism and Sacrality in Thai Royal Imagery." *Digital Philology: A Journal of Medieval Cultures* 8, no. 1 (Spring 2019): 66–85. https:// doi.org/10.1353/dph.2019.0015.

Vickery, Kenneth P. "Shaka Zulu: Creator and Destroyer." The Great Courses Daily. July 18, 2017. https://www.thegreatcoursesdaily .com/shaka-zulu/.

Voller, Peter. "Spartacus Rebellion—Roman Servile Wars." Kings and Generals. February 26, 2020. YouTube, 20:16. https://www .youtube.com/watch?v=RvaXBKUDG-Y.

Voth, H. R. *The Traditions of the Hopi*. Chicago, Field Columbian Museum, 1905. https://www.sacred-texts.com/nam/hopi/toth/index.htm.

Wang, Chang. Nathan H. Madson. *Inside China's Legal System*. Oxford: Chandos Publishing, 2013.

Wasson, Donald L. "Alexander the Great as a God." World History Encyclopedia. July 28, 2016. https://www.worldhistory.org /article/925/alexander-the-great-as-a-god/.

Weatherford, Jack. *Genghis Khan and the Quest for God: How the World's Greatest Conqueror Gave Us Religious Freedom*. New York: Penguin Random House, 2016.

Weatherford, Jack. "Genghis Khan—Hero of Religious Freedom?" OZY. October 31, 2016. https://www.ozy.com/news-and-politics /genghis-khan-hero-of-religious-freedom/72553/.

Webster, Hutton. *Primitive Secret Societies: A Study in Early Politics and Religion*. New York: Macmillan Company, 1908.

Weisberger, Mindy. "Bison vs. Buffalo: What's the Difference?" *Live Science*. December 23, 2017. https://www.livescience.com/32115 -bison-vs-buffalo-whats-the-difference.html.

Whelan, Edward. "Ares: The Greek God of War." Classical Wisdom. July 29, 2020. https://classicalwisdom.com/mythology/gods/ares -the-greek-god-of-war/.

Whitaker, Jarrod L. *Strong Arms and Drinking Strength: Masculinity, Violence, and the Body in Ancient India*. New York: Oxford University Press, 2011.

Wigington, Patti. "Mars, Roman God of War." Learn Religions. December 10, 2018. https://www.learnreligions.com/mars-roman -god-2562632.

Wilentz, Amy. "A Zombie Is a Slave Forever." *The New York Times*. October 30, 2012. https://www.nytimes.com/2012/10/31/opinion /a-zombie-is-a-slave-forever.html?smid=fb-share&_r=1&.

Winkler, Lawrence. *Samurai Road*. Cheyenne, WY: Bellatrix Books, 2015.

Winters, Riley. "The Powerful Valkyries as Icons of Female Force and Fear." Ancient Origins. July 12, 2015. https://www.ancient-origins .net/myths-legends-europe/powerful-valkyries-icons-female-force -and-fear-003407.

Worrall, Simon. "The Templars Got Rich Fighting for God—Then Lost It All." *National Geographic*. September 22, 2017. https://www .nationalgeographic.com/news/2017/09/knights-templar-crusades -dan-jones/.

Yenne, Bill. *Alexander the Great: Lessons from History's Undefeated General*. New York: St. Martin's Press, 2010.

Zhou, Ruru. "Guan Yu." China Highlights. Updated March 18, 2021. https://www.chinahighlights.com/travelguide/china-history/guan -yu.htm.

WEBSITES

Aboriginal Art & Culture: https://www.aboriginalart.com.au/

Aktá Lakota Museum & Cultural Center: http://aktalakota.stjo.org

Amnesty International: https://www.amnesty.org/en/

Ancient Origins: https://www.ancient-origins.net/

Archive for Research in Archetypal Symbolism: https://aras.org/

Australian Broadcasting Corporation: https://www.abc.net.au/

Australian Institute of Aboriginal and Torres Strait Islander Studies: https://aiatsis.gov.au/

Biography: https://www.biography.com

British Broadcasting Corporation: https://www.bbc.com/

Catholic Online: https://www.catholic.org/

Chabad: https://www.chabad.org/

Encyclopedia.com: https://www.encyclopedia.com/

Encylopædia Britannica: https://www.britannica.com/

EuroNews: https://www.euronews.com/

Hawaii Tourism Authority: https://www.gohawaii.com/

History: https://www.history.com/

Human Rights Watch: https://www.hrw.org/

Inti Land Tours: https://intilandtours.pe/inicio.html

Kahn Academy: https://www.khanacademy.org/

Learning for Justice: https://www.learningforjustice.org

Lithuania Tribune: https://lithuaniatribune.com/

Lumen Learning World Civilization: https://courses.lumenlearning .com/suny-hccc-worldcivilization/

Metropolitan Museum of Art: https://www.metmuseum.org/

National Geographic: https://www.nationalgeographic.org/

National Geographic History Magazine: https://www
.nationalgeographic.com/history/magazine/

National Park Service: https://www.nps.gov/index.htm

New World Encyclopedia: https://www.newworldencyclopedia.org

Online Etymology Dictionary: https://www.etymonline.com/

Public Broadcasting Service: https://www.pbs.org/

Realm of History: https://www.realmofhistory.com/

Rosicrucian Egyptian Museum: https://egyptianmuseum.org/

Ruapekapeka: https://www.ruapekapeka.co.nz/

Socialist Republic of Vietnam Government Committee for Religious
Affairs: http://religion.vn/Plus.aspx/en/1/0/

Soka Gakkai Nichiren Buddhism Library: https://www.nichirenlibrary
.org/en/

Thai Tourism Guide: https://blogthaitourismguide.wordpress.com/

The Guardian: https://www.theguardian.com/us

Theoi: https://www.theoi.com/

Un Rincón en la Historia: https://unrinconenlahistoria.wordpress
.com/

United States Conference of Catholic Bishops: http://www.usccb.org/

University of Cambridge Darwin Correspondence Project: https://
www.darwinproject.ac.uk/

U.S. Department of Health & Human Services: https://www.hhs.gov/

U.S. Department of State: Office of the Historian: https://history.state
.gov/

UShistory.org Independence Hall Association: https://www.ushistory
.org/civ/index.asp

Vision Times: https://visiontimes.com/

Yale Law School Avalon Project: https://avalon.law.yale.edu/ancient
/hamframe.asp